The Plays
of
EDWARD BOND

The Plays of EDWARD BOND

Richard Scharine

Lewisburg
Bucknell University Press
London: Associated University Presses

© 1976 by Associated University Presses, Inc.

Associated University Presses, Inc.
Cranbury, New Jersey 08512

Associated University Presses
108 New Bond Street
London W1Y OQX, England

Library of Congress Cataloging in Publication Data
Scharine, Richard
The plays of Edward Bond.

Bibliography: p.
Includes index
1. Bond, Edward—Criticism and interpretation.
I. Title.
PR6052.O5Z9   1975   822'.9'14   74–195
ISBN 0-8387-1538-9

PRINTED IN THE UNITED STATES OF AMERICA

To
Edward Bond:
May This Book Help His Ideas Gain the
Audience They Deserve

and

To
My Wife, Marilyn:
Upon Whose Ability
As Editor/Sounding Board
The Clarity Of This Book Depends

Contents

Acknowledgments	9
You Sit and Watch	13
1 An Introduction to Edward Bond: "If a House Is on Fire and I Cry Fire"	17
2 Little Babe Nailed to a Tree: *The Pope's Wedding*	29
3 *Saved:* Sooner Murder an Infant in Its Cradle	47
4 *Early Morning:* And the Word Was Made Flesh	82
5 Some Problems Have No Solutions: *Narrow Road to the Deep North*	123
6 Madmen, You Are the Fallen! The Incidental Dramatic Works	158
7 *Lear:* "Suffer the Little Children"	181
8 *The Sea:* "You Must Change the World"	223
9 The Edward Bond View of Life: A Summary of Themes and Techniques	255
Works Cited	289
Index	297

Acknowledgments

I wish to thank the following publishers and individuals for having given me permission to quote from published works:

Edward Bond, for permission to quote from his "Censor In Mind," *Censorship,* Autumn 1965; "The Duke in *Measure For Measure,*" *Gambit* 5:17; "you Sit and Watch," an unpublished poem, 1973.

Calder and Boyars, Ltd., for permission to quote from Edward Bond's *Early Morning,* 1968. This play is fully protected by copyright. All inquiries concerning performing rights, professional or amateur or any other use of this material should be directed to Margaret Ramsay, Ltd., 14a Goodwins Court, London WC2, England. Irving Wardle's "A Discussion with Edward Bond" and "An Interview with William Gaskill," *Gambit* 5:17, reprinted by special permission of the publisher, Calder and Boyars, Ltd.

The Dramatic Publishing Company, for permission to quote from the American publication of Edward Bond's *The Sea,* 1974. This play is fully protected by copyright. All inquiries concerning nonprofessional performing rights in North America should be directed to The Dramatic Publishing Company, 86 East Randolph Street, Chicago, Illinois 60601. Inquiries concerning professional or any other use of this material should be directed to Margaret Ramsey, Ltd., 14a Goodwins Court, Saint Martin's Lane, London 2 England.

Farrar, Straus, and Giroux, Inc., for permission to quote from Edward Bond's *Saved*, 1965, *Narrow Road to the Deep North*, 1968, and *Lear*, 1971. These plays are fully protected by copyright. All enquiries concerning performing rights, professional or amateur or any other use of this material should be directed to Margaret Ramsay, Ltd., 14a Goodwins Court, London WC2, England. Reprinted by permission of the publisher, Farrar, Straus, and Giroux, Inc.

Macmillan Publishing Co., Inc., for permission to quote from Elsworth F. Baker's *Man In The Trap*, 1967. Reprinted by special permission, Macmillan Publishing Co., Inc.

Methuen & Co., Ltd., for permission to quote from Edward Bond's *Saved*, 1965, *Narrow Road to the Deep North*, 1968, *Lear*, 1971, *The Pope's Wedding*, 1971, *The Sea*, 1973, and *Passion*, 1974. These plays are fully protected by copyright. All enquiries concerning performing rights, professional or amateur or any other use of this material should be directed to Margaret Ramsay, Ltd., 14a Goodwins Court, London WC2, England. Reprinted by permission of the publisher, Methuen & Co., Ltd.

The New Yorker Magazine, Inc., for permission to quote from Penelope Gilliatt's "Cackle in Hell" (copyright © 1969 by *The New Yorker* Magazine, Inc.).

The New York Times, for permission to quote from Clive Barnes's "Theatre: Openly Cerebral," © 1969, and Charles Marowitz's "A Modern Lear Amid Political Evil," © 1971 and "If a House is On Fire and I Cry Fire," © 1972 by *The New York Times* Company. Reprinted by

Acknowledgments

permission of the publisher, *The New York Times* Company.

The Observer, Ltd., for permission to quote from Ronald Bryden's "Society Makes Men Animals," February 9, 1969. Reprinted by special permission of the publisher, *The Observer,* Ltd.

Penguin Books, Ltd., for permission to quote from Matsuo Basho's *The Narrow Road to the Deep North and Other Travel Sketches,* copyright © by Nobuyuki Yuasa, 1966. Reprinted by permission of the publishers, Penguin Books, Ltd.

Plays and Players, for permission to quote from Peter Ansorge's "Director in Interview: Jane Howell," October 1968; David Benedictus' "Saved Again," June 1967. Reprinted by special permission of the publishers, Hamsom Books.

Theatre Quarterly, for permission to quote from Arthur Arnold's "Lines of Development in Bond's Plays," January-March 1972; Gregory Dark's "Production Casebook no. 5: Edward Bond's *Lear* at the Royal Court," January-March 1972; Roger Hudson, Catherine Itzin, and Simon Trussler's "Drama and the Dialectics of Violence," January-March 1972; Nicholas Hern's "The Theatre of Ernst Toller." Reprinted by special permission of the publishers, *Theatre Quarterly.*

I would also like to thank the following individuals whose personal letters were of invaluable aid in helping me write this book: Bill Bryden, Toby Cole, A. J. Coult, William Gaskill, Peter Gill, Keith Hack, Jane Howell, Peter James, Keith Johnstone, and Margaret Ramsay, and, of course, Edward Bond.

You Sit and Watch

You sit and watch
The stage
Your back is turned—
To what?

I want to remind you
The firing squad
Shoots in the back of the neck

Whole audiences have been caught
Looking the wrong way
Whole nations

I want to remind you
Of what you forgot to see
When you came here
To hear what you were too busy to listen to
Too afraid to believe
Too ashamed to admit

Are you (for example)
Wearing handcuffs while you hold this paper?

If what you see on the stage
Displeases you
Do you run away?

Lucky audience!—in your world
Is there no pain
No waste and cruelty?
No innocence in chains?
No child in the throes of death
Because the whole world is too weak to feed it
And the rich too poor?
The price of your ticket would have fed it. Don't waste it
Run away only if you run into a better world

On the stage actors
Discuss and decide problems
Imitate dying

You must solve the same problems
In your life
Suffer while they are made clear
Perhaps die in solving them
The actors will show you these future deaths

Do you say: No! Our life belongs to the streets
(Like an unclean whore?)
It must not be brought on the stage?

Then you must also make a law
Permitting sufferers to cry
Only within stated hours

And forbid writers to hear them
Finally:
There is still time to learn
Now to hope and build

—EDWARD BOND

The Plays of
EDWARD BOND

Edward Bond
(Photo courtesy of the Royal Court Theatre, S.W.1, London)

1
An Introduction to Edward Bond: "If a House Is on Fire and I Cry Fire"

In the fall of 1971 the master of ceremonies at a Cambridge luncheon introduced the speaker in the following manner: "If England ever went fascist, Edward Bond would be the first writer to be apprehended and jailed."[1] This was rather heady praise for a thirty-six-year-old ex-factory laborer who had been unable to support himself as a playwright and whose plays had been consistently harassed by both the government and the critics. All of Bond's plays had been produced initially at subsidized theaters, and all had lost money. He earned his living as a screenwriter and, although he had been associated with a number of remarkable films —notably Antonioni's *Blow-up,* Tony Richardson's production of Vladimir Nabokov's *Laughter In the Dark,* and Nicholas Roeg's *Walkabout*—he is "not interested in films

1. Charles Marowitz, "If a House is on Fire and I Cry Fire," *New York Times,* 2 January 1972, sec. 2, p. 1.

[because] the capitalist structure of the industry makes it difficult to make good films." [2]

Furthermore, Bond—initially at least—had not been the darling of the critics, while being ignored by the masses. One of the few critics who saw the production of his first play, *The Pope's Wedding* in 1962, called it "too long, too portentious, too elliptical"—a relatively favorable evaluation in light of the controversy raised by Bond's next two plays.

Saved (1965), denied a license by the Lord Chamberlain's office, could not be performed until the English Stage Company was turned into a private club. This did not appease such a reputable critic as J. C. Trewin of *The Illustrated London News* who admitted that "it may not be the feeblest thing I have seen on any stage, but it is certainly the nastiest, and contains perhaps the most horrid scene in contemporary theater." [3] Eventually, the censorship office was able to close the play on the grounds of inadequately observed rules governing private drama clubs.

The police, this time acting in the capacity of inquirers, were much quicker with *Early Morning* (1968) and their unsubtle interest was instrumental in limiting the English Stage Company production to a single performance. That was long enough for critic John Russell Taylor to huff that "though 'good taste' can hardly be invoked anymore as a criterion, relevance I suppose can." [4]

Bond finally achieved some measure of critical success with *Narrow Road to the Deep North* at Belgrade's Coventry Theatre in 1968. That is, he achieved it in England. When *Narrow Road* was presented in New York by Lincoln Center, George Oppenheimer of *Newsday* commented: "Mr. Bond is the author of *Saved,* in which a baby is stoned to death. This time he has given us a play in which the audience is

2. Edward Bond, letter to Richard Scharine, 23 March 1971.
3. J. C. Trewin, "Saved," *Illustrated London News* 249, 13 November 1965: 32.
4. John Russell Taylor, *The Angry Theatre* (London: Methuen, 1969), p. 110.

An Introduction to Edward Bond

bored to death."[5] Even though the retrospective Bond season at the Royal Court in 1969 made critical indignation over Bond unfashionable in England, it could do nothing to ease the irritation felt by those critics to whom he still seemed incomprehensible. Thus, critic-playwright Jeremy Kingston of *Punch* could greet *Lear* (1971) with resignation: "For those who appreciate the works of Edward Bond—I think German playhouses do—his *Lear* presumably establishes the year's quality."[6] Even Bond's first comedy, *The Sea* (1973), inspired in Arthur Thirkell only a massive attack of peevishness.

> [Bond's] latest effort, *The Sea*, washed up [at the Royal Court] last night. Mercifully, it is easier to take than his previous plays. Not easier to understand. That would be asking too much of Mr. Bond.[7]

Nevertheless, if Bond's detractors are legion, he has always had supporters in high places. Lawrence Olivier, Kenneth Tynan, Mary McCarthy, and Penelope Gilliatt placed their very considerable prestige in support of *Saved*, as did Martin Esslin and Ronald Bryden of the London *Observer* for *Early Morning*. Most important, Bond has always had a director and a theater—William Gaskill and the English Stage Company—who were not only willing to stage his plays, but were absolutely committed to them.

Even official reaction to Bond's plays has been sharply divided. On 3 February 1966, the Arts Council awarded Bond a £1,000 bursary as a playwriting grant.[8] Eleven days later, officials of the English Stage Company went on trial

---

5. George Oppenheimer, "Road to Nowhere," *Newsday*, 7 January 1972, p. 24.
6. Jeremy Kingston, "A Good Year in the Theatre Means a Year of Good Plays," *Plays and Players* 19 no. 4 (January 1972): 20.
7. Arthur Thirkell, "Right Royal Mixture," London *Daily Mirror*, 24 May 1973, p. 6.
8. London *Times*, "Arts Council Bursaries to Two Playwrights," 3 February 1966, p. 7.

for having presented one of his plays to a public audience. On 7 April 1968, police pressure prevented the second and last public performance of *Early Morning*. On 30 May 1968, Bond received the George Devine Award for Theatrical Promise for *Early Morning*.[9] This award was later complimented nicely by the John Whiting Award for the Best Play of 1968–69, which was shared by *Narrow Road to the Deep North*.[10]

In September 1968, Parliament at last rescinded the censorship powers of the Lord Chamberlain, powers that had their origins in Elizabethan times and that had remained essentially unchanged for 125 years. Gaskill responded at the Royal Court in early 1969 by scheduling a "Bond season" consisting of *Saved, Narrow Road to the Deep North*, and *Early Morning*.

Although *Saved* was returning to the Royal Court only three years after it had been closed to general approval, and the revival of *Early Morning* followed its original production by less than fifty weeks, a surprising number of critics had reversed their positions. Hilary Spurling of *The Spectator* praised the Royal Court for its policy of "giving what is good until it becomes popular."

> Having disliked *Saved* intensely in 1965 for reasons not now at all clear to me, it is a programme for which I am truly grateful. . . . If *Saved* is a cruelly harsh play, it has a delicacy which makes it anything but bitter.[11]

Irving Wardle of the London *Times*, who has called *Saved* "a systematic degradation of the human animal" [12] and *Early*

---

9. London *Times*, "Devine Award for Edward Bond," 31 May 1968, p. 15.
10. London *Times*, "Whiting Award to Barnes and Bond," 14 April 1969, p. 6.
11. Hilary Spurling, "A Bond Honoured," *The Spectator* 222 (7 March 1969): 313.
12. Irving Wardle, "A Question of Motives and Purposes," London *Times*, 4 November 1965, p. 17.

An Introduction to Edward Bond

Morning "muddled and untalented,"[13] could now say that "Bond writes like a God, holding up the criminal stupidities of a puny species which at any moment he may choose to exterminate."[14] As for the critical reaction to *Narrow Road*, it is perhaps best summed up by John Russell Taylor's reaction to the story that Bond's next project would be a rewriting of Shakespeare's *King Lear:* "After *Narrow Road to the Deep North* he seems ready for anything."[15]

The British Council topped off the "Bond season" by sponsoring a continental tour of *Saved* and *Narrow Road*, but this was by no means Europe's introduction to these plays. Bond's works have been performed in every country on the continent, although Kingston's jibe about Germany is well taken. By 1968, *Saved* had been produced more times in Germany that it had had performances in England.[16] *Early Morning* was voted the best foreign play in Germany during the 1969–70 season, and by the time *Lear* was first performed in England (1971), over forty German theaters were queued up for the European premiere.[17]

Bond has yet to excite such interest either in his homeland or in America, but its formation can be sensed. John Lahr said of the 1970 Chelsea Theater production of *Saved:*

> This writing is hard and full-blooded. . . . The play proves to us our own capacity for compassion and the painful lonely discipline of such responsible love.[18]

Kenneth Hurren of *The Spectator* found himself overwhelmed by the first production of *Lear*.

13. Irving Wardle, "Muddled Fantasy on Brutalization," London *Times*, 1 April 1968, p. 6.
14. Irving Wardle, "The Edward Bond View of Life," London *Times*, 15 March 1970, p. 15.
15. John Russell Taylor, "Edward Bond: Beyond Pessimism?", *Plays and Players* 17, no. 10 (July 1970): 18.
16. Alan Brien, "This Bond has not been much Honoured," London *Sunday Times*, 31 March 1968, p. 55.
17. Marowitz, "If a House," p. 5.
18. John Lahr, "When a playwright is prophetic," *The Village Voice*, 5 November 1970, p. 47.

I have, for example, an instinctive feeling, so strong as to allow of no doubts that Edward Bond's *Lear* was the play of the year. [*Lear*] put not a foot wrong by its lights, and there seemed to me no mistaking the greatness of an achievement that could stand comparison with the late Shakespeare at his most monumental.[19]

Finally, R. B. Marriott called *The Sea* "Edward Bond's best play so far . . . larger in scope, at least in direct human terms, but more deeply affecting and dramatically powerful than any other, not excepting *Saved*." [20]

It is not unusual for a young playwright to have his first efforts receive critical indifference, but the virulent and often personal attacks on Bond demand some explanation. One can always, of course, point to the violence in his plays. A central feature of *The Pope's Wedding* is the murder of an old hermit by a young man who has identified himself so closely with the old man that he must replace him. *Saved* became a fit subject for banning because of a scene in which a baby is smeared with its own excrement and stoned to death. *Early Morning* begins with an incident in a cinema queue where a man and his girlfriend eat the chap who tries to push in front of them and ends with a scene in Heaven where the whole cast reassembles after death for orgies of mutual cannibalism. *Narrow Road to the Deep North* features mass infanticide, a crucifixion, and a ritual hara-kiri onstage. *Lear* has been justifiably described as "a long scream of pain and horror," [21] whose more graphic aspects include the scientific blinding of the title character and the onstage autopsy of his daughter.

This is indeed sickening, but it is a sickness that the author is witnessing, not creating.

19. Kenneth Hurren, "Lord Mansfield's Advice to Judges," *Plays and Players* 19, no. 4 (January 1972): 20.
20. R. B. Marriott, "*The Sea*, Edward Bond's Best Play, Now at the Royal Court," *Stage and Television Today*, 31 May 1973, no. 4,807, 7.
21. John Holmstrom, "Lear," *Plays and Players* 19, no. 2 (November 1971): 42.

An Introduction to Edward Bond

> I write about violence as naturally as Jane Austen wrote about manners. Violence shapes and obsesses our society, and if we do not stop being violent we have no future. People who do not want writers to write about violence want to stop them writing about us and our time. It would be immoral not to write about violence.[22]

Bond believes in the Family of Man, and that makes the crimes men commit against one another fratricide—no matter what "ism" is offered as justification. Bond has a Blake-like view of life as original innocence perverted by the social order. Evil is the offshoot of satanic abstractions called *society, government, Christian tradition,* and, ultimately, *God.* Although Bond denies the existence of God on moral grounds, much in the manner of Dostoevski's Ivan, Christian symbolism pervades all his plays. Particularly, he is haunted by the "slaughter of the Innocents" and the fact that its constant repetition is encouraged rather than prevented by modern society.

> No, I've never heard of a baby being stoned to death, but I have heard of babies being bombed to death. You see, the question of the play is why is it that violence is licensed by society, but only on a political level? When the same thing happens on an individual level, then it's absolutely disgraceful.[23]

Inhumanity respects no national borders in Bond's view and his willingness to attack both existing conditions and revered traditions has multiplied the resistance to his plays. As early as *Saved,* Alan Brien noted the chauvinism that marred the moral indignation greeting Bond's work.

> It appears that British audiences and critics can stomach unlimited helpings of torture, sadism, perversion, murder, and

---

22. Edward Bond, Preface to *Lear* (London: Eyre Methuen, 1972), p. 5.
23. Marowitz, "If a House," p. 5.

bestiality when perpetrated by foreigners upon foreigners in the past. But that was in another country, they say, like Marlowe's "Jew of Malta," and besides the stench is dead. . . . Is it thought that such things cannot happen in this gentle and civilized land?[24]

Early Morning, with its portrait of a lesbian and cannibalistic Queen Victoria presiding over the self-consumption of a surrealistic society, was treated as slander rather than as a satire of the attitudes we have inherited from the Victorians. It is no secret that the critical treatment of Bond improved markedly when he had the grace to place *Narrow Road to the Deep North* in Japan a few centuries in the past. It is also no secret that the resentment shown *Lear* resulted partly from loyalty to Shakespeare as a national monument.

Violence and patriotism aside, moreover, Edward Bond's plays have been misunderstood from the very beginning. With *Saved* this misunderstanding hardened into opposition. *The Pope's Wedding* had pleased some and puzzled many, but the important thing was that a single, Sunday-night performance without decor by an admittedly experimental theater did not require either judgment or commitment. One could merely mention a few stronger moments, note the writer's promise, and commend the Royal Court on its continuing contribution to the nation's dramatic growth. *Saved* was quite something else.

The timing of *Saved* is important in understanding critical reaction both to it and to Bond's work in general. Nearly a decade passed between the first performances of *Look Back In Anger* and *Saved*. What began as a revelation had become a genre. There were highly articulate attacks on the class system (Osborne), highly articulate promotions of socialism (Wesker), and highly articulate "comedies of menace" (Pinter). Furthermore, you could tell what Osborne was

---

24. Alan Brien, "The Monster Within," *New Statesman* 56 (12 November 1965): 735.

against, what Wesker was for, and if you didn't understand Pinter, it was all right because Martin Esslin said he belonged to the Theater of the Absurd. Upper-class accents may have disappeared, but plots (complete with exposition and climaxes) and protagonists (complete with value systems and points of view) had not. In short, the realism of John Galsworthy had not died, it had merely moved to the East End.

In reality, *Saved* was both more than and less than "kitchen-sink" naturalism. The difference lies in the play's focus. Where naturalism supplies us with a detailed background so that we may better understand the motivations of a character, Bond's plays provide a clinically observed set of characters so that we may better understand the motivations of a society.

> Any of Edward Bond's plays requires the actors to put themselves *at the service of the play*; to be extremely logical, simple, and clear and not to allow characterization to stand between the play and the audience—this is bloody difficult.[25]

Therefore, even Bond's so-called naturalistic plays are intellectual rather than psychological. They require, as John Russell Taylor noted about the baby murder in *Saved,* non-naturalistic, technical means of showing the parallels between their violence and the violence of the outer world. In this respect Bond has been hampered by the relatively small size of his "home" theater, the Royal Court. Jane Howell, who has directed *Narrow Road to the Deep North* at three different theaters—the Belgrade at Coventry, the Royal Court, and the Northcott at Exeter—discovered that the wide stage of the Belgrade allowed her to stage scenes pictorally rather than emotionally, like at the Royal Court. Director-critic Charles Marowitz recognized that *Lear* "cries out for the full-scale epic production." Irving Wardle, who

25. Jane Howell, letter to Richard Scharine, 6 July 1971.

was converted from a Bond detractor to a supporter by Miss Howell's Belgrade production, made this comment about a production of *The Sea* at the Freie Volksbühne in Berlin:

> Bond, famously, is a reigning favourite of the German stage; and this production strengthened my feeling that this has much to do with simple physical conditions. In Britain, he is fortunate in his regular director, William Gaskill, but unlucky in having his work cramped to fit the Royal Court stage. Remembering that theatre's premiere of *The Sea* it was fascinating to watch the piece expanding to twice the size at the Volksbühne: the great drapes sweeping apart and mingling with the sound of waves; a whole clifftop dropping in for the funeral scene with glittering white seagulls impaled like moths behind a dazzling sky-cloth; and the arrangement of the draper's shop with a counter facing the audience so that when Hatch draws the blinds and locks up, his fellow vigilantes can steal out conspiratorially from behind the bales of cloth.[26]

In *Early Morning*, Bond used the interrelationship of social institutions and sexual repression to produce a Victorian dream world, thus puzzling those who had defended *Saved* (inaccurately) as naturalism: (1) They were unable, despite copious doses of surrealism, to see beyond historical personages to the attitudes that have been fostered by their images; (2) they were unable to see in cannibalism the symbol of either commercial competition or oral infantile sexuality; (3) they were even incapable of seeing in Siamese twins the representation of a divided personality.

Without question, the major difficulty in understanding what a Bond play means has been in the viewer's preconception. It is not merely because of its merit that *Narrow Road to the Deep North*, featuring a setting and characters that were foreign, has been Bond's most popular play in his homeland.

26. Irving Wardle, "German Theatre: Rolling in Money and Ruled by Directors," London *Times*, 23 May 1974, p. 11.

An Introduction to Edward Bond

To some extent, *Narrow Road* marks a watershed to critical understanding of Bond. Earlier estimates of his work were badly shaken. Nevertheless, this critical confusion has also had its negative side. Those who are deeply opposd to Bond have become "armored" in their opposition. Those who are uncertain seem increasingly reluctant to commit themselves to an honest answer.

To be sure, Bond has not helped himself by choosing to undertake the battle of bardolatry in *Lear*. Nevertheless, the biggest barrier to understanding his work is still that the world Bond writes of is the world we live in. It is the height of irony that when in *The Sea* (1973) Bond used for the first time a *raisonneur* to state explicitly the play's purpose, he was lectured solemnly by critic Irving Wardle because "its positive statement on human regeneration [is] very much at the expense of dramatic quality. Enactment gives way to philosophising." [27] As the old mule skinner said: "First, you've gotta get their attention."

Each of Bond's plays is concerned with the evil that results from the mindless dispensation of a corrupt morality. Yet each play presents the alternative of the man who says no to evil. The "hero" of *Saved*, which Bond has called the parable of a "liberal who is trying to pacify his environment," clutches at the straws of personal relationships available to him because "clutching at straws is the only realistic thing to do." Len chooses neither to be brutalized by his circumstances nor to abandon his responsibilities, the justification for Bond's evaluation of *Saved* as "almost irresponsibly optimistic." [28] In the society of *Early Morning*, Prince Arthur recognizes that men release themselves from the pain of life by preying on their fellow men. Yet he chooses to be eaten, rather than to eat. In *Narrow Road to the Deep North*, Kiro, the Buddhist novice, sees the horror engendered

27. Irving Wardle, "Edward Bond Deals Kindly with his Characters," London *Times*, 24 May, 1973, p. 9.
28. Edward Bond, Preface to *Saved* (New York: Hill and Wang, 1965, p. 5.

by the clash of the two tyrannies and commits suicide. Even as he dies, however, a man who had been drowning drags himself ashore through his own efforts, dries himself off, and begins life anew. After almost unspeakable torment, Bond's Lear learns that the institutions he has built to protect his people are prisons for their souls. Hampered by his social shell, a promising young man drowns in *The Sea*, but his death opens the eyes of a friend who steps forward to fulfill his ideals.

Edward Bond's career as a professional playwright is only a dozen years old. Hopefully, he can look forward to three dozen more. Nevertheless, Bond has already an important body of remarkably consistent work—a collection large enough to reveal patterns and yet small enough to be grasped as a whole. A study of these works will serve not only as an introduction to Bond's dramatic writing from *The Pope's Wedding* through *The Sea*, but also as a context in which his future work may be more readily understood. In the long run, however, Bond's stature may not be determinable by drama criticism at all.

> If a house is on fire and I shout"Fire! Fire!", I don't want people commending my shouting ability, I want them to join in the firefighting.[29]

---

29. Marowitz, "If a House," p. 5

2
Little Babe Nailed to a Tree:
The Pope's Wedding

The Pope's Wedding, the first Bond play to be performed professionally, was initially presented on a Sunday evening, 9 December 1962, by the English Stage Society for a members-only audience at the Royal Court Theatre. It received a single showing without decor, in accordance with the Royal Court's policy of seasoning young dramatists. The Director was Keith Johnstone, himself a Royal Court playwright and well known in more recent years as a teacher of improvisation at The Royal Academy of Dramatic Arts and as a creator of improvisational vehicles.

Although *The Pope's Wedding* was Edward Bond's first professionally performed play, his preparations for his chosen profession were most arduous. Beginning after his military service in 1957, he entered into a deliberately intensive period of playgoing.

> I also saw every play that was put on in London for two years. It was quite an ordeal, it meant going twice most

Saturdays. I saw absolutely everything, the lot: even the Moral Rearmament plays.[1]

It was also during this period that Bond, whom William Gaskill has called the most Chekhovian of modern playwrights,[2] engaged in a line-by-line analysis of *The Three Sisters*. This was to prove invaluable to his understanding of technique, as well as giving rise to his 1967 adaptation of the play for the Royal Court.

Shortly after this time, on the recommendation of Keith Johnstone, Bond was admitted to a writer's group led by Gaskill, then an associate director to George Devine at the English Stage Society.

> The Writers Group which I initiated must have been during 1959. . . . It was a very informal gathering of writers who had come in the second, post-Osborne wave of new writers and included Arden, Wesker, Ann Jellicoe, Keith Johnstone, Donald Howarth, and Wole Soyinka, all of whom had had plays done at the Royal Court and were, in a sense, "established," at least in Sloane Square. My idea behind the work was to give the writers a direct experience of acting and acting techniques rather than attempting any dramaturgical theory. Most of the work was improvisation based on various definite methods, for example, work on objectives in the Stanislavski method, work on the third person narrative in the Brechtian manner, and work on obsessions and humours. We met once a week and each week had special direction or topic. . . . Edward Bond was a totally unknown writer whose work had not been seen even for a Sunday Night prformance and my memory of him is of a quiet intense young man not overawed by the greater reputation or group feeling of the others. I must have run the group for at least a year and when I finished, it was continued by Ann Jellicoe, Arnold Wesker, and Keith Johnstone. I think Edward was there all the time

1. Edward Bond, quoted by Giles Gordon in "Edward Bond," *Transatlantic Review* 22 (Autumn 1966): 12.
2. Hilary Spurling, "A Difference of Opinion," *Spectator* 215 (12 November 1965): 619.

that I arranged the sessions and probably continued afterwards. He was also a regular play reader for the Theatre and was considered by Keith Johnstone, who was head of the Script Department, to be the best reader that we had ever had.[3]

Johnstone's recommendation was based upon a comedy entitled *Klaxon in Atreus' Palace*. He remembers little about it "except that it seemed pretty psychotic, which seemed to me a good thing. I remember saying that we weren't likely to do the play, but that the writer's talent was obvious."[4] Johnstone's approval seems to have been the deciding factor in Bond's admittance, since Gaskill "couldn't make head nor tail of [*Klaxon in Atreus' Palace* and] thought it was very, very difficult to follow."[5] Even now he remembers nothing "except a generalized atmosphere, cold and haunting which could be said to be typical of his work."[6]

Altogether, Bond wrote fourteen or fifteen plays before the production of *The Pope's Wedding* in 1962. Two of these were considered for production by Peter Gill, himself a Royal Court director and playwright. Unfortunately, they were never to be performed. Bond is unwilling to make them available for study,[7] and what we know about them and the situation surrounding their near-production must be gleaned from Mr. Gill's memory of the incident.

> About ten years ago . . . Ann Jellicoe rang me up. She knew I was interested in directing and she knew that Edward Bond had some plays which she felt strongly should be done. . . . One was called, I think, *He Jumped But the Bridge was Burning*, and I can't remember the name of the other. One was rather obscure and apparently influenced by Brecht,

3. William Gaskill, letter to Richard Scharine, 19 March 1971.
4. Keith Johnstone, letter to Richard Scharine, 25 March 1971.
5. William Gaskill, quoted by Irving Wardle in "An Interview with William Gaskill," *Gambit* 5, no. 17: 41.
6. Gaskill, letter, 19 March 1971.
7. Edward Bond, letter to Richard Scharine, 23 March 1971.

which I didn't respond to or understand; in manner it was, I think, a little like *Narrow Road to the Deep North*. The other I liked very much. It had three characters—a tramp and a young man and woman as I remember, very London, set in a wasteland or bombed-site. I suppose people would say it was Beckettian—it was an unmistakable piece of good writing. . . . I wanted really to do only one of the plays and felt strongly about correct casting of it. However, I'd heard John McGrath and someone from the Z. Cars [a popular English TV series] team at the B.B.C. were planning a season of new plays at Oxford. I sent them the script I had, urging them to do the plays, and I never got it back from them. I have felt guilty ever since about the script being lost!—although I imagine Edward had a copy.[8]

For all his doggedly acquired experience as a playgoer, as a playreader, and as a member of the writers' group, Bond's first professionally performed play received a decidedly casual greeting from the critics. The catalogue of charges in an unsigned London *Observer* review included "too long, too portentious, too elliptical."[9] A similarly anonymous reviewer for the London *Times* chided the "unsatisfactory and unrelated street gang scenes,"[10] failing to recognize that these scenes are necessary to define the protagonist's origins and conditioning, and to mark how far he moves away from them. However, Keith Johnstone remembers it as "very well received by most critics."[11] The play's aura of foreboding received especially favorable comments. John Russell Taylor, who was later to dismiss *Saved* as irrelevant and *Early Morning* as only questionably profound, called *The Pope's Wedding* a "powerfully atmospheric piece."[12]

8. Peter Gill, letter to A. J. Coult, 13 may 1971.
9. London *Observer*, "Production Without Decor," 16 December 1962, p. 24.
10. London *Times*, "Play sans Decor but not Theme," 10 December 1962, p. 9.
11. Johnstone, letter, 25 March 1971.
12. John Russell Taylor, *The Angry Theatre* (New York: Hill and Wang, 1969), pp. 108–110.

The Pope's Wedding

Even the London *Observer* admitted that "in every scene ... you felt the presence of a born mood evoker."

The English Stage Company never gave *The Pope's Wedding* a full-scale production. It was, in fact, the only Bond play not reproduced in the 1969 retrospective Bond season at the Royal Court.[13] William Gaskill, the artistic director of the English Stage Society, has called *The Pope's Wedding* "a very fine play,"[14] but admits that "it never crossed my mind to include *The Pope's Wedding* [in the retrospective season] and three is the natural number for such a Season."[15] It is not the first time that a good play has been edged from the repertory by its author's later, more mature work. *The Pope's Wedding*, which contains a number of elements used to better advantage in *Saved*, was particularly susceptible to such displacement.

John Russell Taylor has suggested that the stimulus for *The Pope's Wedding* came from Raleigh Trevelyan's book, *A Hermit Disclosed*,[16] the story of Alexander James Mason, the hermit of Great Canfield in Essex. Trevelyan's book was the source for two other 1962 dramas: James Saunders's absurdist exercise, *Next Time I'll Sing to You*, and Henry Livings's television play, *Jim All Alone*. *The Pope's Wedding*, to some extent, shares with these plays Trevelyan's central image of a hermit as the eye of the hurricane, a still center from which the outside world is viewed objectively without moral comment.[17]

Arthur Arnold has even put forth the possibility that

---

13. The publicity surrounding the revival of *Saved*, *Early Morning*, and *Narrow Road to the Deep North* did lead, however, to the first publication of *The Pope's Wedding* in the April 1969 issue of *Plays and Players*. In the spring of 1971, Methuen published it along with *Black Mass* in book form.
14. Wardle, "Gaskill," p. 41.
15. Gaskill, letter, 19 March 1971.
16. Raleigh Trevelyan, *A Hermit Disclosed* (New York: St. Martin's Press, 1960).
17. John Russell Taylor, *The Second Wave* (London: Methuen & Co., Ltd., 1971), p. 78.

Saunders's play directly inspired Bond's,[18] an unlikely theory considering the proximity of their presentation. Bond himself has not been helpful about pinpointing his sources. When asked by the editors of *Theatre Quarterly* why he chose Essex as the setting for *The Pope's Wedding* and if any of the play's characters were drawn from his experience of country living, he replied:

> Well, I didn't have a car, and it [Essex] was the nearest really rural area I could get to. I went there one weekend and made notes. . . . It's very difficult to remember now what things I put together and in what order. But [I never knew] the hermit, no.[19]

The central character of Bond's work is not the hermit (Alen), but a young man named Scopey who comes from the village. The action is centered around Scopey's gradual withdrawal from village life, his increasing fascination with the hermit's mystery, and his eventual replacement of him.

Scopey is initially indistinguishable from the rest of his mates, a group of unsentimentalized and unexaggerated working-class youths concerned with nothing more demanding than raising the price of a beer the night before payday. It is only when Scopey volunteers to fix the clasp of a handbag broken during the friendly harassment of a local factory girl that he gives sign of a sensibility different from the others. The girl (Pat) is Alen's sole link with the outside world. She does his shopping and some occasional rudimentary cleaning because of a never-explained deathbed request made by her mother. Scopey moves a step closer to an intimate relationship with Pat when her boyfriend is withheld from the cricket competition by his boss. The loss of

---

18. Arthur Arnold, "Lines of Development in Bond's Plays," *Theatre Quarterly* 2 (January–March 1972): 15.
19. Edward Bond, as quoted by Roger Hudson, Catherine Itzin and Simon Trussler in "Drama and the Dialectics of Violence," *Theatre Quarterly* 2 (January–March 1972): 7.

The Pope's Wedding 35

Bill's talents by such a petty trick is, as are all local misfortunes, blamed on "owd Alen's curse." Scopey replaces Bill and wins the cricket match with his alert and daring play. He also wins the admiration of Pat and soon has replaced Bill with her, also.

In courting and marrying Pat, Scopey inherits the problem of Alen. At first, in idle curiosity, he attempts to spy on Alen when Pat is at the shack. Next, seemingly for his wife's convenience, he offers to take over the care of Alen himself.

Brian Capron as Scopey in The Pope's Wedding
(Photo courtesy of the Northcott Theatre, Exeter; photo by Nicholas Toyne, Devon)

Alen first resists, then accepts him, and gradually Scopey's curiosity takes on the tone of emulation. He spends more and more time in Alen's shack, neglecting and losing both job and wife. Seeing, but only dimly understanding, what is happening, Scopey forces Alen to reveal the truth about his withdrawal from society. The truth is simple and mocking, but it is already too late for Scopey to retreat. He kills Alen and takes his place in the shack.

The line of action in *The Pope's Wedding* is ideational. Bond is concerned with the relationship between an inquiring individual and his less-than-perfect society. The London *Times* critic who failed to see the connection between the gang scenes and the subsequent Scopey/Alen relationship did not realize that Bond's main point was that the second could not have occurred without the first. Scopey is successful and accepted within his narrow universe. The hermit existence of Alen, however, mocks Scopey's successes. Alen, through his apparent lack of concern for the values of the village, stimulates in Scopey a suspicion of their hollowness. Scopey hopes unconsciously that in finding the key to Alen's rejection of society, he will be able to understand society and his own vague disappointment in it. In searching out the alternative, however, he becomes enmeshed in it and, finally, in order to give it meaning, he entraps himself in a Pirandellian form.

Scopey is the first of the Bond Innocents,[20] the one character within each of Bond's plays who senses the gap between what is and what should be. The first half of *The Pope's Wedding* is a record of his achievements within his society, culminating in his winning the cricket match and

---

20. The Bond Innocent is an existential optimist, "clutching at straws" in an attempt to preserve his humanity within an inhumane society. Although they are all destroyed or stalemated, their continuing attempts indicate, in whatever debased form, the survival of goodness on the earth. These characters include Scopey, Len in *Saved*, Prince Arthur in *Early Morning*, Kiro in *Narrow Road to the Deep North*, Christ in *Black Mass* and in *Passion*, the title role in *Lear*, and Willy in *The Sea*.

The Pope's Wedding

seducing and marrying Pat. Even in the earliest scenes, however, Scopey's distinguishing characteristic is his curiosity. Although he does not stand out intellectually from his peers, he is the only one who can conceive of a life different from that of the village. When Pat receives a postcard from a girlfriend who has married a soldier and moved to America, Scopey studies intently its picture of a small town with clean-swept streets and clear skies.

> JUNE. Nice.
> SCOPEY. Yoo can't tell.
> JUNE. I like it.
> SCOPEY. Yoo need more. . . . Yoo can't tell. Where's the people an' the corners? (*He turns the card over.*) . . . That don't say a word what's on the front. . . . I'd like a stick postcards all over the room. . . . On the floor an' the ceilin'.
> PAT. Talk about somethin' else. . . .
> SCOPEY. Just pictures.
> PAT. Why?
> SCOPEY. Why? That's what I'd like.[21]

The postcard is significant because it shows both Scopey's distrust of surfaces and his desire for something different from his present experience. It is interesting to note that Scopey's ideal postcard-lined room is symbolically womblike. Such examples of uterine regression are frequent in Bond's work and represent the other side of his social criticism. It is Bond's contention that all children are born full of love and with the capability of giving it, but are distorted and corrupted by the pressures of society.

> Our society is not geared to the protection, love, and care of the child. Now you all live through that experience when you are emotionally developed. You have no mind, but your emotions are absolutely in full display, perhaps more than

21. Edward Bond, *The Pope's Wedding* (London: Methuen & Co., Ltd., 1971). vii, pp. 46–47. Subsequent references to this play will be noted in the text.

at any other life, so you are capable of a greater degree of suffering and of love, perhaps, than you will ever be able to be. Now at that stage where you are most exposed, where you are most neglected, and most acted against; I think this must be a sort of memory that people take with them.[22]

The actions of Bond's moral heroes tend to be innocent and childlike in the view of their societies. Their motivation is frequently an unconscious desire to return to primal innocence or Oedipal nostalgia. The conflicts of these Innocents also tend to be Oedipal. For example, to Scopey, Alen is a father figure. He even initially suspects Alen of being Pat's father. He forces his way into the hermit's shack, which suggests both a womb and Scopey's postcard-lined room, eventually killing the old man and assuming his identity. In later plays, Bond's heroes will resist the temptation to violence, but their motivations will remain the same.

It is convenient to see Scopey's relationship with Pat as a midway point in his gradual withdrawal from his society. His initial disassociation from his group into the traditional dyad of marriage is natural enough, and, had we not already seen evidence of his curiosity about Alen, Scopey's offer to relieve Pat of the responsibility of caring for the hermit might have been interpreted merely as a friendly marital gesture. After the scene in which Scopey makes this offer, however, the easy intimacy between himself and Pat is never resumed. She is quick to misinterpret the reason.

> Doo 'e bring someone with 'im? . . . Nobody wait outside? . . . No one? . . . 'E ent suited a marriage. . . . Soon get tired. I don't see what 'e get out a it, tell you the truth. Yoo know (xii 73–74).

She is soon back with Bill, as unable to understand her husband's loss of interest as she was her own initial fascination with him.

22. Edward Bond, quoted by Irving Wardle in "A Discussion with Edward Bond," *Gambit* 5, no. 17: 22.

The Pope's Wedding

It is Scopey's unspoken quest that is the key to the play's title, *The Pope's Wedding*. It is an evocative image, the playwright's private symbol for Scopey's search, suggesting simultaneously an impossible purity and a blasphemous joke. What Scopey seeks is the former, but what he will achieve is the latter. The "wedding" is ultimately that of Innocent to Innocent, the moment of murder in which Scopey and Alen become one.

Accepting the premise that the action of *The Pope's Wedding* does lie in Scopey's move from integration to alienation, it is plain that Alen's position must be his logical end. In the experience of Scopey and his friends, Alen is the only being who is simultaneously visible yet outside their society. Consequently, they attribute to him the qualities of those who are most alien to human beings: God and the Devil. Alen is somehow, they believe, immune to their own petty failures. For example, he has money on a Thursday night. Although withdrawn from them, he sees their sins and punishes them.

> I reckon owd Alen's put 'is curse on us. Owzat! Our owd telly broke down last Wednesday an' the owd man reckon that's count a 'e cursed us on mum tellin' 'alf the village about Sarah Neat's baby (ii. 38).

Even in crediting the fathering of Pat to Alen, Scopey is granting him the classic characteristic attributed to aliens and devils, excessive sexuality. Ultimately, Alen receives the treatment mankind has traditionally reserved for aliens and gods. He is abused and stoned. He is even murdered by one close to him, and finally, in a sense, he is reborn.

Time after time Scopey attempts to find the key to the mystery of the hermit's withdrawal: the stacks of newspapers Alen needs for his "work"; the relationship with Pat's mother; an old photograph of a high-born lady; etc. All the leads are blind. Even so he is progressing simultaneously toward his answer and his destiny. Scopey becomes more and more immersed in Alen's life as the old man increases his acceptance of him. The effort to learn the hermit's secret and the need to identify with him become personified and unified in the gift from Alen of an old army greatcoat that is a mate to the one the old man wears.

> SCOPEY. I feel bigger. . . . The pockets 'ent 'ere.
> ALEN. They're sewed shut. . . . T' keep the shape.
> SCOPEY. Ent yoo 'ad a look? . . . There might be somethin' inside.
> ALEN. I don't want nothin'.
> SCOPEY. Where's the scissors? . . . Chriss yoo might 'ave anythin' in 'ere (xii, 50).

The sewn-shut pockets of an overcoat purchased fifty years earlier represent both the last stop in Scopey's search and the mystery of the old man himself. To wear the clothes of the father is the Oedipal urge of the child. To be privy to his secrets is to supplant him. Before the pockets can be opened, however, an incident occurs that forecasts their contents. Pat arrives to visit Alen for the first time in months. Her purpose is to pump the old man about Scopey's actions, because, although claiming to work overtime in order to spend more time at Alen's shack, he actually has lost his job because of excessive absences. As Scopey watches from hiding, he sees that the old man is obviously overjoyed at her visit. When Pat leaves, Alen goes to an old stack of papers by the wall, climbs onto them, and peers out after her through a chink in the wall.

> SCOPEY. (*Pause.*) That what yoo use them papers for? . . . Yoo was glad a see 'er.
> ALEN. She say she's comin' back regular.
> SCOPEY. That's what you want. . . . Yoo owd nut! I thought yoo 'ad them papers for keepin'. All yoo want 'em for's t' stare outside. Yoo owd fake! . . . Yoo're at that crack all day! Starin' out! It all goos on outside an' yoo just watch!
> ALEN. I ont said I—

The Pope's Wedding 41

SCOPEY. Yoo're a fake! There's nothin' in this bloody shop!
. . . Look. (*Slight pause.*) What yoo 'ere for? . . . For chris's
sake try t' tell the truth!
ALEN. I forget. My mum an' dad moved all over. We always
stopped just outside places. We were the last 'ouse in the
village. . . . I never stopped gooin' after people. They stopped
gooin' after me. . . . That's all I can bring back.
SCOPEY. (*After a pause.*) Pockets 're empty (xii, 79).

The pockets are empty. In the center of the Chinese box is a mirror. We are eternally alone, imprisoned inside ourselves, and eternally seeking to be united with others. Like the other villagers, Scopey has seen Alen's life as a comment upon his own, a reflection of his solitariness. It is fear of isolation that drives people to accept even demeaning social relationship. Exclusion is the ultimate terror. Nevertheless, Alen had apparently chosen to live apart and, by his own aloneness, made a mockery of the villagers' efforts at communion. Their reaction to his imagined contempt was to despise him and to seek his destruction. Scopey's is to discover the mystery that permits Alen to desire the condition that Scopey unconsciously fears is inevitable. When he discovers that the inevitability extends, not only to solitariness, but to the wish to avoid it, Scopey realizes the irony of his search and the futility of attempting a return to his past life. His murder of Alen and his assumption of the hermit's personality is an existential extreme, an ultimate act of self-recognition.

On still another level, Scopey's murder of Alen is a sacrifice to the society that produced him. The society of *The Pope's Wedding*, like that of all Bond plays, is closed. The presence of Alen served to remind them that there was a way of life other than their own. This apparent contentment served as a goad to those around Alen, reminding them of the inadequacy of their own lives. To Scopey, however, it is another world containing some form of secret self-satisfaction. When he discovers the true reason for the hermit's withdrawal, it has an effect roughly analogous to the loss of religious faith. If Alen's reason for leaving society is not a good one, then Scopey's own withdrawal is meaningless. Scopey's killing of Alen is a fulfillment of the hermit's myth and, therefore, a reaffirmation of society's judgment of him.

Two examples of Christian ritual murder pervade the works of Edward Bond: the Slaughter of the Innocents and the Crucifixion of a Scapegoat. Organized religion is to Bond just another of the bodiless, bloodthirsty abstractions in whose names humanity is destroyed. It is significant that when Scopey terrorizes the old man into singing a hymn, his choice suggests incomparable barbarity rather than a god of love.

> Little babe nailed to the tree
> Wash our souls in they pure blood
> Cleanse each sin and let us be
> Baptized in the purple flood
>
> Bearing thorns and whips and nails
> Wise men kneel before they bier
> Let the love that never fails
> Conquer vice and death and fear
>
> Child they hosts now crowd the sky
> Thou who found love here alone
> Those who nail thee up to die
> Hoist thee nearer to they throne (xii, 79).

Like the baby nailed to the tree, the senile and childlike Alen serves as both Innocent and Scapegoat. In a very real sense the death of innocence is the theme of *The Pope's Wedding*, a theme that covers more than the death of Alen. Scopey is also an Innocent who "dies," in that he ceases to struggle with his situation. Scopey wisely is dissatisfied with a society in which men are alienated. He chooses unwisely, however, in attempting to isolate himself from other men. When he kills Alen, he perpetuates the myth of separateness, while at the same time he seals himself off from the possi-

The Pope's Wedding

bility of change. Scopey's description of the old man's murder bears a strong resemblance to a crucifixion: "I took one 'an on 'is throat and one 'eld 'im up be the 'air" (xvi, 82). Society has triumphed. Scopey has become noncreative, i.e., "dead." He has carried out the judgment of his society and, in the process, become its next victim.

In his first play to be professionally performed, Edward Bond established many of the themes and techniques that were to dominate his subsequent work. To begin with, he revealed himself as a dramatist of action who expresses himself through what his characters do rather than what they say. Never, for example, does Scopey express either a disenchantment with his environment or longing for another. Yet these feelings are there in his abandonment of his wife and his disappointment in Alen's revelation that society had rejected the hermit, rather than vice versa. Moreover, neither Scopey nor any of the other characters are acute enough to recognize their predicament, let alone articulate enough to express it. This led a number of Bond's early critics to accuse him of either confusion or of not having a point of view. In actuality, Bond is an extremely didactic writer, but his refusal to sentimentalize or to provide a *raisonneur*, as does Arnold Wesker, for example, has misled the imperceptive.

Another misleading factor has been Bond's choice of symbols and images. An atheist and a pacifist, he uses, both in *The Pope's Wedding* and in his subsequent plays, images of Christian martyrdom in their most brutally violent light. In *The Pope's Wedding* that means the persecution and slaughter of an old recluse. The revulsion that these images cause in the audience is intended by Bond to force the recognition of the crippling effect of society upon humanity's moral system.

Bond's personal social philosophy is Blakean. He believes that man is perverted by societal pressures: environment, government, religion, etc. Very few people survive these pressures in any spiritual sense. Those who do, like Scopey for a time, intuitively recognize the impurity of their surroundings and set out to find an alternative. With little to choose from, they strive to find or to create some protective environment. Scopey eases himself into Alen's shack, just as Len will later insert himself into Pam's family—not because they are perfect, but because they seem momentarily to offer the best opportunity for survival.

In *The Popes Wedding*, Bond uses sharply contrasting tones in consecutive scenes, a technique featured in all his subsequent works. Sometimes faulted by his critics as an indifferent constructionist, he clearly forecasts early in the play the end result of Scopey's development. In the first two scenes, we see only the young people, full of bravado and quick to respond, in an open environment. The first scene is marked only by an iron railing upstage and the second by an apple on the floor. In the third scene the atmosphere is quite different.

> *Across the stage a black-and-purple corrugated-iron wall. A door centre. A couch right. A table down left. The oil cookers standing on a box down right. Two wooden boxes used as chairs. A stack of newspapers, one foot high, against the wall, right of the door. Three or four smaller stacks of newspapers about the room* (iii, 38).

After the brightly lighted cricket pitch of the previous scene, the interior of Alen's shack is claustrophobic. The old hermit wanders from place to place, unable to concentrate long enough to complete an action. He seems constantly braced against the outside world, alternately fearful and hopeful. Late in the play we see the same setting and similar actions again following a boisterous scene with the young people. This time the solitary figure will be Scopey.

Our first view of Alen also establishes one of the trademarks of Bond's dramaturgy: his ability to devise wordless scenes that nevertheless contribute to plot, thought, and character. He carries that into the cricket-match scene, called by Arthur Arnold "a remarkably successful technical achievement . . . a unique scene."[23] It would be tempting to credit this scene to Keith Johnstone who, earlier that same year, had put together an improvisational comedy and mime troupe, "The Theatre Machine," which still exists today as the best of its kind in London.[24] Johnstone, however, denies this: "The play came in as produced. I altered nothing. Edward wouldn't let me make cuts."[25] He is probably not being modest. Bond's success as a screenwriter attests to his capacity for visualizations, and William Gaskill, who has had more experience with Bond's plays than any other director, credits him with "an extraordinary visual sense. When you actually put on the stage the things that he has said you must do in the stage directions you get fantastic pictures."[26]

While stressing the primacy of action, Bond still reveals himself to be a master of theater language. Catching perfectly the East Anglian dialect, he pares and arranges it into a stage poetry that rhythmically resembles that of the early Pinter plays while avoiding the music-hall flavor that sometimes permeated Pinter's work. As Penelope Gilliatt has noted, Bond's dialogue is not nearly so naturalistic as it may initially seem.

> And though the vernacular language may make the play look like a "slice of life," a phrase that is used to mean a very inferior slab of theatrical fruit cake, the truth is that the prose is skillfully stylized. It uses a hard, curt attack, hardly ever more than five or six syllables to a line.[27]

23. Arnold, "Lines of Development," p. 15.
24. Roger Hudson, Catherine Itzin, and Simon Trussler, "Theatre-survey No. 1: Guide to Underground Theatre," *Theatre Quarterly* 1 (January–March 1971): 64.
25. Johnstone, letter, 25 March 1971.
26. Wardle, "Gaskill," p. 41.
27. Penelope Gilliatt, "*Saved*," in *Contemporary Theatre*, ed. Geoffrey Morgan (London: London Magazine Editions, 1968), pp. 42–43.

The structure of *The Pope's Wedding* is pyramidal. We are first shown the broad base of an Essex village and only gradually is detail stripped away to reveal the focus of the playwright to be a single young man's search for purity. The episodic structure is an attempt to cope with the fragmentation of our contemporary perception.

> I think a well-made play is death anyway, simple because it tells lies; that sort of competent structure deforms the content so that you can't make a play well in that sense . . . because that sort of thing just wouldn't tell the truth about our sociey and life.[28]

At the same time, Bond follows two theatrical conventions in *The Pope's Wedding* that he sometimes ignores in his later plays. First, he places the play's intellectual climax in its most emotionally moving scene, then places that scene relatively late in the play. Second, he builds that scene up to the point of violence and then does not show it. Bond is able, thus, to complete the theatrically effective denouement for which he prepared us earlier in the play. In our first view of Alen in his shack, a scene that was discussed earlier in terms of Bond's mastery of the visual, the hermit is uneasy, fearing every outside sound, but unable to concentrate long enough even to confirm or allay his fears. He begins an action, then switches to another without so much as recognizing his change. He wanders aimlessly, focusing only briefly and without purpose. In a scene following the climax, we see Scopey alone in the shack, wearing the old man's coat. He tries to sweep the floor, but must stop to repair the broom. He puts down the broom to check the stove. He looks at his watch. It isn't running. He gets a knife in order to open it. He cannot. We are not told that the old man is dead. We do not need to be.

---

28. Wardle, "Discussion with Bond," p. 33.

3

Saved:
Sooner Murder an Infant
in Its Cradle

In fall 1965, William Gaskill returned from the National Theatre to succeed the late George Devine as artistic director of the English Stage Company. He immediately revived the repertory policy that Devine had abandoned early in the theater's history and used it to inaugurate three new plays, two by established Royal Court playwrights and one by a relative newcomer.[1]

The first two plays were Ann Jellicoe's *Shelley* and N. F. Simpson's *Cresta Run,* both of which received mixed and generally disappointing reviews. Nevertheless, the critics' real ire was reserved for Edward Bond, whose only previous professionally performed play, *The Pope's Wedding,* had been seen in a Royal Court Sunday-night production with-

---

1. John Russell Taylor: "Ten Years of the English Stage Company," *Tulane Drama Review* 11, no. 2 (Winter 1966): 130.

out decor three years earlier. His *Saved* joined the repertory on November 3.

After the Independent Theatre produced Ibsen's *Ghosts* in 1891, its manager, J. T. Grein, described himself as "the best-hated man in London." On the morning of 4 November 1965, Edward Bond must have felt that he had inherited the title. Penelope Gilliatt opened a favorable review in the London *Observer* by saying, "I spent a lot of the first act shaking with claustrophobia and thinking I was going to be sick." [2] The *unfavorable* reviews were predictably more severe. The reasons for the condemnation varied, although most critics cited several. Herbert Kretzmer began in *The* [London] *Daily Express* with the "characters who, almost without exception, are foul-mouthed, dirty-minded, illiterate, and barely to be judged on any recognizable human level at all." [3] J. C. Trewin of *The Illustrated London News* admitted:

> It may not be the feeblest thing I have seen on any stage, but it is certainly the nastiest, and contains perhaps the most horrid scene in the contemporary theatre. (Even as I write that hedging "perhaps" I delete it: nobody can hedge about *Saved*.)[4]

Irving Wardle of the London *Times* declared that "the writing itself, with its self-admiring jokes and gloating approach to moments of brutality and erotic humiliation amounts to a systematic degradation of the human animal." [5] The outcries of offended critics were followed shortly by

2. Penelope Gilliatt, "*Saved*," in *Contemporary Theatre*, ed. Geoffrey Morgan (London: London Magazine Editions, 1968), p. 42.
3. Herbert Kretzmer, "*Saved*," in *Contemporary Theatre*, ed. Geoffrey Morgan (London: Magazine Editions, 1968), p. 45.
4. J. C. Trewin, "*Saved*," *The Illustrated London News*, 249 (13 November 1965): 32.
5. Irving Wardle, "A Question of Motives and Purposes," London *Times*, 4 November 1965, p. 17.

those of aroused patrons who formed "representative organizations" in order to combat "pornographic, sadistic, filthy, unfunny, and obscene" drama.[6]

Initially, the "slaughter by the critics just emptied theatre."[7] However, the Royal Court continued to present the play and it soon generated support among England's most influential members of the theatrical profession. Irene Worth wrote to Bond endorsing *Saved*. In the letter columns of the London *Observer*, Sir Laurence Olivier praised the play as one in which "we can experience the sacramental catharsis of a very chastening look at the sort of ground we have prepared for the next lot."[8] On 14 November, Kenneth Tynan organized a teach-in at the Royal Court at which Mary McCarthy praised *Saved* for its "remarkable delicacy" and stated that the play was concerned with "limit and decorum."[9] Bond himself responded with an open letter to the critics in the London *Observer*. In December and January the box office "picked up enormously." The opposition, however, still had a legal ace in the hole.

The English Stage Company was not unaware of the problems that might be caused by *Saved*. They had commissioned a play from Bond as a result of their pleasure with *The Pope's Wedding*. *Saved*, however, had come as something of a shock and it was given to the director of *The Pope's Wedding*, Keith Johnstone, for another Sunday-night production without decor.[10] At this point, Gaskill, who was planning his first season at the Royal Court, read *Saved* for the first time.

6. Mary V. Thom, letters on *Saved*, *Plays and Players* 13, no. 5 (February 1966): 8.
7. Edward Bond, quoted by Giles Gordon in "Edward Bond," *Transatlantic Review* 22 (Autumn 1966): 13.
8. Laurence Olivier, quoted on the cover of *Saved* by Edward Bond (New York: Hill and Wang, 1965).
9. London *Times*, "Critics Hold Teach-in on *Saved*," 15 November 1965, p. 14.
10. Keith Johnstone, letter to Richard Scharine, 25 March 1971.

I remember reading it straight through and being absolutely convinced that it should be done and that I should direct it myself. I had some doubts about the extremes of violence but I knew the play had to be done.[11]

On 24 June, 1965, Gaskill submitted the play to the censorship office of the Lord Chamberlain, an office that *Saved* and its successor, *Early Morning*, were to be instrumental in closing. The Lord Chamberlain's representative, the Assistant Comptroller, recommended a considerable number of cuts, including all of one scene and a major part of another. On 3 August, Gaskill and Iain Cuthbertson, a Royal Court associate director, discussed the case with the Assistant Comptroller. Gaskill promised to deliberate the proposed cuts with the author. Eight days later the Lord Chamberlain's office received a letter from the author stating that the changes would be too damaging to the play and that a decision had been made to present it to a club-audience only.[12]

The action of the Royal Court in limiting showings of *Saved* to private audiences seemed momentarily to reduce the possibilities of a legal conflict. Technically, under the Theatres Act of 1843, it was an offence to act plays anywhere "for hire" without a license from the Lord Chamberlain and the payment of anyone connected with a production defined it as a play acted "for hire." However, with some exceptions, the Lord Chamberlain had turned a blind eye to productions that were to be viewed by private groups, such as the English Stage Society, the Royal Court's private club.[13] Nevertheless, in December several performances of *Saved* were attended by police officers acting on behalf of the Lord Chamberlain's office.[14] On 14 February, eleven days

11. William Gaskill, letter to Richard Scharine, 19 March 1971.
12. London *Times*, "Censored Play Summonses," 15 February, 1966, p. 13.
13. Richard Findlater, *Banned!* (London: MacGibbon and McKee, Ltd., 1967), p. 150.
14. "Drama in Court—Act One," *Plays and Players* 13 no. 8 (May 1966): 66–67.

after Bond had been awarded a £1,000 writer's bursary by the Arts Council and two days after a motion in the House of Lords was introduced to review the stage censorship laws,[15] summonses were served on Gaskill and Alfred Esdaile, the Licensee of the Royal Court, for presentation of a play before it had been licensed.[16] The complaint was based on the failure of Royal Court door attendants to check for membership cards at performances of *Saved*. In actuality, the censor may have been more irritated by the fact that the play was running in repertory with licensed productions. Lord Cobbold, then Lord Chamberlain, expressed his philosophy on this practice in a 1964 interview:

> Whether or not they could strictly be brought under the Lord Chamberlain's jurisdiction—which has never actually been tested in the courts—my predecessors and I have never wished to interfere with genuine theatre clubs. Where a management uses them for a different purpose, e.g., to put on for a long run a play part of which had been refused a licence, I think rather a different position arises. The arrangement is then really being used more as an attempt to evade the law.[17]

If *Saved* was intended by the Lord Chamberlain to serve as a legal test case, it must have been a disappointing one. The English Stage Company was convicted, but the trial served as an excellent forum for both the merits of *Saved* and the censorship system. The fine was a nominal £50.[18] Nevertheless, productions of *Saved* were forbidden in England for the time being. The Royal Court had scheduled performances for 21 and 22 February, and Gaskill initially announced that these performances would take place, despite

---

15. London *Times*, "Censorship Review may be accepted," 12 February 1966, p. 12.
16. London *Times*, "Censored Play Summonses," p. 13.
17. Lord Cobbold, as quoted in *Banned!* by Richard Findlater, p. 173.
18. Findlater, *Banned!*, p. 173.

the impending legal action.[19] However, he later relented, perhaps through fear of alienating the court.

Outside of England, *Saved* received more favorable treatment. By March of 1968 Bond could legitimately claim to have "had more productions of *Saved* in Germany than I've had performances in England." [20] A production by the Cinoherni Klub of Prague intended "to illustrate the point that when personal freedom is frustrated by external authority it takes a very ugly secondary course" received Bond's personal commendation.[21] The American premiere, under the direction of Jeff Bleckner, was presented at the Yale Repertory Theater 5 December 1968. The audience's response was typical, but reviews reflect a new respect for the work itself.

> Mr. Bleckner and his cast were able to unearth the complexities of the play, and, more importantly, to sound its astonishing verbal music for us, especially in the second half. One was able to perceive that Bond's use of dialogue, seemingly the simplest realism, actually had a density and richness close to that of Chekhov. . . . The work communicated itself with complete success: the walkout rate after the first half was the highest the theatre has ever had, and I have never seen an audience at a traditional play so disturbed and stimulated.[22]

Six days later, *Saved* had its Canadian premiere at McGill University in Montreal.[23]

Meanwhile, back in England, attitudes toward Bond's work were beginning to shift. The critical success of Jane Howell's production of *Narrow Road to the Deep North* at the Belgrade Theater of Coventry in June 1968, prompted

19. London *Times*, "Saved continues next week," 16 February 1966, p. 16.
20. Alain Brien, "This Bond has not been much Honoured," London *Sunday Times*, 31 March 1968, p. 55.
21. Irving Wardle, "A Discussion with Edward Bond," *Gambit* 5, no. 17: 22.
22. Michael Feingold, "Ensembles," *Plays and Players* 16, no. 8 (May 1969): 65.
23. Toby Cole, letter to Richard Scharine, 7 June 1971.

some grudging aesthetic reassessments of the earlier plays. Stressing "the legitimate points they make about political morality or class dereliction," Irving Wardle admitted to making a complete about-face in reference to *Saved* and *Early Morning*.

> Even for those who still hate his work, Bond has become one of the facts of theatrical life, no longer to be dismissed with a bored yawn or an outraged howl. And it is now time for the guilty reviewers to queue up and excuse their past arrogance and obtuseness as best they may. As one of the guiltiest, I am glad to acknowledge that my feeling toward the plays has changed, and that if I had originally responded to them as I do now I should not have applied words like "half-baked" and "untalented" to *Saved* and *Early Morning*.[24]

The retrospective "Bond season" at the Royal Court opened 7 February 1969, with *Saved*. The performers were different and a few other details had altered, but nothing was so significantly different as the reaction from the dark side of the footlights.

> After the grotesque antics in which the moral health of the nation was supposedly to be preserved by the imposition of a fine and the banning of the play, less than four years later it is staged, received with quiet respect, and recognized to be a moral tract for the times, no less. Can anyone be proved to have been depraved or corrupted by it? Has it led to sadistic orgies? Or riots in the streets of Chelsea? Where, then, are all the arguments which maintained stage censorship in being for decades? "Oh well, old boy, if you allowed that sort of thing, who knows what might happen?" Well, now we know the answer. *Nothing* except that some people emerge from the theatre with a deeper insight, a greater compassion for the sufferings of some of their fellow human beings.[25]

24. Irving Wardle, "The Edward Bond View of Life," London *Times*, 15 March 1970, p. 21.
25. Martin Esslin, "Bond Unbound," *Plays and Players* 16, no. 7 (April 1969): 33.

Finally, Peter Roberts, the editor of *Plays and Players*, called the European tour staging of *Saved* the best English production of 1969.[26]

Saved is made up of thirteen scenes: six in the living room of a South London flat; two in a bedroom of that same flat; three in a park near it; and one each in a cell and in a café. An intermission is recommended after the seventh scene. As human possibilities are reduced, the scenes become increasingly interior and restrictive. All of the park scenes occur in the first act, and four of the living-room scenes occur in the second act.

The play opens with the seduction of a South London working-class boy named Len by a girl named Pam. She brings him to the flat of her parents who haven't spoken to one another for years. There Len settles in happily, falls in love with Pam, and even plans to marry her. She soon tires of him, however, and takes up with a young "stud" named Fred. Pam is devoted to Fred and has his baby, but Fred grows restive even before the baby is born and is anxious to break off all ties. Len, doggedly devoted, alternates between trying to reawaken Pam's interest through the tender care he takes of both her and the baby, which is otherwise ignored, and a genuine attempt to patch up affairs between her and Fred. One such attempt in the park is followed by an argument between Pam and Fred, after which she exits angrily, followed by Len, and leaves behind the baby. In the first scene banned by the Lord Chamberlain, Fred's mates, later goading Fred into taking part, begin with playing with the baby and end by smearing it with its own excrement and stoning it to death. From a distance Len sees the killing, but he does nothing. The act ends with Fred being visited in a jail cell by Len and a tearful, still-infatuated Pam.

Act Two chonicles the deteriorating relationship between

26. Peter Roberts, "A Last Look at 1969," *Plays and Players* 17, no. 4 (January 1970): 24.

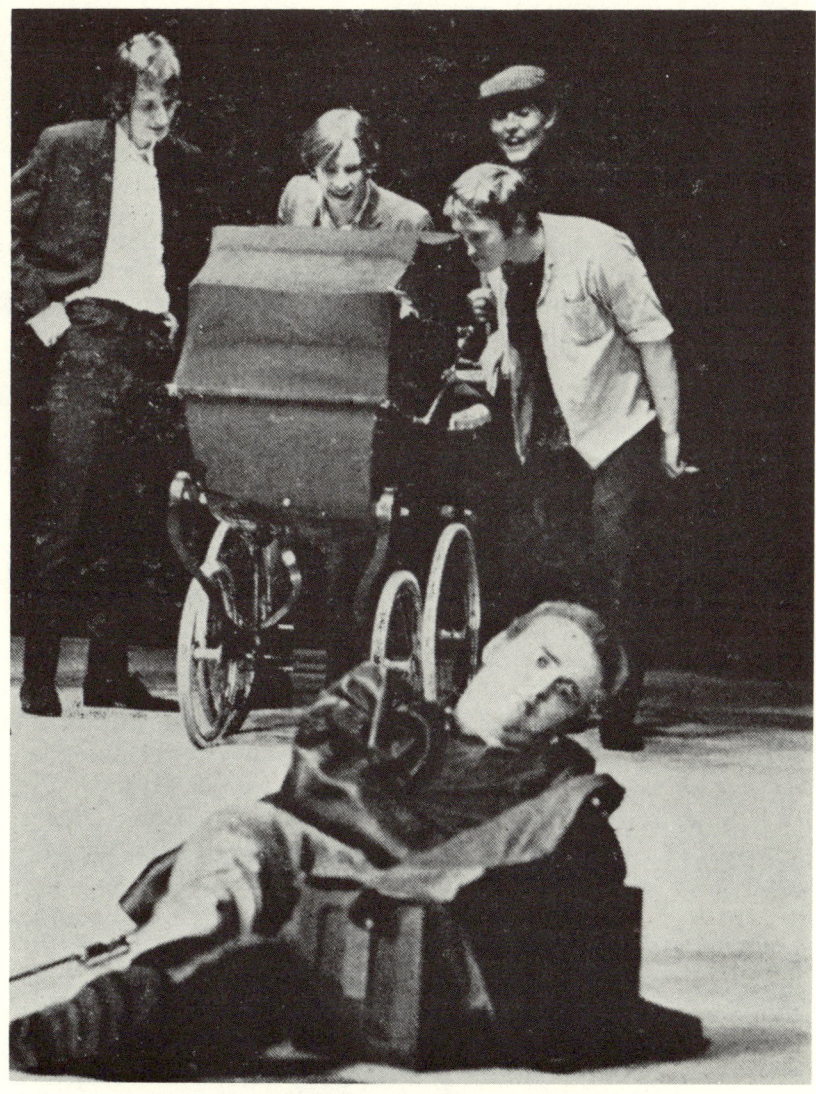

The baby-killing scene from Saved
(Photo courtesy of the Royal Court Theatre, S.W.1, London; photo by Zoë Dominic)

Pam and Len, on whom she blames all her troubles. It is the repeat of the pattern of gradual and continuing estrangement suffered by Pam's parents, Harry and Mary. In the second scene banned by the censor, Len's sexual frustration drives him to Mary, and what begins as a simple case of stocking-mending very nearly turns into a seduction scene. It is interrupted by Harry, who leaves without comment. Fred's release from prison is the occasion for a celebration breakfast given by his friends and co-murderers. Len and Pam attend uninvited, and when she tries to force herself on Fred, she is humiliated and dismissed. Len makes one more effort to reunite himself and Pam. An argument between Mary and Harry over Len ends with the latter's being bashed by a teapot. Len, entering, tries to help but is drawn into the fight and finally agrees to leave. Harry visits Len in his room. He talks about his past with his wife and convinces Len that things would be just the same elsewhere. The play ends in a silent stalemate with all four household members in the same room. None speak with the exception of Len, who asks for a tool to help him in his attempt to fix a chair that was broken earlier in the fight. No one answers. No one helps.

Edward Bond has called *Saved* "formally a comedy" and "almost irresponsibly optimistic." [27] These two statements define simultaneously Bond's view of the universe and the cool objectivity with which he explains it. In Bond's universe, tragedy is possible because of the strict limitations placed on man, but the gods play no part—except as rationalizations for inhumane action—in defining limits and punishing the disobedient. This responsibility belongs to man himself, acting in the name of social, governmental, and religious abstractions, abstractions that man himself has created, which corrupt him and which are totally antithetical to his human needs. *Saved* is a comedy, not because its pro-

---

27. Edward Bond, Preface to *Saved* (New York: Hill and Wang, 1965), p. 7.

Saved

tagonist, Len, is victorious, but because he refuses to recognize defeat. It is also an Oedipal comedy. On one level, Len is in opposition to Harry, the father of Pam and the owner of the flat where Len boards. Harry is also the man whom Len will obviously become, and Harry's wife is sexually attracted to Len. Yet, despite these Freudian implications, Len and Harry do not destroy one another.

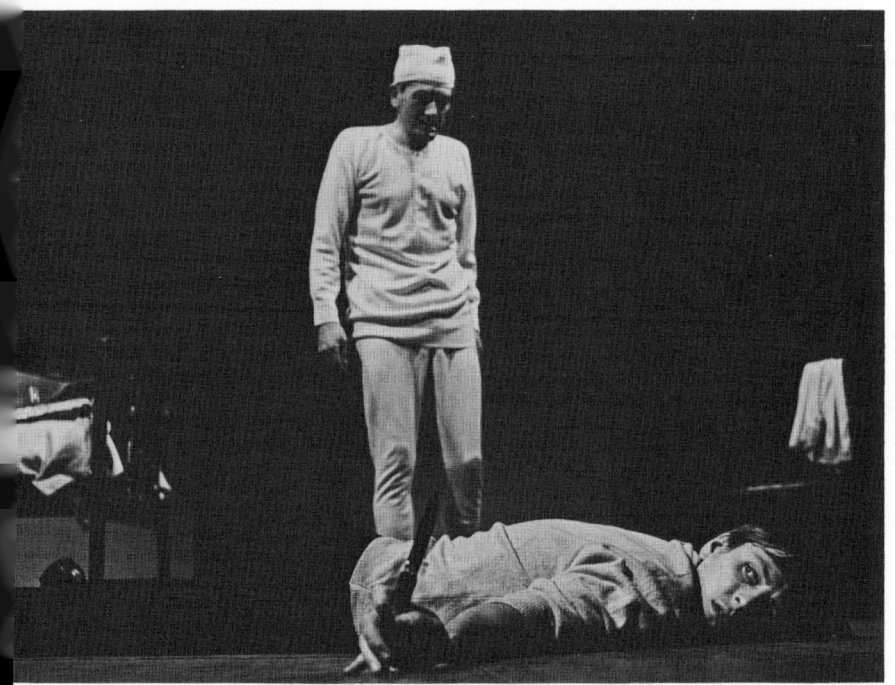

Harry and Len in Saved
(Photo courtesy of the Royal Court Theatre, S.W.1, London; photo by Donald Cooper, London)

The Oedipus outcome should be a row and death. There *is* a row and even a struggle with a knife—but Len persists in trying to help. The next scene starts with him stretched on the floor with a knife in his hand, and the old man comes in dressed as a ghost—but neither of them is dead. They talk, and for once in the play someone apart from Len is as honest and friendly as it is possible for him to be. The old man can only give a widow's mite; but in the context it is a victory—and a shared victory. It is trivial to talk of defeat in this context. The only sensible object in defeating an enemy is to make him your friend. This happens in the play, although in fact most social and personal problems are solved by alienation or killing.[28]

Saved, however, is an Oedipal comedy on yet another level. Its characters are the children of their society, sacrificed for the preservation of the industrial society Blake characterized as the "Dark Satanic Mills." Yet even the awesome restrictions of society have not destroyed Len's basic goodness. At the same time, Len has not triumphed over his society. The play remains, at final curtain, ambivalent in its attitude.

William Gaskill, Bond's chief interpreter, has said of *Saved:* "Whatever Edward may say I cannot find its ending optimistic." [29] If the synonym for optimism must be ambivalence, it is difficult to dispute him. Len has "saved" humanity from defeat, but Bond has traced the patterns of deterioration too clearly for us to believe in any kind of ultimate triumph. The path followed by Len and trod by Harry before him is that of Beckett's *Endgame,* circular and reductive as long as life lasts. Nevertheless, there is a significant difference between the philosophies of Beckett and Bond. Beckett's heroes are condemned to hope, a pain from which they would be gladly released. They continue to live because their humanity allows them no other choice. Bond's heroes cling stubbornly to their humanity, accepting even their pain as a sign of life.

The authenticity of Bond's dialogue is without question,

28. Bond, Preface to *Saved,* pp. 5–6.
29. Gaskill, letter, 19 March 1971.

but it is never naturalism for its own sake. In form, as much as in content, it conveys the play's motivations and themes. It is richly comic and, surprisingly, capable of carrying several levels of meaning simultaneously.

The earliest critics of *Saved* credited Edward Bond ungraciously with the power to reproduce South London speech.

> It is fluent and, so far as an outsider can tell, an accurate transcription of South London speech: but a tape recorder could reveal almost as much. . . . It strikes the audience like a handful of gravel thrown against the window (an effect I imagine Bond intended); its only departure from literal naturalism being a suspiciously conniving attitude towards the audience.[30] The author's single asset, if this is the word, is an ear for the loose lingo of vicious teenagers and the semiarticulate banalities of their elders. He reproduces the dialogue faithfully and (so it seems) without bothering to select: a recording of the slovenly, obscene horrors of everyday speech that might have been caught on tape.[31]

A few, like Mollie Panter-Downes, found *Saved*'s authenticity of language "magnificent";[32] the majority, like Hilary Spurling, found it merely "excessively boring."[33] That its authenticity might cause difficulties was admitted by the English Stage Company when it preceded its revival of *Saved* in 1969 with a neardocumentary of the same milieu, *Life Price*.[34] The publishers of the *Saved* text have supplied no fewer than twenty-seven footnotes to explain the meaning of a word or phrase, a precaution that is far from excessive and that must be unparalleled in a contemporary play being

30. Irving Wardle, "The Wrong Quarrel over the Wrong Play," *New Society* 56 (25 November 1965): 27.
31. Trewin, p. 32.
32. Mollie Panter-Downes, "Letter from London," *New Yorker* 41 (11 December 1965): 231.
33. Hilary Spurling, "A Difference of Opinion," *Spectator* 215 (12 November 1965): 619.
34. Wardle, "The Edward Bond View of Life," p. 21.

published in its own country. Beyond the words themselves is the even greater problem of accent. The first American production of *Saved* at the Yale Repertory Theater suffered from the "problem—perhaps inevitable . . . of lapsing accent or New York inflection." [35] William Gaskill was speaking in First Precepts when he discussed the casting of the revival of *Saved*.

> As a director casting Bond text, the speaking of it is almost the first essential. It's got to sound right. And certainly in *Saved* it was essential to have a high proportion of London-born people in it to speak it properly. Because it's extraordinarily inflected with a London ear. We have had Northerners in it in some of the parts, and they can get away with it, but you have to have some Cockneys in it. When you hear people read it you know that some of them will never get the sound right however good they may be as actors.[36]

The basic mode of speech in *Saved* is the attack, but it is seldom sustained and reflects no particular personal aggressiveness. It is the attack of the teased, trapped animal, striking at anything that comes too close to it out of fear or the momentary relief that comes from inflicting pain that it cannot feel itself. It jabs, then retreats with bared fangs in fear of both retaliation and, surprisingly, of the damage caused. Even when the intent does exist, that intent is hidden, possibly even from the attacker. For example, Pam's wish for Len to leave the flat before Fred is released from prison is expressed in an incessant quibbling over the location of her copy of the *Radio Times*.

To this atmosphere of pared-down communication, Bond has brought the perfect form: a pared-down line of five or six syllables that screams for verification even as it denies it

35. Feingold, "Ensembles," p. 65.
36. William Gaskill, quoted by Irving Wardle in "An Interview with William Gaskill," *Gambit* 5, no. 17: 41.

Saved

to others. The people of *Saved* mistrust words, as they mistrust any human symbol or extention that might reveal them to themselves. Len stands apart from his mates in a manner that recalls Cincinnatus in Nabokov's *Invitation to a Beheading*. While Cincinnatus is condemned for obliqueness, Len is condemned for questioning obliqueness, for searching and suggesting by his questions the possibility of answers and reasons. In *Saved*, language as a tool functions only to hold others at a distance. For example, Pam, having picked up Len and brought him to her parents' flat, is willing to share her body, but avoids all other contact.

> LEN. Wass yer name?
> PAM. Yer ain' arf nosey.
> LEN. Somethin' up?
> PAM. Can't I blow me nose? (*She puts her hanky back in her bag and puts it on the table.*) Better. (*She sits on the couch.*)
> LEN. Wass yer name?
> PAM. Wass yourn? . . . .
> LEN. 'Ow often yer done this?
> PAM. Don't be nosey.[37]

Bond claims to share his characters' distaste for words:

> I dislike anybody who imagines the answers to life are cerebral and that the problems are cerebral. . . . I dislike that sort of cerebral activity that imagines problems exist somewhere out *there* and don't exist *here*. One lives in the world and one must find one's way of living in the world.[38]

This attitude toward intellectualisms is illustrated by having the baby-killing Fred present the play's only plea for law and order. "I don't know what'll 'appen. There's bloody gangs like that roamin' everywhere. The bloody police don't do their job" (vii, 58).

37. Edward Bond, *Saved* (New York: Hill and Wang, 1965), i, pp. 11–12. All subsequent references to *Saved* will be noted in the text.
38. Wardle, "A Discussion with Edward Bond," pp. 18–19.

The ironic humor of the speech is, of course, not accidental. In the gang scenes and in Len's first scene with Pam, Bond has captured the "kind of cockney badinage which is disappearing in the streets but finding a loving home in the theatre, where it has always half-belonged." [39] Nevertheless, Bond's technical proficiency with language in *Saved* extends beyond a tape-recorder accuracy. An early reader of the play noted with surprised pleasure the importance of rhythm: "Edward Bond has all of the fascination of a metronome with all of those four-word speches." [40]

MARY. . . . I could a gone t'bed, an' I will next time 'e arsts me.
HARRY. Now 'e's caught a sniff a yer 'e'll be off with 'is tail between 'is legs! (*She hits him with the teapot. The water pours over him. Pam is too frightened to move.*) Ah!
MARY. 'Ope yer die!
HARRY. Blood!
PAM. Mum! . . . .
HARRY. Doctor.
MARY. Cracked me weddin' present. 'Im. (*Len comes in.*)
LEN. Blimey!
HARRY. Scalded!
PAM. Whas's 'appenin'? . . . .
HARRY. Yer saw 'er.
MARY. 'E went mad.
LEN. 'E's all wet.
PAM. (*To Mary.* Why? . . . .
HARRY. Blood.
PAM. (*To Mary.*) Whas's 'e done?
LLEN. 'E's all wet.
MARY. Swore at me!
PAM. Why?
HARRY. Doctor.
MARY. There's nothin' wrong with 'im.
HARRY. Scalded.

39. Hugo Williams, "Theatre," *London Magazine* 6 (January 1966): 67–68.
40. Sheilah Ling, letters on *Saved*, *Plays and Players* 13, no. 5 (March 1966): 8.

MARY. I 'ardly touched 'im. 'E needs a good thrashin'!
LEN. *(To Pam.)* Get a towel.
HARRY. I ain't allowed t' touch the towels.
MARY. I kep' this twenty-three years. Look what 'e's done to it!
PAM. *What 'appened?*
LEN. *(Looking at Harry's head.)* Yer'll 'ave t' wash that cut. It's got tea leaves in it (xi, 85–87).

Even as Bond's sense of rhythm enables him to generate unforced laughter from a potentially ugly domestic scene, it can also give a seemingly naturalistic speech a number of levels of meaning—a virile and nonacademic poetry. While Len and Fred are fishing in the park, Len makes an attempt to convince Fred to return to Pam. This effort is interrupted by Fred's realization that the bait is gone from his hook.

LEN. Gone? They've 'ad it away. . . .
FRED. More like wriggled off.
LEN. I mounted it 'ow yer said.
FRED. *(Winds in.)* Come 'ere. Look *(He takes a worm from the worm box).* Right, yer take yer worm. Yer roll it in yer 'and t' knock it out. Thas's first. Then yer break a bit off. Cop 'old a that. *(He gives part of the worm to Len.)* . . . Now yer thread yer 'ook, but yer leave a fair bit 'anging off like that, why, t'wiggle in the water. Then yer push yer top bit down off the gut and camer-flarge yer shank. Got it?
LEN. Thas's 'ow I done it.
FRED. Yeh. Main thing, keep it neat. *(He casts. The line hums.)* Lovely. *(A long silence.)* The life. *(Silence.)*
LEN. Down the labour Monday. *(Fred grunts.)* Start somethin'. *(Silence.)* No life, broke.
FRED. True. *(Silence. Len pokes in the worm box with a stick.)* Feed 'em on milk.
LEN. *(Silence.)* I'll tell 'er yer ain' comin' (vi, 39).

The undertones are sexual and understood by the audience, if not by the characters. Fred stresses not only the superiority of his sexual technique to Len's, but the irrevocability of his break with Pam. His purely physical interests are over and he feels no moral responsibility for their consequences.

An actual physical environment plays a more important part in *Saved* than in any other Bond play. The characters are exhausted by the inhumanity of their setting. Its unchanging and unhospitable sterility is reflected in the characters' relationships with time, their world, and with one another.

> I always get the impression, whether it's true or not, that it's [South London] more industrialized. I've got a feeling, too, that it's physically flatter there—and those miles and miles of long straight streets that always look the same. I used to call it the brick desert, and this feeling of being in a desert of bricks seemed to be absolutely right for the play.[41]

The events of *Saved* must take years, but time makes no changes in the atmosphere of the play. The "desert of bricks" is as immune to change as it is barren. The men in *The Pope's Wedding* at least saw the variation of the seasons and felt some satisfaction in their work.

> RON. I oiled that owd Ferguson this mornin'. Yoo should a seen 'er. My life! . . . .
> LORRY. (*Wiping scythe blade.*) Beautiful owd thing, ent she. 'Ung 'er up in owd apple tree t' take the rust out on 'er.[42]

In contrast, the factory workers of *Saved* never see the end product of their labor and think of their jobs only as disapreeable but inevitable interludes.

> COLIN. Workin'?
> LEN. Worse luck (iii, 26).

. . . .

41. Edward Bond, as quoted by Roger Hudson, Catherine Itzen, and Simon Trussler in "Drama and the Dialectics of Violence," *Theatre Quarterly* 2 (January–March 1972): 7–8.
42. Edward Bond, *The Pope's Wedding, Plays and Players* 16, no. 7 (April 1969): ii, 36 and ii, 38.

Saved

LEN. 'Ow's the job?
FRED. Don't talk about it (iv, 33).

. . . .

FRED. *(Shrugs, to Len.)* 'Ow's the job?
LEN. Stinks.
FRED. It don't change (x, 77).

Mechanical devices exist in the world of *The Pope's Wedding*, of course, but they are personal and immediate extensions of human beings. When the wringer on his mother's washing machine breaks, Bill can—and must—fix it himself. When the television set in *Saved* doesn't work, "the man'll 'ave to come an' fix it" (iv, 29).

Sex, which in *The Pope's Wedding* is treated as a mutual and pleasurable activity, is reduced to a calculated and impersonal hunt in *Saved*.

> They opened that new church on the corner. . . . Best place out for'n easy pick up. . . . I done it before. There's little pieces all over the shop, nothin' a do. . . . The ol' bleeder shuts 'is eyes for prayers an' they're touchin' 'em up all over the place. Then the law raided this one an' they 'ad it shut down. . . . If there's nothin' in the church, know what? . . . Do the all-night laundries. . . . Yer get all them little 'ousewives there (vi, 48, 50–51).

Even the violence of *Saved* is impersonal and unmotivated. It is basically defensive, the sociologically verifiable effect of too many people crowded too close together.[43]

> If you cage an animal so that it can't behave in a normal way, so that it always feels threatened by the things around it, it becomes violent: And if you threaten human beings all the

---

43. For example, in 1959, a French husband and wife sociology/psychology team, the Chombart de Lauwes, found that the optimum number of square meters per person was ten to fourteen per housing unit. When the space available was below ten square meters per person, social and physical pathologies doubled. Edward T. Hall, *The Hidden Dimension* (Garden City, New York: Doubleday & Company, Inc., 1966), p. 172.

while, they become violent. No animal can be subjected to too much noise, for instance, because noise means danger. We have the same function in us—we don't like noise. We are living on top of motorways. Biologically we cannot function. There are H-bombs in the air all the time. The human being today is always in a state of tension and of being scared and frightened, and is therefore aggressive.[44]

To Edward Bond, industrialization is political as well as economic and social. Its society has enforced upon humans strictures that can only lead to violence. It then calls that violence an inherent part of human nature and uses it as an excuse to add still more strictures. To Edward Bond, the son of North London working-class parents and a man who left school for work at the age of fifteen, the end product of the assembly line is dehumanization.

> Well, my background is typical of 75% of the people in this country and that is that I was brought up in very much the same sort of society as *Saved*. . . . They destroy people because I mean our society could not exist unless we were destroyed. A human being was not designed to work in a factory, I mean, just as a tool. You're not made to stand at a bench day after day doing these mechanical jobs. A human being is not designed for that. Now we live in a mechanical society. We make sure if we design a machine it carries out its function absolutely right with total efficiency. The grotesque thing is that human beings are used so inefficiently, they aren't made for that sort of thing, so that nobody can be happy. Human beings are adaptable, they can survive in prisons, but at a cost.[45]

It is possible that Bond's very success in recreating a naturalistic South London environment has hampered the acceptance of *Saved* in England. Bond's play is about the corrupting effect of society upon its children—a point

---

44. Bond, quoted by Hudson, *et al.*, "Drama and the Dialectics of Violence," p. 9.
45. Wardle, "A Discussion with Edward Bond," pp. 17–18.

Saved

missed by many for whom the realistic production of *Saved* made it seem to be only a specific instance, lacking in symbolic overtones. John Russell Taylor has suggested that showing the brutal murder of the baby in the park as merely the release of similar tensions to those already on view in the flat requires a less naturalistic production, in which setting, costuming, etc., could provide parallels that would suggest the other great atrocities of our century.[46] That *Saved* has had its greatest successes in non-English speaking countries, thus doubly removing them from its original milieu, supports Taylor's assessment.

The stoning of the baby is on one level the explosive release of the aggressions created by the dehumanizing restrictions of an industrialized society. On a more poetic level, however, the stoning is a metaphor for the restrictions themselves. Whether the method be murder or unnatural conditions and control, the end result is the same: the loss of innocence and humanity.

All of Bond's characters are children of society and all are more or less battered by it. In turn, they have become the instruments of society, destroying others. They are murdered Innocents, incapable of feeling or responding, capable only of murdering others.

> Clearly the stoning to death of a baby in a London park is a typical English understatement. Compared to the "strategic" bombing of German towns it is a negligible atrocity, compared to the cultural and emotional deprivation of most of our children its consequences are insignificant.[47]

Allowing for the already discussed pressure of environmental differences, the gangs in *The Pope's Wedding* (Bill, Joe, Byo, Len, Lorry, and Ron) and in *Saved* (Fred, Barry, Pete, Colin, and Mike) seem very nearly interchangeable.

---

46. John Russell Taylor, *The Second Wave* (London: Methuen and Co., Ltd., 1971), pp. 82–83.
47. Bond, Preface to *Saved*, p. 7.

They are witty, playful, and brutal by turns. The gangs function as a chorus to the action of Bond's central characters, the matrix out of which these characters arise. The gangs supply the societal norm and it is in their context that we must see the actions of Scopey and Len. In the later plays, when the spine of the action is the development of the protagonists's understanding of his environment, the chorus will be eliminated.

Bond's handling of the chorus in *Saved* shows a marked improvement in technique over *The Pope's Wedding*. Without sacrificing its collective environmental identity, Bond has used individual gang members to illustrate the mores and values of their society. Pete, the one gang member in *Saved* who has no parallel in the earlier play, effectively epitomizes what Bond believes to be the logical end result of the enmity between society and humanity. A brutal child-killer twice over, he is not ostracized by his peers but is the recipient of their adulation and envy.

COLIN. What a giggle, though.
MIKE. Accidents is legal.
COLIN. Can't touch yer.
PETE. This coroner-twit says 'e's sorry for troublin' me.
MIKE. The law thanks 'im for 'is 'elp.
PETE. They paid me for comin'.
MIKE. An' the nip's mother reckons 'e ain' got a blame 'isself.
COLIN. She'll turn up at the funeral.
PETE. Rraammmmmmmmm!
COLIN. Bad for the body work.
MIKE. Can't yer claim insurance? (iii, 24).

Whether or not Pete is actually guilty of the manslaughter for which he was exonerated is beside the point. He seeks and receives favor for both the act and the evasion of responsibility—a measure of both the man and his society. Pete is, at the beginning, what we will see Fred become in the course of the action. The norms of his society are legal and economic rather than moral and humane. Therefore, they are essentially restrictive rather than inspiring and the human reaction is to evade their consequences. Even in rebellion, their lesson has been internalized. The success or failure of an act depends upon whether or not you get caught and whether or not "yer 'ave t' make yer time up." Therefore, Pete not only feels no remorse for his actions, he has no sympathy for Fred who, in effect, took the blame for the entire gang: "Yer made yer own decisions, didn't yer? ... We ain' got a crawl up yer arse.... 'E ain' swingin' that one on me" (x, 79).

Furthermore, if Pete is considered as the model member of his society, those who would be successful can only attempt to surpass him in inhumanity. In *Saved*, Barry reacts jealously to Pete's intentionally running the boy down with his truck and because of his jealousy, he is made the focus of the gang's contempt.

> MIKE. Yer creep.
> COLIN. Yer big creep. . . . 'E don't know nothin'.
> MIKE. Big stingy creep.
> COLIN. Yer wouldn't 'ave the guts. . . . What yer scratchin'?
> MIKE. 'E's got a dose.
> PETE. Ain' surprisin'.
> COLIN. Ain' it dropped off yet?
> MIKE. Tied on with a ol' johnny.
> COLIN. It's 'is girl.
> MIKE. 'Is what?
> PETE. Gunged-up ol' boot (iii, 24–25).

Not surprisingly, it is Barry who first begins to tease the baby in the park. It is either he or Pete, whom he longed to emulate, who initiates each new stage in its destruction. In the end it is Barry who cannot bear to leave the scene and he is the last to cease his attack.

> Juss this one! (*He throws a stone as Peter pushes him over. It goes wide.*) Bastard! (*To Pete.*) Yer put me off! . . . I got

a get it once more! (*The others have gone up left. He takes a stone from the pram and throws it at point-blank range. Hits.*) Yar! . . . Bleedin' little sod! (*He hacks into the pram. He goes up left.*) (vi, 56).

It is a classic case of what is defined in the next chapter as social morality. Pete has learned his values from his environment and has passed them on to Barry. Barry is a successful man at last.

It is tempting to picture Fred as the villain in *Saved*. He fathered Pam's child, eventually abandoning her, and finally took a leading part in their child's death. On the other hand, there is no reason to believe that Fred's advances to Pam were unsolicited and his abandonment of her is certainly no more callous than her treatment of Len. Fred would have been perfectly willing to return Pam to Len, but he understands why this is impossible. He is possibly even sincere when he says that he failed to recognize Len's seriousness concerning her.

What d'yer expect? No—they're like that. Once they go off, they go right off. . . . 'Appens all the time. . . . I thought she was goin' spare. . . . I reckon it was up t' you t'say. Yer got a tongue in yer 'ead (vi, 40–42).

Fred's attitude toward the baby and, especially, his actions toward it are difficult to condone but not impossible to explain. As with the other characters in the play, the baby was never a human being to him. Still, he tries half-heartedly several times to halt the teasing and even refuses initially to take part in the stoning. It is not until he is convinced that "it's done now" (vi, 55) and the baby's death is inevitable, that he throws a stone. It misses, but with the act he is caught in the escalating, Oedipal frenzy of his mates. The killing happens because some kind of release from environmental pressures has to occur and this is available. Afterwards, Fred insists that the blame for the crime belongs elsewhere: to a passing gang; or to Pam for leaving the baby there, for bringing it in the first place and, ultimately, for having it.

> Blamin' me? Yer got bugger all t'blame me for, mate! Yer ruined my life, thas's all! . . . Why the bloody 'ell bring the little perisher out that time a night? . . . Yer got no right chasin' after me with a pram! Drop me right in it! . . . Never know why yer 'ad the little bleeder in the first place! Yer a bloody menace! (vii, 57).

Through its example, society teaches its members to ignore the needs of others: "I ain' gettin' involved. Bound t'be wrong," says Harry in a response to a plea from Pam (iv, 32). "I don't wan'a get involved, mate" is Len's reaction to a question about Pam's intentions (x, 80).

In his own mind, Fred is not guilty of any crime: "It was only a kid" (vii, 59), and besides, "I wer'n the only one" (x, 82). After his release Fred explodes in anger when Len questions him as to his feeling during the killing. To admit feeling would be to admit the humanity of his victim and to admit humanity would be to admit his own culpability. Yet, the effect of his crime on Fred is central to an understanding of *Saved*.

> I wanted to show that violence and what you could call misdirected sex cannot be indulged in in an interlude from normal life and then forgotten; the agent is affected as well as the victim. These effects change the structure of his life in less obvious but more far-reaching ways than the effects of social exposure or punishment. They force compromises and give psychological wounds that often turn the remainder of his life into tragedy.[48]

For all Fred's denial of his guilt, he has subconsciously accepted both it and the definition of himself that guilt provides. He has killed, is capable of killing, and will kill again. This is evident from his own words.

48. Edward Bond, "Censor in Mind," *Censorship* 4 (Autumn 1965): 9.

> Yer're arstin' for trouble. I don't wan'a go back juss yet. . . . So I gets 'im on the landin' an' clobbers 'im. . . . Keep yer 'ands off me! So 'elp me I'll land yer so bloody 'ard they'll put me back for life! (x, 76, 78, 83).

We never see Fred again after this scene, but Len clearly predicts his future: "Yer ain' seen what it done t' 'im. 'E's like a kid. 'E'll finish up like some ol' lag, or an ol' soak. Bound to. An' soon. Yer'll see" (xii, 91). Like Pete, Fred has become socially moralized. That is, pressured by his environment (the gang) into committing a crime, he has accepted the definition of himself given by the social institutions that created his environment. He is a criminal and therefore must act as one.

It has been previously noted how Bond used contrasting scenes for structural effect and group characters as representative of environment. He also uses individual characters to show the way in which his protagonists might have developed. Seen from that viewpoint, the structural differences between the natures of Bill and Fred may well stem from the differences between Scopey and Len. Although both Scopey and Len function as thinkers and questioners of their respective societies, the former initiates action and follows it through. Dimly aware, as is Len of the shortcomings of the accepted life-style, he seeks an alternative in the hermit existence of Alen. In contrast, Bill is passive, pursued by Ol' Man Bullright's wife, ousted by Scopey from Pat's affections, and inheriting her again when Scopey drifts away from society. Len, on the other hand, initiates no action. Picked up by Pam, he loses her to Fred without protest and thereafter acts only in her behalf or in reaction to her. Unlike Scopey, who confronts his situation and ultimately is defeated by it, Len avoids confrontation and attempts, within a steadily narrowing range of opportunities, to continue existing relationships. Scopey *takes* Alen's place in society, but Len does not try to supplant Harry. He merely becomes part of Harry's household and, by his presence, keeps that household alive.

> Harry acts as the *representative* of the family when he comes to Len's room. All the members of the family need Len in some way because he's the only human being they know—the only one who's learned anything from the park killing. When Len stays, it's a moral act, though its effect is limited to one house.[49]

Other than the young man, the most obvious character similarities in the two plays lie between Alen, the hermit, and Harry, Pam's father. Both exist in an isolation that has gradually increased over the years, and both, to some extent, have that isolation penetrated by the Innocent figure (Scopey/Len). The isolation of Alen is external and obvious. His contact with others is limited to the absolute minimum required to keep him alive. Indeed, he fears anything else. This fear is not the cause of his isolation, however, but the result. Within his limits, Alen becomes friendly with Scopey, despite the fact that Scopey virtually forces his company on the old man, and his reaction to Pat's return after a long absence is touching. Under the layers of legend and time, the reason for Alen's living apart is simple: His parents always lived apart from others, which made them different. The passage of time made it increasingly difficult to bridge that difference. Ironically, Alen remains unharmed only so long as he maintains the isolation that is his curse. To be different is a singular thing and Scopey learns Alen's identity only at the cost of his own identity and Alen's life.

As Alen's isolation is external, Harry's is internal. To some extent, Harry is a functioning member of his community: he lives in a South London flat with his wife, his daughter, and a lodger; he is a war veteran; he holds a

---

49. Edward Bond, letter to Richard Scharine, 2 October 1974.

regular job; and he faithfully fills out his coupon for the football pools. Yet he has not spoken to his wife for as long as his daughter (who is twenty-five) can remember, and he breaks this silence in only one scene, which results in his being hit on the head with a teapot. He very quickly exits when he comes across his daughter bedding down with a strange young man in the living room and leaves just as quickly later in the play when he discovers the same young man in the same living room with his hand up his wife's dress. He ventures no opinions on anything but the most concrete of subjects and yet, over the years, his position within the household has become more and more tenuous.

> HARRY. She thinks she's on top. I'll 'ave t' fall back a bit—buy a few things an' stay in me room more. I can wait. . . . I left 'er once. . . . I come back. . . .I worked it out. Why should I soil me 'ands washin' an' cookin'? Let 'er do it. She'll find out.
> LEN. Yer do yer own washin'.
> HARRY. Eh?
> LEN. An' cookin.
> HARRY. Ah, *now* (xii, 90–93).

Harry's isolation differs from Alen's in that it is still evolving. It is similar, however, in that it prefigures the course of action for the Innocent character. At the beginning of *The Pope's Wedding,* Alen is completely alone in the shack. At its close he has been replaced literally and symbolically by Scopey. Alen's position was defined and fixed by time and circumstance; Scopey's act of murder fixes his position just as unchangeably. In the course of *Saved,* Harry makes just one more step toward a complete separation from those in his house: a reduction of his domestic privileges by Mary.

> Yer can leave my things alone for a start. All this stuff come out a my pocket. I worked for it! I ain' 'avin' you dirtyin' me kitchin. Yer can get yerself some new towels for a start!

An' plates! An' knives! An' cups! Yer'll soon find a difference! . . . An' my cooker! An' my curtains! An' my sheets! (xi, 85).

To watch the baby-stoning scene in *Saved* is horrifying, but far worse are the implications of society's condoned violence. "None of the people in *Saved* do anything they couldn't get a medal for under other circumstances."[50] Domestic restrictions dehumanize and cause violence, an excuse society uses for more restrictions. Under given circumstances, however, society licences dehumanization and violence and rewards it. When asked if he killed anyone during the war, Harry's answer shows no consciousness of any humanity among his country's political enemies.

Must 'ave. Yer never saw the bleeders, 'ceptin' prisoners or dead. Well, I did once. I was in a room. Some bloke stood up in the door. Lost, I expect. I shot 'im. 'E fell down. Like a coat fallin' off a 'anger, I always say. Not a word. (*Pause*.) Yer never killed yer man. Yer missed that. Gives yer a sense of perspective. I was one a the lucky ones (xii, 92).

In his relationship with Mary, Harry has passed through the same circumstances as have Len and Pam. Furthermore, by his example, he suggests their likely future. First there was premarital sex: Harry and Mary have been married twenty-three years, and Pam is twenty-five-years old. Even earlier there was a little boy who, like Pam's child, died in the park. Second, Mary, like Pam, has been periodically unfaithful. Now they merely coexist, embodying the lifetime of implacable silence that awaits Len and Pam. At the close of the play, Harry still nurses visions of leaving, but they are as hollow as Len's stated intention to Pam not to emulate her parents: "I won't turn out like that. I wouldn't arst yer if I didn't know better'n that" (ii, 21). The fact is that Len

50. Charles Marowitz, "If a House Is on Fire and I Cry Fire," *New York Times*, 2 January 1972, sec. 2, p. 5.

will turn out like that and Harry will be his teacher. Presuming that he cannot continue to question without receiving answers, Len has only two other choices: he could adopt the ethic of society, become brutalized, and strike out against individuals; or he could see society as the true villain and become revolutionary. To both these alternatives he is temperamentally and intellectually unsuited.

Yet, Len is not a saint among sinners. His motivations and his actions are simetimes ambivalent. For example, he claims parenthood and responsibility for the child primarily as an excuse to stay near Pam. Later, he returns to the park in time to have prevented the baby's death, but does not. The first is forgivable, because it results, at least, in the only interest shown in the child during its lifetime. The second is harder to understand, but the key may be found in the morbid curiosity Len exhibits about the sensations of the murderers.

> LEN. What was it like?
> FRED. No, talk about somethin' else.
> LEN. No, *before.*
> FRED. Yer 'eard the trial. . . .
> LEN. What was it like?
> FRED. I tol' yer.
> LEN. No. before.
> FRED. Before what?
> LEN. In the park.
> FRED. Yer saw.
> LEN. Was's it feel like?
> FRED. Don't know.
> LEN. When yer was killin' it.
> FRED. Do what?
> LEN. Was's it feel like when yer killed it? . . . Whas's it like, Fred?
> FRED. (*Drinks.*) It ain't like this in there.
> LEN. Fred.
> FRED. I tol' yer.
> LEN. No, yer ain'.

Saved

FRED. I forget.
LEN. I thought yer'd a bin full a it. I was—
FRED. Len!
LEN. Curious, thas's all, 'ow it feels t'—
FRED. No. (*He slams his fist on the table.*) (x, 80–81).

Bond suggests that "the murder of the baby shows the Oedipus, atavistic fury fully unleashed,"[51] the destructive force released when severe restrictions and inhibitions are even momentarily removed. Society has taught men that they must be restricted or they will kill. Therefore, when the restrictions are lifted, they *do* kill. Len sees this fury and, recognizing it instinctively, is both afraid of it and fascinated by it. He is witness and accomplice, but he is not alone. The audience witnesses with him—as it witnesses a thousand worse atrocities daily—and, like Len, it does nothing.

"This sort of fury is what is kept under painful control by other people in the play, and that partly accounts for the corruption of their lives."[52] The silence between Harry and Mary is frustration and controlled rage, and its effect is felt as much by Pam as by her parents. In his theory of child and personality development, psychologist Abraham Maslow postulates that a child advances by the process of choosing between the need for safety and the delight of new experiences that lead toward change and growth. If the child does not feel safe in the present, it will turn inward and will not feel free to contemplate change in the future.[53]

Because Len questions things as they are, he represents a threat to Pam. It is painful for Pam to admit that her family life might have been different; for to admit the possibility of love is to admit the certainty of rejection. There-

51. Bond, Preface to *Saved*, p. 6.
52. Bond, Preface to *Saved*, p. 6.
53. See Maslow's concept discussed in Kim Giffin and Mary Heider, "The Relation between Speech Anxiety and the Suppression of Communication in Childhood," in *Basic Readings in Interpersonal Communication*, eds. Kim Giffin and Bobby R. Patton (New York: Harper & Row, 1971), pp. 52–53.

fore, she responds to his constant questions about her parents' mutual silence with an equally constant series of negatives and evasions.

> Never arst. . . . Never listen. It's their life. . . . Yer can't do nothin', yer know. No one'll thank yer. . . . Never know'd no difference. . . . No need. . . . Nothing t' say. . . . I never 'eard 'em. . . . *No!* (ii, 20–21).

Pam's whole life has been a struggle to adapt to existing conditions. To question their validity at this late date is beyond her stunted emotional capacities.

For Pam, Fred is a welcome relief. Len is searching and sincere; Fred is determinedly casual and plays the game on an easily understood and undemanding physical level. However, as Bond has pointed out, the effects of misdirected sex are just as pernicious to the agent as violence. Both "force compromises and give psychological wounds that often turn the remainder of life into tragedy." [54] As Fred's life is warped by casual violence, Pam's is warped by casual sex. The depth of her feeling is as much a factor in driving away Fred as was Len's searching in frightening her. It is a modern exercise in tragic irony. Both Len and Pam have exceeded the limits of feelings as defined by the forces that shaped their world. Fittingly, it is Len that Pam blames for her loss of Fred: "'E started this. . . . Somebody's got a save me from 'im" (x, 82). To be saved within the existing society is to be stunted as an emotional being. Pam cannot be "saved" because she loves Fred. The passion cuts her off from both the emotional numbness that is the mark of her society and the one man who could appreciate her love, Len.

Pam's tragedy is traceable to Mary and Harry, but as it did not begin with them, it does not end with her. According to Maslow, one of the consequences of a child's sense of rejection is a reduction in communication. These communications and the subsequent responses to them are ultimately

---

54. Bond, "Censor in Mind," p. 9.

the foundation of self-identity. The lack of a self-identity leads to a further insecurity and defensiveness, and, finally, to the withholding of recognition and interpersonal trust from others.[55] Thus, her parents withdrawal from one another and from Pam precipitated Pam's withdrawal from Len. The pattern comes full cycle with Pam's treatment of her own baby.

Pam's baby was never recognized as a human being. In the first scene following the baby's birth, it cries incessantly and without comfort offstage while onstage, Pam, Len, and Mary argue over the responsibility of seeing to it. Harry says nothing. The others, ultimately, do nothing. We do not even know that it is a boy until the gang takes away its diaper in the murder scene. Pam kept the baby doped with aspirin to reduce its emotional demands on her. When the doped baby fails to respond to their teasing in the park, the boys increase their violence upon it. The baby is killed because it never received what Pam lacked from her own parents—a human identity. In an obvious Bondian parallel, the baby stoned to death in the park is as much a victim of society-condoned actions as Mary's son who died in the park during wartime bombing. The program for the original production of *Saved* included a quotation from William Blake: "Sooner murder an infant in its cradle than nurse unacted desires." It is fitting epigram, but one that was widely misunderstood. For society to deny to humans their basic needs to love, create, protect, and enjoy is to murder the humanity in them as surely as if they had been stoned to death in their cribs.

What ultimately defines Len's goodness, as indeed it defines the characters in all Bond's plays, is his actions. He is sincere in his love for Pam, to the point of trying to reconcile his rival to her because that is the way she wants it. At the end of the play, he alone persists in trying to reverse the growing social malaise that infects the household. He mends the chair.

55. Giffin and Heider, p. 53.

(*Len gets off the chair and crouches beside it. His back is to the audience. He bends over the chair so that stomach or chest rest on the seat. He reaches down with his left hand and pulls the loose rear leg up into the socket. . . . Len slips his left arm round the back of the chair. His chest rests against the side edge of the seat. The fingers of his right hand touch the floor. His head lies sideways on the seat.*) (xii, 96).

It is a powerful theatrical image, the first physical evidence of Bond's fascination with crucifixion representations. Nevertheless, for a resurrection we must wait until *Early Morning*.

Saved clearly is one of the most important English plays of the 1960s, just as John Osborne's *Look Back in Anger* was probably the most pivotal English play of the 1950s. Osborne unintentionally revolutionized the English theater. Bond intentionally aims to revolutionize English society. Written twenty years after Great Britain's socialization, *Saved* is the first great dramatic self-indictment of the welfare state. Jimmy Porter was a university man who chose to run a sweetstall in protest of a bourgeois society. Ronnie Kahn was a leftist intellectual who saw in the education of the working classes a Utopian tomorrow. The characters of *Saved* have no such spokesman, no such intellect, no such alternative, and no such vision. They are a stunted, inarticulate, dehumanized people whose very condition speaks volumes. They are rendered with accuracy and seeming clinical detachment—not because their creator lacks compassion for them, but because he detests the sentimentality that would allow his audiences to accept, without changing, the conditions that created them.

Saved established Edward Bond as more than just a documentarist with a tape recorder. If he showed an unparalleled ear for common speech, he also displayed a selective ability that allowed him to move easily from low farce to high lyricism. If his structuring seemed naturalistic and undisciplined, it included nothing unnecessary to his themes. If his characters were not always sympathetic, they were never unbelievable. More than anything else, Edward Bond is an artist who uses his art as a prosecuting attorney uses his brief: the defendant is the social order; the crime is perversion of the innocent; and the evidence is *Saved.*

4
Early Morning:
And the Word Was Made Flesh

On the day of the opening of *Early Morning*, 31 March 1968, Alen Brien summed up the progress Edward Bond had made in five and one-half years of being a produced playwright.

> His first play, *The Pope's Wedding*, was given only a single Sunday-night production at the Royal Court in 1962. . . . His third play, *Early Morning*, a comic fantasy about a civil war over the succession to the throne in the time of Queen Victoria, opens tonight at the Court for *two* Sunday productions. Such is the progress toward fame and fortune made in London's swinging theatre by one of Britain's most original and uncompromising playwrights.[1]

Even in his irony, however, Brien proved to be overly optimistic about Bond's staying power on the Royal Court stage.

---

1. Alen Brien, "This Bond has not been much Honoured," London *Sunday Times*, 31 March 1968, p. 55.

Early Morning 83

The proposed second performance of *Early Morning*, scheduled for 7 April was canceled by the office of the Lord Chamberlain—the last play to receive this honor before the office was stripped of its responsibilities.

The brief light of *Early Morning* had been a long time in coming. In February 1966, while one arm of the government was engaged in the removal of Bond's *Saved* from the English Stage Company's repertory, another—The Arts Council —was awarding Bond a £1,000 bursary to enable him to write more plays. The product of this grant was delayed, however, by a screenwriting stint (*Blow-up* for Michelangelo Antonioni) and a commissioned adaptation of Chekhov's *The Three Sisters*, which opened at the Royal Court in June 1967. Nevertheless, the public had not forgotten Bond nor were they unaware totally of what awaited them in *Early Morning*. As early as 4 August 1967, the London *Times* headlined its first story on the production, "Lesbian Charge in Victoria Play." The English Stage Company had anticipated the official reaction and had already limited the showing of the play to a member audience. Asked for its reaction, the Lord Chamberlain's office would only say that it wouldn't "comment upon a play unless it comes within our jurisdiction." [2] This was presumed to mean, as it had earlier been presumed with *Saved*, that the Lord Chamberlain would take no action against a play to be presented to a private audience. Again, this presumption proved to be incorrect.

Early Morning was originally intended to open on 23 January 1968, for a three-week season, but was delayed when William Gaskill contracted pneumonia.[3] As the delay extended, outside pressures mounted. Eventually the decision was made to limit the production to a pair of showcase performances—an action that could be interpreted in

---
2. London *Times*, "Lesbian Charge in Victoria Play," 4 August 1967, p. 2.
3. London *Times*, "Gaskill Strikes Again," 21 March 1968, p. 10.

light of subsequent happenings as either brave or cowardly.

The combined circumstances of a Sunday-night production and certain predispositions toward the author and his subject matter limited the sheer quantity of criticism actually directed toward the play itself. In quality, however, it rivaled that of *Saved,* and, as before, the pack was led by Irving Wardle of the London *Times.* In his review, entitled, "Muddled Fantasy on Brutalization," Wardle took Bond to task for his use of historical figures and the English Stage Company for its production of the play:

> But what I regret is that the Royal Court's just and necessary fight for theatrical free speech should be conducted on behalf of a piece as muddled and untalented as this. . . . Mr. Bond regards politicians as gangsters and has every right to portray them as such. But what on earth is being proved by taking a group of well-known historical figures and inventing an action fantastically at variance with their lives. It would not be necessary to ask this question if *Early Morning* were simply a joke at the expense of not-so-sacred British cows. . . . But on the whole *Early Morning* is not, and is not intended to be, funny.[4]

Kenneth Tynan, who had personally conducted a teach-in in defense of *Saved* two and a half years earlier, neatly potted both the play and the production in a single shot: "if only it had been better done, we would have realized how bad a play it was."[5] Sean Day-Lewis, who admitted to not being present for the entire performance, chastized the Lord Chamberlain for "his persistence in inflating the reputation of Edward Bond far beyond the present deserts of that muddled playwright."

> Mr. Bryden declares that Mr. Bond's *Saved* . . . is "now generally recognized as one of the finest, most serious plays

---

4. Irving Wardle, "Muddled Fantasy on Brutalization," London *Times,* 8 April 1968, p. 6.
5. Kenneth Tynan, "Shouts and Murmurs," London *Observer,* 7 April 1968, p. 26.

by a young British writer to appear in the sixties." If this is right then presumably we should thank the Lord Chamberlain for getting this play so much extra publicity through refusing it a license. . . . We should thank him for finding "gross insults" to respected characters of recent history in *Early Morning* and refusing that play a license. We should thank him for informing the Director of Public Prosecutions about the proposed Sunday-evening performances of the play at the Court. . . . If the Lord Chamberlain has achieved one thing by his intense reaction to Mr. Bond it is to ensure that as soon as his censorship powers are abolished, productions of both *Saved* and *Early Morning* are put on immediate offer to the public. Personally I am convinced Mr. Bryden is wrong and that the Lord Chamberlain should have used his surplus energy to establish the career of some more promising dramatist.[6]

Early Morning was, as John Russell Taylor summed up the critical reaction, "in general . . . not felt to be very successful." [7]

In vain Bond defenders argued that judgments on the play were based on totally irrelevant criteria. Martin Esslin dismissed as ridiculous the assertion that the play was in any way a slander on the Royal Family.

Indeed, from the very first scene it is clearly established by the author that we are in the realm of fantasy. But fantasy is free from the shackles of logic or factual proof. *Nothing that is stated in the vein of fantasy can possibly threaten the foundations of real institutions.*[8]

Ronald Bryden went still further and denounced the banning as an act of political suppression.

6. Sean Day-Lewis, "Rude Noises from St. James's Palace," *Plays and Players* 15, no. 9 (June 1968): 58.
7. John Russell Taylor, *The Angry Theatre* (London: Methuen, 1969), p. 110.
8. Martin Esslin, "A Bond Honoured," *Plays and Players* 15, no. 9 (June 1968): 26.

I can say that it is a serious and passionate moral play, and that a country which forbids its performance is unfree to an extent we should not countenance a day longer.[9]

It was predictable that the Lord Chamberlain would refuse a license to *Early Morning*. That there would be Scotland Yard "inquiries" about further performances was surprising. Alfred Esdaile, the licensee of the English Stage Society and codefendant in the *Saved* case, compromised sensibly and the 7 April performance was changed into an afternoon "dress rehearsal" and discussion to which critics and reporters were admitted through a side door.[10]

The Lord Chamberlain's office remained adamant, however, and obtained a court ruling that required the Arts Council to suspend subsidies to any theater producing an unlicensed play,[11] thus ending any possibility of *Early Morning* being produced so long as the censorship office remained in power.

Parliament removed the duties of theater censorship from the office of the Lord Chamberlain on 26 September 1968, and shortly afterward William Gaskill began planning the special three-play Bond season at the Royal Court Theater. *Early Morning* joined the repertory on 13 March 1969, and the three plays were alternated until 12 April.

The second time around *Early Morning* played to a generally more respectful audience. It still suffered from being simultaneously the longest and the least easily understood of Bond's plays and for those who, like Jeremy Kingston of *Punch,* lost the thread early, "the dense and cluttered canvases . . . rapidly cease to be interesting." [12] Bond made some transpositions and omissions for the 1969 pro-

9. Ronald Bryden, "Making Bond a Test Case," London *Observer,* 14 April, 1968, p. 27.
10. Day-Lewis, p. 58.
11. Bryden, "Making Bond a Test Case," p. 27.
12. Jeremy Kingston, "At the Theatre," *Punch,* 256 (19 March 1969): 430.

Early Morning

duction, but the latter were only made to meet the limitations of the short rehearsal period. In a display of unity, favorable critics Ronald Bryden and Martin Esslin concluded that the production, not the play, was at fault. Both suggested that the play required more emphasis on fantasy.

> Its quality isn't fully revealed by William Gaskill's production, which handles it with a Brechtian sparseness better suited to a play making a logical statement than one trying, as this one does, to impose a vision. It needs to compel, like a dream: I'd have liked more visual fantasy, and more farcical elaboration in the first two acts.[13]

Esslin, who preferred the original production without decor, had more specific suggestions about production.

> In William Gaskill's present production the scenery and costumes are more elaborate and force one to see the play in their terms. And their terms are far too naturalistic, far too genuinely historical, and indeed far too sober; they therefore again and again inhibit the play from taking off into its own region, that of high, extravagant, childish fantasy. The historical characters being mere "Images d'Epinal" (primitive woodcuts of historical figures sold at county fairs), they ought to look like such primitive images: there should be backdrops in the style of the Douanier Rousseau or, indeed, of children's drawings. Likewise in the style of acting and production there ought to be a wilder vein of naive fantasy.[14]

Bond spent over a year writing *Early Morning* and obviously prefers it to either *Saved* or *Narrow Road*.

> I knew that it [*Early Morning*] was a much better play than *Saved,* because I'd written it. One can obviously deceive

---

13. Ronald Bryden, "Bond in a Wild Victorian Dreamworld," London *Observer,* 16 March 1969, p. 26.
14. Martin Esslin, "Early Morning," *Plays and Players* 16, no. 8 (May 1969): 26.

oneself about that, I've got to admit that, but I was reasonably confident that this was so, so when I had to write this other play [Narrow Road], I thought, well, I'll dash off a play in a couple of days just to show them I can do it.[15]

William Gaskill prefers *Saved,* but he agrees with Bond that *Early Morning* is far superior to *Narrow Road.* However, it is an appraisal he arrived at only after a period of rehearsal: "My feeling finally about *Early Morning* was just that you have to live with it. It's one of the strangest experiences in the theatre." [16] To "live" with a play is asking a lot of any audience, of course, and it is possible that *Early Morning* has yet to receive a production that best expresses its particular qualities. Gaskill feels that the central problem of producing *Early Morning* lies not in style as a separate entity or even in interpretation, but in finding a way to tell the play's story clearly.

> It can be looked at allegorically, but I think you have to take every play as something that happens. As a director you can never work on the symbolic level. That's what's so difficult about allegory. You can always read a psychological meaning into any play. But, say, with the three Witches in *Macbeth* it's really of no value to me that they represent the darker thoughts of Macbeth's mind. That's nothing to me in the theatre; that is an interpretation of the play. But to an audience, the Witches are the Witches. When it says "enter three Witches," three Witches must enter or the play doesn't exist. What an author says happens, happens even on the level of the supernatural.[17]

The following is what "happens" in *Early Morning.* Divided into twenty-one scenes, it was presented at the

---

15. Edward Bond, quoted by Irving Wardle in "A Discussion with Edward Bond," *Gambit* 5, no. 17: 32.
16. William Gaskill, quoted by Irving Wardle in "An Interview with William Gaskill," *Gambit* 5, no. 17: 41.
17. Wardle, "An Interview with Wiliam Gaskill," p. 42.

Early Morning

Royal Court in three parts with intervals after scenes five and fifteen. At the outset Prince Albert and Disraeli plot to overthrow Queen Victoria, who hopes to pacify the people by announcing a wedding between George, Prince of Wales, and Florence Nightingale. This prospect distresses Arthur, George's Siamese-twin brother, whom their father wants to recruit for the revolution. In the excitement following the trial of a Cockney couple who killed and ate a man guilty of pushing ahead of them in a cinema queue, Victoria rapes Florence. Albert picks the Cockney boy, Len, to serve as Victoria's assassin at a picnic. The job is botched; Victoria kills Albert; George is seriously wounded; and George and Arthur are captured by Disraeli. Faced with an attempt by Disraeli to cut them apart, Arthur and George escape. At their father's grave the ghost of Albert attacks and kills George. Arthur uses George's body and the threat of plague to rescue Len from an execution party led by Joyce, Len's former girlfriend, and William Gladstone. Len reveals the whereabouts of the Princes to Victoria who, in planning to execute Arthur, accidentally revives George. Disraeli plans to execute them all, but he is shot by his own men under orders from Gladstone. Gladstone, in turn, has a heart attack, and George shoots himself. Arthur goes mad and concludes that the chief goal of civilization is the destruction of mankind. He devises a plan by which he uses Victoria's treachery to destroy both armies; then he commits suicide. At the moment of Arthur's death, George appears from among the army's ghosts and reattaches himself to Arthur. The final scenes take place in a heaven populated entirely by cannibals who consume one another constantly and painlessly. Arthur is tried and freed from George, but is repulsed by the idea of cannibalism. His refusal to eat makes it impossible for George to eat either. Seeing their revulsion, the heavenly mob suspects poison and revolts. In order to quell the rebellion, Arthur's family eats him, thus finally freeing him.

"The events of this play are true," says Edward Bond in his one-sentence preface to the printed version of *Early Morning*. Yet, other than the admitted existence of some of the historical personages of the play, there is scarcely a literal fact in it. Beginning with the title, we are in analytical difficulties. Interpretations vary.

The German translation of *Early Morning* is *Trauer Zu Frueh (Mourning Too Soon)*.[18] In France the play is known as *Demain La Veille (The Eve of Tomorrow)*.[19] The confusion over the meaning of the title is more than merely lingual, however, and is as prevalent among the play's defenders as it is among its detractors or its translators. William Gaskill, who twice directed the play, does not even attempt to link the title to his interpretation of the play.

> The title *Early Morning* is partially a pun and in Germany is translated as meaning "early mourning," i.e., don't think someone's dead until you are absolutely sure. The play is very concerned with the child's relationship with its parents and the three acts could be seen as Act I Childhood, Act II Adolescence, Act III Adulthood. In the first act the mother and father fight for the loyalty of the child. Each tries to persuade the child to hate the other. In the last act when the child is grown up the mother is the more dominant memory, the father has become an amiable figure, but the mother is still destructive and nails him into the coffin.[20]

Jane Howell, who played Joyce in Gaskill's first production and who later became known as a director of Bond plays, has ventured a highly personal interpretation of the title.

> For me it is as though one was lying in bed early in the morning having read the night before a book on Victorian

18. Esslin, "Early Morning," p. 25.
19. Marie-Claude Pasquier, "La Place d'Edward Bond dans le Nouveau Théâtre Anglais," *Bref*, no. 136, p. 3.
20. William Gaskill, letter to Richard Scharine, 19 March 1971.

Early Morning

England and somehow in an early morning dream one's personal problems and the book on Victorian England synthesized together. This may be totally wrong.[21]

Martin Esslin also saw the play in terms of a child's view of adults. His interpretation of the 1968 production was essentially Freudian and led him to make comparisons with Genet's *The Balcony* and Ionesco's *Exit the King*.

> Why, incidentally, is it called *Early Morning*, if not in a reference to early childhood? . . . Now cannibalism is . . . the expression of the earliest infantile sexuality, oral eroticism. We are, quite clearly, in a dream world of infantile sexuality. Hence, equally clearly, the Queen and the Prince, and Florence, the archetypal nurse, can be seen as grown-ups, figures of authority from the angle of vision of a very young child. The other central image of the play, that of the Siamese twins, painfully tied together, then reveals itself as an image of childhood, too: sibling rivalry, the hatred of the other baby in the double pram. The cruelty and wholesale slaughter—with the dead coming to life at the drop of a hat—also fit into this picture: infantile fantasies of cruelty and power. Arthur's brilliant speech about Hitler and Einstein (both his models as authors of wholesale slaughter, Aushwitz, and the atom bomb), his desires to be like them, mirrors infantile fantasies of omnipotence. And Arthur's final Christ-like ascension is interpreted as signifying the process of growing out of the primitive cannibalistic phase of oral eroticism.[22]

In his review of the 1969 production, Esslin modified his interpretation only slightly. Taking Bond's preface as his cue, he commented on the play's relation to history.

> Yet, the events of the play *are* true. They are true insofar as they mirror establishment politics and history as they might

---

21. Jane Howell, letter to Richard Scharine, 6 July 1971.
22. Esslin, "A Bond Honoured," pp. 26, 63.

appear to a child exposed to the history of teaching practiced in most of our schools, where stereotypes and idiotic clichés of history are paraded before working-class children who are barely able to understand the vocabulary of battles, civil and external wars, dynasties, and the whole panoply of terms in which politics and power are discussed.[23]

In the publishers' preface to *Early Morning* is the suggestion that Bond's work "is a play, not about Queen Victoria, but about her reign and its influence on us today." This is a reasonable interpretation, but one that can only be understood with Bondian principles in mind. No matter what his subject matter, Bond is always writing about the same thing: the attempt of the individual to preserve his humanity in a society alien to the human condition. In *The Pope's Wedding*, Scopey recognizes the limitations of his environment and moves toward another that is equally hopeless. In *Saved*, Len survives by finding alternatives to the forces that oppress him. In *Early Morning*, Arthur begins as a partially socialized being who is unable to understand his society because he is a part of it. As Marshall McLuhan has said: "We don't know who first discovered water, but we're pretty sure it wasn't a fish." George represents the socialized part of Arthur. Although Arthur possessess the heart that powers them both, it is George who is the heir-apparent of society (Victoria). Arthur can only dimly understand his problem because he approaches it initially with the standards of his society. The action of *Early Morning* is Arthur's progression from acceptance to rejection of that society. Only when he has totally rejected the socialized part of himself can he be completely free and fully human. In short, Arthur awakens to the causes of the human condition and passes beyond them. Regarding the events of the play as steps in Arthur's progress illuminates our own perceptions of Bond's theme.

23. Esslin, *Early Morning*, p. 25.

Early Morning

At the outset of the play Queen Victoria describes the conditions of her kingdom.

> Our kingdom is degenerating. Our people cannot walk on our highways in peace. They cannot count their money in safety, even though our head is on it. We cannot understand most of what is called our English. Our prisons are full. Instead of fighting our enemies our armies are putting down strikers and guarding our judges. Our peace is broken . . . the anarchist and immoralists say that the monarchy must end with our death, and so they shoot at us. They are wrong. . . . Our line began at Stonehenge, and we shall not fall till Stonehenge falls.[24]

The situation that Victoria describes is contemporary and clearly is meant to be so. It is the result of an unjust society, justice being defined by Bond as "allowing people to live in the way for which they evolved." [25] Man is a biologically successful animal. He multiplied and prospered and, in order to protect his success, he developed social institutions and leaders to guide them. In times of crisis for the community, leaders were given special privileges and, because nonconformity was a danger to the group's survival, the leaders were given the power to punish it. These privileges and powers were justified, but when they continued beyond the period of crisis or were passed on to the next generation, they became unjust. The control of power became its own justification and people became dissatisfied. This dissatisfaction initially expressed itself in petty ways, including the infringement of minor regulations set up by the leaders. The leaders viewed these infringements as disruptions of society's fabric and established controls to punish the disruptors. This led to more disruptions and, subsequently, to more stringent

---

24. Edward Bond, *Early Morning* (London: Calder and Boyars, 1968), iii, 14. All subsequent references to *Early Morning* will be noted in the text.
25. Edward Bond, Preface to *Lear* (London: Eyre Methuen, 1972) p. 12.

controls. The leadership originally created to solve the problems of the people had become the source of these problems. The unjust had become the definers and administrators of justice.

> I think that society as it exists is primitive, dangerous, and corrupt—that it destroys people. . . . It's superstitious, neolithic in its origins. At the end of the Old Stone Age, people found themselves with surplus energy set free by specialization. They used it to control their fears—fear of the dark, that summer wouldn't come back. So they built Stonehenge, and all it implied: a caste of priests and leaders to cope with their fears for them. You have to have people to do it, so you give some men power over others, and fear them instead.[26]

In *Saved* Bond recorded the dehumanizing effects of being trapped at the bottom end of society. The picture was shocking but somehow not unexpected. In *Early Morning* he notes the scarcely less rigid strictures at the top. The pressures involved in the act of controlling society are equal in their dehumanizing potential to those resulting from being controlled, and the greatest of these pressures is the fear of the people asserting their natural right to freedom. Albert accurately recognizes the fear that motivates Victoria, and his revolution is planned to free the people from it. The revolution is doomed from the start, however, for Albert believes that society is changed by changing its leader. His answer to the people's frustration is to give it a new focus. Basically, Albert intends to retain Stonehenge and found a new line of descent from it.

> She sould have been a prison governess. She's afraid of people She thinks they're evil, she doesn't understand their energy. She suppresses it. . . . Hate destroys, I want to build. The people are strong. They want to be used—to build

26. Edward Bond, quoted by Ronald Bryden in "Society Makes Men Animals," London *Observer*, 9 February 1969, p. 27.

empires and establish law and order. I know there'll be crimes but we can punish them. The good will always outweigh the bad—in the end perhaps there won't be any bad, though I don't believe that. Arthur, I can't do this alone. That would be tragic. You must promise to carry on my work (ii, 10–11).

At the outset of the play, Arthur is aware of the impending revolution but is determined not to become involved in it. He extracts his father's false promise that there will be no purge and that no harm will come to his mother and brother. Despite Albert's urging, he refuses to do more than remain aloof during the coup. Arthur is induced to change his mind, however, by the trial of the working-class couple, Len and Joyce, for cannibalism. They killed and ate the man who pushed ahead of them in the queue outside the State Cinema on Kiburn High Street. In an interview, Edward Bond once gave a rough explanation of this scene and its importance.

> During that play *[Early Morning]* there is an interlude in which *Saved* appears in the play. The character Len is brought in from the earlier play, and there is a trial of *Saved* in the first act of *Early Morning* and in this Arthur has made a great advance on the world of *Saved,* because he is able to see much more clearly the nature of Len's activity than Len could when he was himself in that play, but he is still very much tied up in that sort of character himself, and that's why Len kicks the clothes over him.[27]

The key to Arthur's acceptance of Albert's plan of revolution is the pair of handcuffs holding together Len and Joyce. The handcuffs provide a parallel for the attachment between Arthur and George. Arthur recognizes himself in Len, even as the Len of *Saved* recognized the Oedipal violence in himself through Fred.

27. Wardle, "A Discussion with Edward Bond." p. 14

LEN. She likes t'keep an eye on me.
ARTHUR. Why did you kill him?
LEN. 'E pushed in the queue. . . .
ARTHUR. Why did you kill him—
LEN. No fany questions. I ain' being mucked about! . . . .
ARTHUR. Why did you kill him—
LEN. I said it ain' I? 'Is shirt! 'Is shoes! 'Is vest! (*He kicks the exhibits at Arthur.*) I done it! Thas's that! Get, mate, get! They're 'is! I got a right a be guilty same as you! (iv, 25–26).

Arthur can see that the difference between his class and Len's is only circumstantial. In killing and eating the man, Len and Joyce were merely punishing a rule breaker. In turn, they are being hung by Victoria for this action, which broke another rule. Len and Joyce are not antisocial. On the contrary, they are so completely socialized that they have adopted society's morality as their own. They have made themselves the punisher of the deviant.

> Social morality is a form of suicide. Socially moralized people must act contemptuously and angrily to all liberalism . . . because these are the things they are fighting in themselves. . . . So other people's happiness becomes their pain, and other people's freedom reminds them of their slavery. It is as if they had created in themselves a desoluate, inhospitable landscape in which they had to live out their emotional and spiritual lives. This landscape reflects, of course, the inhospitable unjust world in which they first suffered; and it exacerbates and reinforces their aggression and seems to give it added depths of bitterness. By calling the unjust world good, they re-create it in themselves and are condemned to live in it.[28]

Len is society as much as Victoria. He has "got a right a be guilty." The difference is that the leaders are the definers of guilt. Len's actions are a parallel of Victoria's. However, Victoria, from her position of power, chooses to see Len's

28. Bond, Preface to *Lear,* pp. 9–10.

actions as social deviations and, thus, as another sign that men require social control.

Arthur sees that Victoria is the cause of Len's aggressions. Therefore, he agrees to the plan to overthrow her, not realizing that revolution can be itself just another form of socialized aggression. The changes that Arthur desires will not come from a change of leaders, because leadership as a form is itself hopelessly corrupt. By plotting violent overthrow, Arthur is still "working within the system" and punishing deviants. He is still half-asleep, still in the "early morning" of his understanding of the problem.

> Men did not suddenly become possessors of human minds and then use them to solve the problems of existence. These problems were constantly posed and solved within an inherited organization or social structure, and this structure was redeveloped to deal with new problems as they arose. . . . As men's minds clarified, they were already living in herds or groups, and these would have evolved into tribes and societies. Like waking sleepers they would not know dream from reality.[29]

The revolution fails to achieve even its basic objective, the dethroning of Victoria, because it is inefficient from a societal standpoint. Albert hesitates because he is unwilling to admit to Arthur his murderous (inhuman) intentions toward Victoria. She, however, *is* society and, as the first rule of morality is the preservation of the society that defines it, any action that she takes is automatically morally correct. She poisons Albert and strangles him in Windsor Park.

Disraeli, who assumes leadership of the revolution that Albert has botched, plans to kill the wounded George by cutting him free from Arthur and to set up Arthur as a figurehead king. However, in the chaos surrounding the uprising, Arthur and George escape. In a parody of *Hamlet*, they are confronted by the ghost of Albert, complete with

29. Bond, Preface to *Lear*, p. 6.

Victoria strangles Albert in Early Morning
(Photo courtesy of the Royal Court Theatre, S.W.1, London; photo by Douglas H. Jeffery)

Early Morning

shroud, draped chains, military sword, and crowing cock. Albert, too, wants Arthur to cut off George and make himself king, a position that Albert insists is Arthur's natural right: "You were first in the womb. Your mother screamed and struggled and your brother thrashed his way out in front" (viii, 50).

Society always struggles against those who would dispute its power. Nevertheless, Arthur cannot cut off George. He persists in seeing the problem from within the social order in which he was raised, and he still believes in the need for a system; therefore he cannot eliminate the socialized part of himself. On a more wakeful level, he recognizes that the evil of the system is in that it kills; therefore he refuses to perpetuate the system by killing to obtain power. Still beyond his comprehension is the realization that he cannot be freed from society by killing, for killing is the most characteristic societal action and power is the most characteristic of its goals.

George drives Albert back into his grave by crowing like a cock but is fatally wounded in the process. Later, Arthur tricks Victoria into using the Queen's power to revive George. George, like Lazarus, does not want to be brought back to life. At the earliest opportunity, he seizes a gun and shoots himself.

> Yes, I remember. . . . We weren't joined together there, we were free . . . when you die *you*'ll be . . . free and happy . . . when you die (x, 66).

Arthur is driven mad by George's suicide. If humanity can only be free in death, there can be no justification for its continued existence. However, Arthur has mistaken the social order for humanity. To George, Arthur's socialized self, "freedom" means liberty from the compulsion to behave humanely that Arthur's presence requires. Heaven is for George, as it is for Victoria, Len, and Albert (once he conquers his weakness for Arthur), pure society, a place of constant aggression without emotion and without consequence.

The sanity of an Edward Bond character may be defined by his attitude toward life. Arthur is mad because he sees the aim of humanity as death. This disturbs him only because men do not realize this fact and persist in believing they are pursuing life.

> D'you dream about the mill? There are men and women and children and cattle and birds and horses pushing a mill. They're grinding other cattle and people and children: they push each other in. Some fall in. It grinds their bones, you see. The ones pushing the wheel, even the animals, look at the horizon. They stumble. Their feet get caught up in the rags and dressings that slip down from their wounds. They go round and round. At the end they go very fast. They shout. Half of them run in their sleep. Some are trampled on. They're sure they're reaching the horizon. . . . Later I come back. There's a dust storm. There's white powder everywhere. I find the mill, and it's stopped. The last man died half in. One of the wooden arms dropped off, and there's a body under it. . . . Some of my dreams are better. In one, each man slaughters his family and cattle and then kills himself (xi, 68).

Arthur's madness is a metaphor for the socialized morality that results from accepting as necessary the constraints society places on men.

> That is, he is so desperate under the pressures, pressures that everybody lives under, that he becomes schizophrenic, he really does go mad and he swallows the Victoria line, that's the law-and-order bit, completely and he says, "So we are violent, so what we must do is we must have law and more law and law enforcement, law control and more and more of the pressure just to keep the animal in control," and then he says, "well, if this is true what is the point of life, if we are wicked or aggressive in that way there is no evolutionary

advantage in carrying on this sordid business of life, so to hell with the whole thing."[30]

Many in our culture share Arthur's conception that men are originally and unchangeably sinful. Few, fortunately, share his intellectual honesty and determination. Arthur is naturally good, a representative of Bond's Innocent in that he does what he thinks is best for others. His madness does not alter this facet of his personality; it merely changes his perceptions and, thus, reverses his objectives. The philosophy of Bond's Innocents is the same as his: "The natural condition in which people are born is love, the aptitude for loving, and being loved."[31] In his madness, Arthur sees the natural condition for man as hatred, but not merely hatred of one another or of their own lives—hatred of life itself.

> It's a matter of conscience, like duty in the blood: they stay alive to kill. They can't die in peace till they've seen the world dead first. That's why they have doctors and drugs and anti-famine weeks and scientists and factories and comfort to keep them alive—when their only happiness is being dead. It's tragic. But not for long. They're clever. They'll soon learn how to grant their own wishes (xi, 69-70).

It is an explanation that has its own logic, for it makes society and its heroes comprehensible. Both have been created for the purpose of destroying life. They are to be measured by the efficiency in that action and all other moral considerations are irrelevant:

> Heil Hitler! Heil Einstein! Hitler gets a bad name, and Einstein's good. But it doesn't matter, the good still kill. And the civilized kill more than the savage. That's what science is for, even when it's doing good. Civilization is just bigger heaps of dead (xi, 69).

30. Wardle, "A Discussion with Edward Bond," p. 14.
31. Bryden, "Society makes Men Animals," p. 27.

The result of Arthur's mad logic is an absurdly simple syllogism. If the measure of goodness is the efficiency of murder and, if Arthur is basically good, then he, too, must find a way to murder efficiently.

> But even Hitler had his limitations. He pretended—in my dark moments I think he pretended to himself—that he killed for the sake of something else. But I've discovered the logical thing for men to do next. It's a real step in human progress. For the first time in my life I can be useful. Hitler protected his own people. What we need now is the great traitor: who kills both sides, his and theirs. I'm surprised no one's seen it. It lets you kill twice as many (xi, 70).

So that he can betray the army opposing Victoria, Arthur puts himself at its head. He goes to her with a plan for a tug of war to decide the victor. Both sides will put every human, animal, and fowl in their groups on opposite ends of a line. Arthur's army will be lined up with a precipice behind them. At a prearranged signal, Victoria's side will drop the rope, and Arthur's group will rush backward over the cliff.

Although Arthur justifies his betrayal of his side by citing the socially acceptable definition of men as vile, an anagram of "evil" and "live," Victoria realizes that he is mad.[32] That his thoughts and actions are a reflection of her own is beside the point. Even as Len and Joyce were to be hung for punishing a wrongdoer, Arthur is to be executed for betraying the rebels. Society may sometimes license inhumane actions by individuals but they must be actions of society's own devising. Nevertheless, Arthur is more clever in his madness than Victoria is in hers.

> When my men go over the side what will hers do? What

[32]. The Queen in Bond's one-act play *Passion* speaks and thinks like a badly programmed computer. After she precipitates a nuclear disaster, her prime minister also speaks and thinks like a robot. She immediately recognizes that he is mad. Society defines antisocial behavior, but it does not accuse itself.

can you trust them to do? What would you expect them to
do? Whats the natural thing, the normal thing, the human
thing to do? Run to the edge and watch the others die. Her
whole army will stand along the edge. That's why I chose it.
It's weak, it'll give, and her men will fall down on top of my
men, and they'll all be killed, both lots together (xiv, 79).

The tug of war itself is a triumph of Bondian horror-
farce. The stage is filled with soldiers lining up on either end
of the rope, some on crutches and some in wheelchairs or in
splints. It is a microcosm of warfare in any age, done in the
name of all the satanic abstractions with which men have
justified killing throughout history, topped by the most
ironic of stated military ideals.

HERS. Onward!
HIS. Forward!
HERS. Upward!
HIS. To the future!
HERS. The dawn!
HIS. Freedom! Justice!
HERS. Culture! Democracy!
HIS. Science! Civilization!
HERS. Our future! Our past!
HIS. Our children! Our home!
HERS. Fraternity! Brotherhood! Love! Mankind!
VICTORIA. Peace (xiv, 79–80).

The line of ghosts rises up to meet Arthur as he wanders
among the bodies at the base of the cliff. As he shoots himself, they move apart to reveal that they "are joined together
like a row of paper cut-out men" (xv, 81). George appears
from among the ghosts and attaches himself to the dying
Arthur. At the moment of his death, Arthur's madness leaves
him and he will soon realize that the "freedom" George has
promised him is quite different from what he wants or
expects.

William Gaskill has said of the heaven sequence in *Early*

Morning: "The last act is almost like a separate play in itself. Bond didn't lodge any preparatory hints for it in the first act." [33] This is literally true, of course, but in another sense the entire play to that point is the preparation. Bond merely accepts the common definition of heaven as the ultimate in men's desires, the perfect society, and by showing us the voraciousness of society on earth, prepares us for an environment in which its "virtues" exist without opposition. Men are not joined together in this heaven. They do not even touch in love. The habits of humanity—fatigue, pain, imagination, and all other factors related to the consequences of human interaction—are forgotten there. As human beings the inhabitants of this heaven are dead; as representatives of society they continue to thrive.

At Arthur's trial, Victoria sums up his heavenly qualifications.

> We call no evidence. (*She grabs her papers.*) Members of the jury, we speak to the mothers among you. (*They are all men.*) My son used to be a disappointment to me. But then he killed us all. For the first time I was able to call him son. The defense confidently asks for a verdict of guilty. (*She puts her papers away.*) (xvi, 86).

Arthur is put to trial by ordeal. Albert stabs him with a sword to find out if he is still capable of feeling pain. He makes no reaction despite a suspicious smell of burning and is found guilty and admitted to heaven. At the announcement of the verdict, Arthur is introduced to another feature of heaven.

> (*Albert cuts Arthur free from George with the sword. There are loud shouts from the crowd at the pulley. Len runs downstage carrying a leg. It is torn off at the thigh and still wears its sock and shoe. The stump is ragged and bloody. Len chews it. The crowd fight round him like sparrows*). . . .

33. Wardle, "An Interview with William Gaskill," pp. 41–42.

Early Morning

> LEN. 'Old on, 'old on. (*He turns to Arthur.*) Yer once did me a good turn. Welcom t' 'eaven. It's all yourn—(*He wrenches a bite from the leg.*)—was's left of it. (*He puts the leg into Arthur's hands and steps back shyly. Then he shyly rubs the palms of his hands on the seat of his trousers. Shyly and pleasantly.*) An' I 'ope it chokes yer (xvi, 87).

Since the consumed part of the body rapidly regrows, the people in heaven eat one another without pain or consequence. The ghosts of *Early Morning* do literally in heaven what their competitive society has forced them to do metaphorically on earth. They consume one another, a horror made doubly tragic on earth because there is nothing inherent in the human condition that requires such competition and mutual destruction.

> I mean we would be much saner if we were cannibals. . . . cannibals are much more civilised than we are, because if you eat somebody, it's some sort of magical nonsense, but it makes some sort of sense, more sense than the slaughtering holocaust that for instance I have lived through, which makes no sense at all.[34]

Arthur is, of course, the exception. Eating human flesh makes him retch. This is because he is still alive and still capable of feeling, as the smell of burning when Albert stuck him with the sword might have warned us. This makes "life" in heaven difficult for not only Arthur but for those around him. Arthur and George are the moral and social halves respectively of the same character. Like Siamese twins, the moral and social elements of human beings are, or ought to be, inseparable. If the social element is allowed to function unchecked, society will always determine the conduct of the individual, rather than the other way around —as it should be. In the presence of its conscience, however, the social aspect of a character operates morally or suffers

---

34. Wardle, "A Discussion with Edward Bond," p. 13.

for its actions. Therefore, when Arthur cannot eat, George starves.

"The living haunt the dead" (viii, 49). Albert tells Arthur this when Albert returns from the grave to demand the deaths of George and Victoria. What Arthur does not realize then is that it is not physical death that Albert speaks of. It is the death of humanity, the "slaughter of the Innocents" that figures in every Bond play.

> Most people die before they reach their teens. Most die when they're still babies or little children. A few reach fourteen or fifteen. Hardly anyone lives on into their twenties. . . . Bodies are supposed to die and souls go on living. That's not true. Souls die first and bodies live. They wander round like ghosts, they bump into each other, tread on each other, haunt each other. That's another reason why it's better to die and come here—there *must* be peace when you're dead. Only I'm not dead (xix, 101).

George's starvation is a metaphor for the inability of a humane society to thrive through the consumption of its own kind. However, because the justification of society lies in the necessity to control the aggression that its conditions provoke, society as a form is threatened by the survival of humanity. Yet, those who retain humanity must continue, like Arthur, to contend for the souls of their brothers who remain in society. Indeed, that very concern defines their humanity. Therefore, society, whose first concern must be its perpetuation, persecutes the humane, as it has done with the Ghandis, the Martin Luther King, Jr.s, and the Berrigans throughout history. The presence of the "living" forces the "dead" to consider alternatives to the society for which they have sacrificed their humanity.

> FLORENCE. You talk about life when you mean pain. That's why you cause trouble—you can't let them die in peace. The mob, your mother—where ever you go—someone will always want to kill someone, and they can't and so it goes on and

> on! I'm hungry! They're hungry! We're all dead and hungry! And it's the same where ever you go!
> ARTHUR. You keep me alive.
> FLORENCE. You're not alive! This is heaven! You can't live or laugh or cry or be in pain! You can't love! You can't torture people! Let me alone! You're a ghost! Ghost! Ghost! You're haunting me—O stop it!
> ARTHUR. You're crying. . . .
> FLORENCE. Nothing to cry for. Too late. Why didn't you tell me this before? What d'you think I did while I waited? I'm not crying. Perhaps I'm alive, perhaps we needn't be like this. I'm trying to think (xix, 102–103).

Even on a lesser level, the presence of a live soul is dangerous to the stability of a lesser environment. By exhibiting the possibility of disgust and pain, it restimulates one of those human habits forgotten in heaven—imagination. Seeing Arthur and George vomit, the mob imagines that human flesh is poison to it, which in a moral sense, it is. They adopt Arthur as their messiah. Ironically, this is just what Bond would not advocate. He believes that once people canonize a natural instinct and select a leader to do their thinking for them, their impulse is as dead as the movement it replaces.

> We go on building Stonehenge all the time. What must be done is to get rid of the awful business of teaching some people to be leaders and others to be led. We've got to get men out of their uniforms, from behind their desks, away from their flagpoles. No, I've no Utopia, no image of the society I want to see emerge. It would simply be people being themselves, happy in their own way—what could be more natural.[35]

The final scenes thus become a parody of the Passion. The mob follows Arthur, as the mob followed Jesus, because it believes that he can protect them from the pain it imagines

35. Bryden, "Society Makes Men Animals," p. 27.

to be there. They cannot completely follow his commandments not to eat one another, for that exposes them to the very real pain that is the natural result of caring for one another. Arthur's enemies, like those of Jesus, are more resolute than his followers. They find him meditating alone, with Len, Joyce, and his other disciples sitting apart complaining about food. Florence, whom Arthur loves and wants to save, lures him to where Victoria can strangle him and the others can eat him.

Arthur is eaten, but George's pain persists, for Arthur's head remains alive and is hidden under Florence's skirt. Soon, however, George smells out the head and snatches it from its hiding place. Arthur's head laughs as it is consumed. He has at last been freed from his society without sacrificing his humanity.

Irving Wardle purports to find a relationship between Bond's social beliefs and uterine regression: That is, Scopey retreats into Alen's womblike shack; Len burrows deep into Pam's South London flat; Kiro in *Narrow Road to the Deep North* hides his head in a sacred Buddhist vessel, etc.[36] Bond ridicules such interpretations.

> Arthur doesn't feel safe because he's under Florence's skirt —she hides him there because there is no where else to hide him—but because he's found someone else capable of a humane act in heaven/hell. That's why he laughs when he's discovered. He's found that life exists in the universe—like Willy [the central character of *The Sea*]. If he'd been plucked out of the womb . . . he should have cried, shouldn't he? If you like, it's Florence who cries because she's still in the womb/coffin.[37]

Edward Bond has suggested that society makes god in its own image. Christianity, with its Father who sacrifices

---

36. Irving Wardle, "The Edward Bond View of Life," London *Times*, 15 March 1970, p. 15.
37. Edward Bond, letter to Richard Scharine, 2 October 1974.

Early Morning 109

his son to save those who believe in him, makes a perfect Bondian parallel for a society that sacrifices its children to preserve its own structure.

In the final scene of *Early Morning*, a combination of the Last Supper, the Pieta, and the Ascension, Victoria twists the murder of Arthur so that it justifies society's interpretation of morality. She presents the refleshed, but now completely dead, body of Arthur to the multitude. He committed suicide, she tells them, taking upon himself the sin of their eating so that they might sin and not go hungry.

> That's why he killed himself. . . . He told you not to eat each other. . . . But he knew he was asking something unnatural and impossible. Something quite, quite impossible. And because he loved you—and he only attacked you out of love— he wouldn't ask you to eat yourself, as he did. (*Len puts his arm behind his back.*) So he died, to let you eat each other in peace. . . . His last words were, "Feed them" (xxi, 117).

The food is laid out on the coffin lid that Victoria nails shut with her teeth. The entire cast sits around the coffin taking the communion of Arthur's body. Only Florence sits to one side, facing the audience and crying silently. Arthur steps out onto the lid of the coffin, dressed in a long white smock. Half lifting his hands to his chest, he rises up into the sky.

The ending is, as usual, ambivalent. Arthur has passed beyond society, but even he does not know where he is going. Florence is crying, a clear sign that she feels the pain that is the mark of humanity. Nevertheless, she accepts the meat from Victoria and, although we do not see her eat, she has never been able to resist Victoria's urging before. The survival of any humanity is a triumph in this context, of course, but in the long run we are tempted to declare society and its personification, Victoria, the victor. "There's no dirt in heaven. There's only peace and happiness, law and order, consent and cooperation. My life's work has borne fruit. It's settled" (xxi, 120).

If Arthur is the child of society who achieves salvation by denying his parent's influence, Florence is the whore of society who acquiesces to society's every whim. Nevertheless, it is the question of Florence's salvation that determines the optimism of *Early Morning*.

Florence is the vestal virgin of *Early Morning*, simultaneously the bride of society and a sacrifice to it. Even as Victoria is the archetype of the absolute monarch, Florence epitomizes the eternal nurse. Victoria is total control; Florence is complete servitude. Initially planned to be the bride of George (society's heir), her character changes completely when she literally is raped by society in the form of Victoria: "I've started to have evil thoughts" (v, 28). Soon she progresses from being accomplice and tool in the killing of Albert to a more official position as the first public hangwoman in history.

Florence's actions in *Early Morning* are not, in fact, inconsistent with her archetypal image. She is society's servant. Society needs her ("you've seen my maids of honour") and makes use of her on a number of levels. Her actions are not immoral, of course, because society defines morality. They are, however, in contrast to her normal needs and functions.

> One way or the other the child soon learns that it is born into a strange world and not the world it evolved for: we are no longer born free. So the small, infinitely vulnerable child panics—as any animal must. It does not get the assurance it needs, and in its fear it identifies with the people who have power over it. That is, it accepts their view of the situation, their judgment of who is right and wrong—their *morality*. But this morality—which is social morality—now has all the force of the fear and panic that created it. Morality stops being something people want and becomes what they are terrified to be without. So social morality is a form of corrupted innocence, and it is against the basic wishes of those who have been moralized in this way. It is a threat, a weapon

used against their most fundamental desire for justice, without which they are not able to be happy or allow others to be happy.[38]

Typically, Florence's rebellion against the unnatural demands of society initially takes petty, seemingly arbitrary forms. For example, she refuses to masquarade any longer as John Brown. Not until she watches the mad Arthur, George's bones still attached, outline his plan of betrayal to Victoria does Florence begin to awake to the shortcomings of society: "That's why I've been unhappy. I knew it when I saw those bones. Men are dying. They need me" (xii, 74).

The next scene is a parody of the "Lady with a Lamp" legend. Set in a wartime field hospital, it deals rather shortly with any sentimentality.

> (*Florence comes on. She carries a lamp.*)
> VOICES. Bless yer mum. God bless yer mum. Angel a Mons. Angel a mercy. "Underneath the lamp light dum-di-dum-di-dum."
> FLORENCE. Good evening, boys. (*To Griss.*) You're the new man?
> GRISS. Permission t' touch yer skirt, lady.
> NED. 'Or! They're scrapin' the barrel—they're sendin' out fetishists. Another one t' jerk off in 'er shadder (xiii, 76).

Recognizing that her natural function is alleviating suffering rather than causing it, Florence has donated her body to the troops. For purely practical purposes she has limited actual participants to those on the brink of death, an inducement that has greatly increased death's popularity.

Florence's voluntary prostitution is a mistake comparable to Arthur's endorsement of the revolution. She does not realize that in making it easier for men to die, she is still working within the system. In *Early Morning*, Florence's sexual allure is used to encourage men to die, even as the image of the historical Florence, lovingly caring for the

---

38. Bond, Preface to *Lear*, pp. 8–9.

wounded heroes by the soft glow of lamplight has been used for a hundred years to sentimentalize and glamorize warfare.

Bond uses the hospital scene to introduce a contrast to Florence's ambiguous values: Ned, whose cliché role as a "dying drummer boy" is somewhat altered by his obsessive satyriasis.

> I got a lot a give thanks for. If I was 'ome I'd still be developin' the muscles in me right wrist. 'Ere I've 'ad more 'ole than the ol' fella ever 'ad off the ol' lady, an' they're celebratin' their silver bunk-up (*He drums a roll.*) (xiii, 75).

Whatever one may think of his needs, Ned is total in his pursuit of them. He is natural and uninhibited by the restraints of society, "the purest person" Florence knows. This does not put him beyond the effects of the social order (he dies of his wounds *before* Florence can reward him for them), but it does free him from its aftermath. Ned is the only character from the earlier scenes not to reappear in heaven.

Despite her motives, Florence continues on the battlefield to be as much society's whore as she was in Windsor Park. After Victoria, Arthur, and the opposing armies die, she literalizes her function.

> People thought I was invalided, but in fact I'd opened my own brothel, and business was so brisk I didn't have time to get up. I catered for ministers, probation officers, WVS hierarchy, and women police chiefs (xvii, 89).

Eventually, Florence expires in the service of her country (beneath the overexcited Gladstone and Disraeli) and is admitted immediately to the next world, apparently none the wiser for her experience.

Even as the sight of Arthur's suffering on earth awakened Florence's sense of responsibility to the soldiers, his self-denial for the sake of humanity stimulates her discontent in heaven. Her initial response is characteristic: she offers herself to be eaten. Arthur's answer is to ask of her the one thing most difficult for her to do: deny herself to society, refuse to eat.

From this point, Florence's relationships with society and Arthur are ambivalent. Victoria, George, and Albert discover them before Florence can gather the courage to give her promise to Arthur. She protests the eating of Arthur, but nevertheless joins in because "Victoria was watching" (xx, 109). She seems about to surrender to the appeals from Arthur's head when the others return and George discovers and eats the head. Florence continues to be Victoria's servant, but she is much less efficient. For example, she forgets to bring the hammer and nails to close Arthur's coffin. In the previously cited Last Supper/Ascension scene, Florence cries while accepting the meat from Victoria, and we do not see her eat.

Florence is a corrupted Innocent, the product of a social morality she no longer believes in but cannot live without. For her, Victoria will always be watching, but Arthur will always be remembered. It remains to be seen whether or not this will be her tragedy or her salvation. For the moment, she is in limbo, a reborn child in heaven unable to serve either humanity or society.

Ronald Bryden has rightly called *Early Morning* "a gargantuan Swiftian metaphor of universal consumption." Nevertheless, the focus of the play frequently narrows from the cannibalism society practices on its own to an attack on the concept of leadership in general. As the actions of society are primarily self-preserving, leaders exist primarily to extend their own power. For the people, life remains the same. In *Early Morning* the civil war begins with the revolt against Victoria by Albert and Disraeli. After Albert's death, Disraeli teams with Gladstone until the latter has him assassinated. Arthur takes command of the mob after Gladstone's heart attack and kills Victoria, both armies, and himself. Somehow Disraeli and Gladstone are revived by these deaths and the war continues against an unnamed foe. At the play's end, both Disraeli and Gladstone are in heaven. We are not shown either their successors or the progress of the war, but the implication is clear. The leaders are interchangeable and as unnecessary as the problems they raise.

Victoria *is* society on a metaphorical level, of course. Notwithstanding, she provides a number of excellent examples of how leaders use governmental and religious institutions to promote their own needs against those of their people.

> VICTORIA. I'd like to pardon him, but it's too late. Governments must *keep their word.* Officer! (*She takes Florence aside.*) Listen, Florence. I'll tell them not to hit George.
> FLORENCE. If Arthur dies, he dies!
> VICTORIA. Will he? The doctors say he will—that means he probably won't. And if he does I'll bring him back to life. . . . (*She turns away and goes to the squad.*). . . . Shoot them both. (*Aside.*) I shan't resurrect him. I'll say my power's gone. Florence has only herself to blame. I can't share her—certainly not with my son. It's worse than incest, and I'm head of the church (x, 61–62).

Bureaucracy, too, is a justification for preying on the people. In a scene that neatly parallels the stoning of the baby in *Saved,* Gladstone, Joyce, and members of the mob argue over what credentials are required in order to participate in the execution of Len by kicking.

> GLADSTONE. (*Griss gives Len a kick.*) Do my mincers see right? Yer can't do that, brother. Where's your uniform?
> GRISS. What uniform? I got a right a do me duty same as 'im. Change the rules. . . .
> GLADSTONE. 'Oo uses a nose rag. (*Joyce gives him a handkerchief.*) Thank yer, sister. I like me women folk t' be clean in their 'abits. (*He ties the handkerchief round Griss's arm.*)

> Yer'll do now yer got yer armband up, brother. . . .
> JOYCE. I'll give yer a 'and.
> GLADSTONE. Dodgy, darlin'.
> JOYCE. Fair shares for—
> GLADSTONE. (*Explaining.*) It's the uniform, ain' it?
> JOYCE. I ain' got no armband, but I got a legband. (*She shows him the top of her stockings.*)
> GLADSTONE. It's stretchin' a point, but it'll do for an emergency.
> JONES. It'll do for my emergency. . . .
> JOYCE. (*Lining up.*) Ain' it a giggle?
> GLADSTONE. One, two, three! (*They kick Len.*) (vii, 45–47).

The scene recalls the status of the Professor in Ionesco's *The Lesson* whose procession of forty-one coffins will go unnoticed as long as he wears an armband. Any violence, no matter how hideous, that society initiates and that is carried out by society's officially designated representatives is acceptable.

The metaphor of society battering its children is made literal by the fact that Len is Gladstone's son: "When 'e dies I'll be the first t'cry. I ain' ashamed a tears. Till then 'e lives by the book. Rule 5" (viii, 53). A father's sacrifice of his son to meet the needs of his society has, of course, an illustrious precedent. It is the basis of Christianity and Christian tradition, and, as Alan Brian reminds us, it is to Bond the work of a monster.

> He remembers walking the North London streets as a boy— "terrified to think how God was love and he killed his son for us and hung him up and tortured him and washed us in his blood." But he resents the Resurrection rather than the Crucifixion. "We need love to overcome life, not to overcome death. Only among bodies can love exist. And God has no body."[39]

---

39. Brien, "This Bond has not been much Honoured," p. 55.

A constant thread running through *Saved*, the Oedipal instinct, is present in *Early Morning*, but receives reduced emphasis. One facet, uterine regression, was already discussed in relation to the Bondian hero's need to regain his innocence. A second, only hinted at in *Saved* when the possibility of a sexual relationship arises between the twenty-one-year-old Len and the fifty-three-year-old Mary, becomes factual with the liason between the eighteen-year-old Len and the fifty-year-old Joyce. Arthur's unwillingness to aid his father's revolution against his mother also could be given Oedipal significance: "He's peculiar about his mother" (iv, 18).

The most strikingly Oedipal scene occurs when Arthur retches at eating human flesh and triggers a similar reaction in George. The mob, fearing poison, turns against the Royal Family. Albert is eaten in a bacchanalian frenzy in which Arthur takes part.

> Stop it! No more! I'll eat! I'll eat! (*George runs from the hamper, eating a piece of Albert. Arthur takes a piece of Albert from the hamper. He bites from it. . . . Eats.*) Eat and be good. Be good and die. Die and be happy. (*They chew in silence for a few moments.*) O God, let me die. Let me die. Let me die and everyone will be happy (xvii, 94–95).

The consumption of the father is a characteristically Oedipal fantasy indicating a desire to replace the father in the affections of the mother. In context, however, it indicates an acceptance of Victoria's ethic by Arthur. After a period of rebellion, Arthur is now acting in a socially acceptable manner, even as is his father who also once rebelled. Arthur is yielding to his mother and replacing, or at least becoming equivalent to, his father. Such an act should accomplish his spiritual death, but it does not.

> My beard grew overnight. The night my father was eaten. I ate some of him. I don't know what. When I woke up I was

old. My hair was white and I had a beard. It was white when it came, and wet—I must have been crying. I felt very tired, as if I'd been born with a beard. . . . I've tried, but I can't die! Even eating didn't kill me. There's something I can't kill—and they can't kill it for me. Pity—it must be nice to be dead (xix, 100, 102).

Arthur's extreme age after eating his father can be triply interpreted. On one level, it is a manifestation of the son's anxiety for wanting to replace his father. The son identifies with the father whom he imagines to be much older than he, in fact, is. On another level, it is Arthur's punishment for having sinned against humanity. He regains his youthful spirit and vigor only after he has expiated for his sin by being eaten by his family. A third interpretation, however, is required to explain the second part—Arthur's recognition of the immortality of his innocence. In consuming his father, Arthur is encompassing within himself his father's experience. He "digests the past" in order to build upon it an understanding of the present.

> How d'you escape from the past? By becoming old yourself in the sense of taking possession of the experience of the past. And how d'you escape from foolishness? By accepting responsibility for what you've done. So the beard is a conventional sign for wisdom and of maturity—and of freedom, escape from the past.[40]

Early Morning is very tightly written on an allegorical level, so much so that the play's theatricality may have been hindered. Meaning follows upon multiple meaning, each so important that the problem of dramatic build and emphasis becomes insurmountable. All the Bond themes are present, albeit they are subordinated to the literalized relationship of society and its children. To follow the plot on other than an allegorical level is possible, but to have other than the

40. Edward Bond, letter to Richard Scharine, 2 October 1974.

haziest notion of nineteenth-century English history will probably hinder rather than help understanding. Sides in the revolution change as quickly and as improbably as a music-hall version of Shakespeare's *Henry VI*, a play with which *Early Morning* has been frequently and unfavorably compared. Yet, as Gaskill has pointed out, there is nothing literal in the complex earth scenes to prepare the audience for Bond's heaven. Peter James, who directed *Early Morning* in Liverpool in 1969, confirms William Gaskill's contention that the greatest problem of production is clarifying the story line.

> One of the difficulties as well as one of its great interests is the problem of style. Scenes like the attempted execution of Victoria, etc., are burlesque. . . . So, too, is the picnic, but made very difficult by the fact that several things happen on the stage at once—according to Bond by design. But it makes the focus difficult to arrange since the audience is expected to glean almost everything from each incident. If they do not, the plot becomes exceedingly difficult to follow. In a letter which Bond wrote to me after the Royal Court production he emphasized that I should get the *story* of the play clear above all things. This proved extremely difficult. . . . Bond has eschewed his very fine naturalistic ear in *Saved* and attempted a more condensed style. This is so tight that the narrative becomes obscure. "There is no room to move in it." [an actor] One important sentence follows hard upon another too quickly. Somehow the style lacks the ability to emphasize and throw away, build to crux, etc. Read it to see whether you think it has an undertext. I think not. I think it *is* the undertext which is why the play is not naturalistic.[41]

Technically *Early Morning* is tremendously demanding. The handling of the acts of cannibalism is designed to tax the ingenuity and dexterity of costumers, actors, and prop

41. Peter James, letter to A. J. Coult, 27 May 1971.

men alike. The tug of war, the hanging and dismantling of Albert, Arthur's head under Florence's skirt, and the like, can all be both hilarious and tragic for entirely the wrong reasons if the technical aspects are not precise. The style of acting must also be such that it can remain consistent within scenes that vary from heightened realism to pure burlesque to macabre fantasy.

Characterization is on quite a different and decidedly less naturalistic level than *Saved*. The lower classes still speak the authentic South London idiom, but they do so on the plane of Cockney comedians. Indeed, Len's attempt to testify through Joyce's constant interruption at their trial would be perfectly in place on a BBC goon show routine. Fittingly, when they are sentenced to hang, they break into a song-and-dance number, complete with comic clumsiness induced by their being handcuffed together. The comedy, of course, does double duty. The lower classes of *Early Morning* have been so socially moralized that they take great glee in discovering and punishing infringements of social mores. All deviations being equally punishable, all deviations are punished equally. Therefore, Len and Joyce, assisted by the rest of the crowd, eat a man who pushed ahead in the cinema queue and the accusing jury in heaven treats social crudities with the same intensity they devote to capital crimes.

(The Jurors raise their hands one after the other and say one of the following lines. Some say more than one line, but not two lines consecutively. They smile and nod at Arthur while they speak. One waves.) He rapes little girls. He rapes little boys. He rapes grey-haired grannies. He rapes grey-haired grandads. He rapes dogs. He rapes anything. He rapes himself. He likes to flog. He gives babies syphilis. He drinks before breakfast. He wastes electricity. He's mean. He gives gonorrhea syphilis. He kills. He's a nose picker. He looks at dirty pictures. He picks his nose while he looks at dirty pictures. He kills. He can't control his natural functions.

He's only got unnatural functions. He kills. He eats dirt. He is dirt. He dreams about killing. They ought to name a venereal disease after him (xvi, 84–85).

The nobility—new to Bond's work in *Early Morning*—is no more naturalistically portrayed than are the commoners. With the exception of Arthur, they have no intellectual consistency and a number of critics have noted a resemblance to the characters of *Alice in Wonderland*. Certainly, Victoria, for whom words, ideals, and actions have exactly the meaning she gives them and no more, could pass for a Lewis Carroll queen if it were not for the results of her efforts. Peter James may have come close to the performance requirements with the suggestion that the nobility must be "cartoonlike." Our primary reaction to them must be humorous if we are to fight off a wave of revulsion at their actions.

Despite the remarks of Ronald Bryden and Martin Esslin, it does not appear that either setting or acting should be unduly exaggerated. The people in *Early Morning* are very ordinary in that they have a strict—one might even say "Victorian"—code of conduct. There is, unfortunately, nothing in it about killing people. When asked whether she helped butcher the man she and the others eventually ate, the otherwise forgetful Joyce can say convincingly: "I know I stripped him. I kep' 's knickers on. I don't 'old with this rudery yer get" (iv, 23).

The most remarkable factor about the evil in *Early Morning* is its sheer banality. All that is required of a system of morals, says Bond, is that it teach people to act humanely toward one another. This is just the point where contemporary morals stop. We stand, like Victoria and Florence, amidst a *grand guignol* of corpses of our own making, spouting virtuous trivia and plotting more massive murders.

(*The long walk at Windsor. Three corpses hang on a gallows upstage. Another corpse is tied to a gallows-post. And two other corpses to the other gallows-post. These last three have*

Early Morning 121

>been blindfolded and shot. . . . Arthur comes on. George is still attached to him, but a leg, an arm, and half the ribs are gone.)
>ARTHUR. (Looks at the gallows.) Who were they?
>VICTORIA. They were all called Albert. I can't take chances.
>FLORENCE. I didn't shoot the ones on the posts, but I hanged the others
>ARTHUR. (Looks across at them.) Good, good.
>FLORENCE. I'm the first hangwoman in history—public hangwoman, that is. It's part of our war effort. And if we're being emancipated we must be consistent. So we take over any man's job that's suitable.
>ARTHUR. I'm sure *they* prefer it.
>FLORENCE. Victoria knits the hoods.
>VICTORIA. I run a knitting circle for ladies. They like to be useful.
>FLORENCE. I use a new hood each time. It adds that little touch of feminine sensibility. That's very precious in war.
>ARTHUR. What d'you charge?
>FLORENCE. Just pin money. (*Arthur goes to the gallows. He unblindfolds one of the shot men. He looks at him. A long silent pause. Florence tiptoes to the gallows. She takes hold of the feet of one of the hanging men and swings the body so that it kicks Arthur.*) Penny for them (xii, 71–72).

In *Early Morning* Edward Bond has indicted contemporary society by distortion. The social culture of our age is personified in Queen Victoria, the archetype of monarchy and repression. We see, like in a fun-house mirror, the slaughter of our children to preserve a national image, the rebellion created by oppression, and the corruption of those who try to work within the system. The events in *Early Morning* are true; they are distilled from our own experience and they make a potent and bitter brew.

Arthur is the hero of *Early Morning* because he says *no* to society. He is not a tragic hero because in violating the moral order of his universe, he is saved rather than destroyed. He is not a Christian hero because he lives for the virtues of men rather than dying for their sins. He is not an existential hero because he keeps faith with something greater than himself. Arthur stands with Ionesco's Berenger and refuses to become a rhinoceros. He hears the call of Dostoevski's Grand Inquisitor for peace and cries for life. Arthur is humanity—unexpurgated.

5
Some Problems Have No Solutions: *Narrow Road to the Deep North*

The spring of 1968 must have been a depressing time for Edward Bond. *Early Morning*, which had taken more than a year to write and had awaited production for more than six months, had only one performance before a Sunday-night club-audience. That production seemed improvised even to friendly critics, and a few staunch supporters of *Saved*, such as the influential Kenneth Tynan, switched camps. For the most part, however, the play itself had been lost in a plethora of Royalist and anti-Royalist trivia.

Ironically, since Bond is an avowed atheist, it was the Church of England that eventually provided relief. An unexpected commission to write a play for the international conference on People and Cities came from Coventry Cathedral Canon Stephen Vernay. The play was to provide a springboard for discussions on the nature of what a city should be and was to be presented in the Belgrade Theater of Coventry. Fearing ecclesiastical reactions, Bond delayed in delivering his script.

They asked somebody else and nobody else could do it, so I did it and I then produced the play at the last moment when it was too late for them to say they wouldn't have it.[1]

Bond's caution proved unnecessary. Relationships with Coventry Cathedral were amicable and he was later invited to preach a sermon there. Nevertheless, Bond's caution was probably justified. The initial reaction to the unperformed play, which was written in two-and-a-half days, did little to excite any optimism. Even William Gaskill had little interest in it: "Edward wanted me to direct the play but I had very little response to it and suggested that Jane Howell, who was my Associate Director, should direct it instead."[2] Miss Howell, who had been the assistant director on *Saved* and who had played Joyce in the only performance of *Early Morning*, proved to be an excellent choice as producer; but, before rehearsals had even gotten underway, Bond was once again in trouble with the Lord Chamberlain.

With the start of rehearsals less than a week away, the Lord Chamberlain required five alterations in the text of *Narrow Road*. Predictably, Bond publicly refused to make any changes, and what was to have been the first Bond play to be presented to a nonprivate audience seemed about to be the last play banned by the Lord Chamberlain. Happily, thanks to what has been described as a "week of the most concentrated backstage diplomacy the Belgrade has known,"[3] this honor remained with *Early Morning*. As the management prepared feverishly to substitute an alternative production, Canon Vernay and Miss Howell made a last bid to salvage the production. Armed with some slight concessions by the author, they met representatives of the Lord Chamberlain at St. James's Palace in London. From this

---

1. Edward Bond, quoted by Irving Wardle in "A Discussion with Edward Bond," *Gambit*, 5, no. 17: 31.
2. William Gaskill, letter to Richard Scharine, 19 March, 1971.
3. London *Daily Mail*, "Drama of Bond Premiere and the Censor," 30 June 1968, p. 14.

meeting emerged a compromise and a license, and rehearsals began only one day late. The alterations were minor in the extreme and Bond has admitted: "We ignored them all in performance."[4]

The play ran only a week to half-empty houses but received surprisingly good critical reception. A few, like Ronald Bryden of the London *Observer*, might have been expected to be sympathetic.

> It hasn't the shock or directness of the two previous plays, but it's easily Bond's most accomplished work so far. Far from seeming an imitation or masquerade of his talent, it presents the most balanced expression of its full range, from tenderness through ironic comedy to despairing anger, that we've seen yet.[5]

His impressions were reinforced by Gareth Lloyd Evans of the Manchester *Guardian*.

> Its depth of dramatic perception drowns all overt thoughts of sin, sex, and censor . . . the history of the world is the history of cruelty where what is needed is love.[6]

More startling was the reaction of two critics for whom Bond's plays had previously only served as objects of disgust and contempt: Irving Wardle and John Russell Taylor:

> The work of a playwright with a confident method and an unmistakable voice . . . new is the admirably disciplined dialogue and the capacity for scene building and story telling.[7]

4. Edward Bond, letter to Richard Scharine, 2 October 1974.
5. Ronald Bryden, "Bond goes to Japan," London *Observer*, 30 June, 1968, p. 27.
6. Gareth Lloyd Evans, "Narrow Road to the Deep North at Coventry," Manchester *Guardian*, 25 June 1968, p. 6.
7. Irving Wardle, "Confident Voice of Violence," London *Times*, 25 June 1968, p. 13.

> *Narrow Road to the Deep North* . . . showed a new certainty of touch and purposeful economy in its dialogue. Again its climax is an outbreak of carnage, but the lead-up is cool and controlled, and the resolution pulls the whole thing into shape.[8]

The Belgrade Theater was physically an excellent choice for *Narrow Road* because of its width. As Jane Howell described it, this width strengthened the play's narrative quality by permitting the use of two centers of action.

> We could set part of the action on one side and part on the other. The picture-book element in the play was thus brought out in the right way—the actors were able to work in *demonstrated* relationships. At the Royal Court we work on a very narrow stage, one can't get two centers of action in the sight-lines at the same time. We have to work up and down stage—in doing this actors tend to work in an *emotional* relationship to each other. Edward Bond's plays have always previously been done at the Court and, I suspect, a wide stage would help all his works in a similar way.[9]

For the 1969 Bond revival season, designer Hayden Griffin was not able to add width to the Royal Court stage, although he did add a small thrust stage.

The critical reaction to the English Stage Company's *Narrow Road* remained generally good and, a better measure of the changing times, always respectful. Herbert Kretzmer of the London *Daily Express,* one who was most vehement in his condemnation of the first production of *Saved* and who was utterly stupefied by *Narrow Road,* found himself forced to qualify even his expressions of displeasure.

> Edward Bond . . . is an English playwright with a reputation totally out of proportion with his actual output. His career

8. John Russell Taylor, *Anger and After* (London: Methuen, 1969), p. 110.
9. Jane Howell, quoted by Peter Ansorge in "Director In Interview: Jane Howell," *Plays and Players* 16, no. 1 (October 1968): 70.

is a reminder that it is possible in this country to become famous for having achieved nothing much at all. . . . This, I respectfully hasten to add, is not to deny Mr. Bond's undoubted qualities as a playwright.[10]

More favorably impressed and probably more honest was Peter Lewis of the London *Daily Mail:* "I might as well say straight out that though I think Edward Bond is a good writer, I don't know what he's driving at most of the time." [11] More frequent than those who were hostile or confused, however, were those critics who, like Hilary Spurling of *The Spectator,* had been antagonistic to Bond's work initially, only to find that seeing the plays produced together was an aid to understanding them individually.

> *Narrow Road to the Deep North,* set in Japan two or three hundred years ago, could scarcely be farther from the mean and dingy London streets of *Saved;* but, though its colours are lighter and brighter, and dashed on with a bolder hand, its themes are the same—what Coleridge called "the vulgarity of all bad passions"—and it has the same clarity and economy of line.[12]

The following September *Saved* and *Narrow Road,* supported by the British Council, toured Eastern Europe, appearing in Belgrade, Venice, Warsaw, and Prague. The audience reception was sometimes glowing and sometimes hostile, but it was never passive. *Narrow Road* was the most controversial production at the Venice Theatre Festival, culminating in a lively polemical debate between Bond, Jane Howell, and sixty-odd international students of the theater in Venice's Palazzo Grassi. The press was divided on the

10. Herbert Kretzmer, "Too deep—Bond's Noh play," London *Daily Express,* 20 February 1969, p. 13.
11. Peter Lewis, "Georgina was not the only one to wind up haunted," London *Daily Mail,* 20 February 1969, p. 6.
12. Hilary Spurling, "Bond Honoured," *Spectator* 222 (7 March 1969): 313.

production, and a central feature of the debate was the possible influence of Brecht. Bond denied any influence, labeling "Brechtian theatre outdated," [13] a position he has since modified. Despite the great popularity of *Saved* on the continent since its first German production in 1966, William Gaskill found that *Narrow Road* was more readily accepted in Eastern Europe.

> The interesting thing about reactions in countries like Czechoslovakia and Poland was that the allegory of *Narrow Road* was much easier for them to "read" as they spend their lives creating allegories when censorship prevents a more direct realistic approach. *Saved* was more remote because the social conditions which produce crimes of violence of that kind are not found to the same extent in their countries and the obsession with infanticide seems to be a very English obsession.[14]

The stimulus for the play, its title, and the setting for the opening scene all came to Bond as he was reading, "The Records of a Weather-exposed Skeleton," by Matsuo Basho, the seventeenth-century Japanese haiku poet, in his *The Narrow Road to the Deep North and other Travel Sketches*.

> As I was plodding along the River Fuji, I saw a small child, hardly three years of age, crying pitifully on the bank, obviously abandoned by his parents. They must have thought this child was unable to ride through the stormy waters of life which run as wild as the rapid river itself and that he was destined to have a life even shorter than that of the morning dew. The child looked to me as fragile as the flowers of bushclover that scatter at the slightest stir of the autumn wind, and it was so pitiful that I gave him what little food I had with me.

13. John Francis Lane, "Resounding Success," London *Times*, 25 September 1969, p. 8.
14. Gaskill, letter, 19 March 1971.

> The ancient poet
> Who pitied monkeys for their cries,
> What would he say, if he saw
> This child crying in the autumn wind?
>
> How is it indeed that this child has been reduced to this state of utter misery? Is it because of his mother who ignored him, or because of his father who abandoned him? Alas, it seems to me that this child's undeserved suffering has been caused by something far greater and more massive—by what one might call the irresistible will of heaven. If it is so, child, you must raise your voice to heaven, and I must pass on, leaving you behind.[15]

Basho had concluded that heaven was responsible for the condition of the child, and heaven, if anything, must come to his aid. Bond concludes that human beings created the child and his misery and the human action to take would be to save him. This did not happen historically and it does not happen in Bond's play. *Narrow Road* is the story of what Bond perceives to be the results of this kind of inhumanity.

Narrow Road to the Deep North opens with the incident described above. Basho, the seventeenth-century Japanese poet and priest, is planning a journey to the north in search of enlightenment. He discovers an abandoned infant by the river but leaves it there. Thirty years later he returns to the river to find a great city ruled by a tyrant named Shogo. On the spot where he left the baby, Basho finds a young man named Kiro, who is also seeking enlightenment. Basho refuses to accept Kiro as a disciple, telling him to join the local seminary. Two years pass. One day while Basho is hoeing in his garden and dictating haiku, soldiers come to

15. Matsuo Basho, "The Records of a Weather-exposed Skeleton," *The Narrow Road to the Deep North and Other Travel Sketches*, trans. Nobuyuki Yuasa (Harmondsworth, Middlesex, England: Penguin Books, Ltd., 1966) p. 52.

take him to Shogo. Basho suspects that Shogo, who rules by atrocity, is jealous of his enlightenment. On the way to Shogo's palace, Basho and the soldiers meet four young priests, one of whom has his head stuck in a sacred vessel following a drinking bout. It is Kiro, who is sad because he has learned nothing in the seminary. Basho realizes that the vessel cannot be safely removed from over Kiro's head and takes him to Shogo. He plans to challenge Shogo to remove the vessel, thus demonstrating that even a tyrant's powers have limits. Meanwhile at the palace, Shogo is interrogating a peasant who witnessed an assassination attempt. He does not harm Basho and designates him as guardian for the infant son of the emperor Shogo has overthrown. After sentencing the peasant to death, he breaks the sacred vessel and frees the suffocating Kiro. Kiro becomes devoted to Shogo, but Basho is appalled by the affront to religion and returns north to find the barbarians he encountered there on his earlier trip. Basho plans to use the barbarians, an English Commodore and his Salvation Army sister, to overthrow Shogo in the name of the infant emperor. Under the leadership of Georgina, the Salvation Army sister, the barbarians capture the city, but Shogo and Kiro escape into the north.

In Act Two Georgina converts the city to Christianity and establishes rule by morality as restrictive as Shogo's rule by atrocity. When the Commodore's ships and big guns are away, Shogo returns from the north and recaptures the city. When Georgina refuses to tell him which of the children in her charge is the child emperor, Shogo has all the children killed, thus driving Georgina mad. Shogo sends for Kiro, but by the time he arrives from the north, the Commodore's forces have returned and defeated Shogo once more. As Kiro watches, Shogo is revealed to be the baby Basho had refused to save on the river bank thirty-odd years earlier. Shogo is hacked to pieces and then crucified. Kiro commits hara-kiri on the river bank, ignoring the nearby

Narrow Road to the Deep North

cries of a drowning man. The man saves himself by his own efforts and, as he dries himself, angrily asks why no one came to help him.

Narrow Road to the Deep North was commissioned for the Coventry Conference on People and Cities. As Brecht does in *The Caucasian Chalk Circle,* Bond poses a question in the prologue to *Narrow Road* that the play subsequently answers: What should be the relationship between a social system and its people? Basho believes that a social system should teach its members to venerate traditional religion so that they may live in the hope of an afterlife. Shogo believes in the necessity of imposing social order for the good of the people. Georgina also believes in strict social order, but would impose it from within by manipulating the people's moral code. All argue their cases with sincerity and implement them with conviction. From this implementation comes war, death, and madness. The successive examination of these points of view makes up the story line of *Narrow Road.* Kiro, the traditional Bond Innocent, watches diligently, but despairs of finding enlightenment and commits suicide. Even as Kiro dies, however, Bond's answer to the question presents itself.

Basho's philosophy is elitest. He believes that all fates, lucky or unlucky, are dispensed by heaven and that he is one of heaven's chosen ones. Basho continues to believe in the omnipotence of heaven and the relative unimportance of men, despite the fact that the only good (the care taken of the begging, meditating poet) and the only evil (the abandonment of the baby) he sees are clearly the actions of men rather than gods. Preoccupation with humanity, in Basho's all too familiar view, is totally incompatible with a religious vocation and it is by this criterion that he refuses Kiro the right to be a disciple.

BASHO. (*Looks closely at Kiro.*) How many feet has god?
KIRO. (*Hesitates.*) Two?

> BASHO. How many hands has god?
> KIRO. (*Slighter hesitation.*) Two.
> BASHO. How many eyes has god?
> KIRO. Two.
> BASHO. How many ears has god?
> KIRO. Two.
> BASHO. How many lips has god?
> KIRO. Two.
> BASHO. How many hairs has god?
> KIRO. How many hairs . . . ?
> BASHO. (*Losing patience.*) How much patience has god?
> KIRO. I. . . .
> BASHO. Kwatz! You don't know anything about god. You've only been looking at men.[16]

Since Basho sees himself as superior to other men, his reaction to their problems is detached. For instance, shortly after returning from the north, he moves from his home near the river where Shogo regularly drowns his prisoners. It is not, however, that Basho is either sensitive or humanitarian. He is merely practical.

> My old hut was by the place where they throw people in the river. Their friends and relatives used to come and stand quietly on the bank, with Shogo expressions on the faces. But when it was over they ran round looking for somewhere quiet to cry, and they always ended up behind my hut, crying on my vegetable and treading on them (I, ii, 13).

Basho believes in a monarchy of divinity and intellect as unassailable as Victoria's heaven. As priest and poet of this enlightenment, Basho's self-preservation is an act of piety. Those who contribute themselves to his preservation are engaged in religious sacrifice; those who oppose it are sacrilegious. For example, when he challenges Shogo to remove

---

16. Edward Bond, *Narrow Road to the Deep North* (New York: Hill and Wang, 1968), I, i, pp. 10–11. All subsequent references to the play will be noted in the text.

the sacred vessel from Kiro's head, he has no concern for Kiro, who he is sure will die. Basho merely hopes to divert Shogo to the philosophical question of a ruler's limits. If Shogo cannot separate the religious symbol from the live man, how can he presume to destroy Basho, the human representative of god on earth? In this argument, Basho presumes that Shogo's attitude toward god and religious symbols is the same as Basho's. Shogo, however, has little reverence for religious abstractions and breaks the vessel, thus saving Kiro and earning Basho's undying enmity.

> He's imprisoned innocent women, orphaned children, made the men soldiers, and killed them. His city is hell, ruled by atrocity. I could put up with that if I could still hope. But how can I hope if he destroys religion? He knew the pot was sacred. Of course, that's only a symbol, but we need symbols to protect us from ourselves. If he destroys them, there's no future. A fool destroys men, but a fanatic destroys their hope—and he's a fanatic (I, iv, 27).

Willing to accept murder but unable to tolerate sacrilege, Basho returns to the Deep North. There he makes an alliance with the barabarian British in order to overthrow Shogo and place the infant emperor on the throne in the name of traditional religion.

Basho, Bond has told us forthrightly, is the villain of *Narrow Road*.[17] He does not object to Shogo's atrocities, and he believes men must be controlled in the name of abstractions. Further, Basho believes in the cult of the leader. That is, he believes that his enlightenment endows him with the privilege to make decisions that will alter the lives of those around him.

Basho and Shogo, despite their different views of god and religion, both believe that men are basically evil. Bond believes that this attitude is far from historical. Society, the

17. Wardle, "A Discussion with Edward Bond," p. 26.

creator of violence, teaches its young that violence is inherent in them.

> I was talking to some students the other night. To a man, they believed in original sin—not the old religious version of it, but the new doctrine of natural aggression. People are not born violent by nature. The natural condition in which people are born is love, the aptitude for loving and being loved. This has to be knocked out of them to make them fit in. Society takes hold of them at school and tampers with their minds, teaches them that human nature is unworthy, bestial, needs to be controlled. All the schools do it. Children are made competitive, aggressive—society does not control the beast in men, it makes men animals in order to control them. The students did not like it when I said this to them, it made them afraid. They had been got at, taught to fear themselves.[18]

Like most men with strong beliefs, Basho is unable to understand a point of view different from his own. As he had done earlier with Shogo, Basho makes the mistake of judging the English by his own standards of intellect: "He's so stupid I *think* I can control him. . . . She's possessed" (I, v, 31–32). Although he allied with the British for their military power, Basho does not realize that this power, once in effect, will be come its own reason for being. The fate of the child-Emperor remains unchanged, and the status of traditional religion has deteriorated.

> COMMODORE. This Go-slow chappie worked out a little scheme for its education, I hear? . . . Georgina thinks we ought to stick with it: bring him up as a peasant. Open air, healthy sort of life. . . . No use getting the little fellow involved. Wouldn't do it to one of my own. . . . Bring the little fella up to the quiet life. If he never knows what he is, he'll never know what he's missed. Is that right? Haw, haw. In England we have a saying: ignorance is bliss. That's a favourite of

18. Edward Bond, quoted by Ronald Bryden in "Society Makes Men Animals," London *Observer*, 9 February 1969, p. 26.

mine. . . . I'll make you—er—Minister for—er, orphans.
GEORGINA. Three cheers for Jesus (I, vi, 34–35).

Some critics have been troubled by Basho's failure to protest when Georgina establishes Christianity as the city's official religion. This inconsistency is more apparent than real for two reasons: first, Basho has a very strong sense of self preservation. Second, the difference between the two religions as presented seems limited to technology.

Basho has no strong ideals concerning temporal power. What he cannot change or manipulate, he will accept. Essentially, his philosophy and art is extraneous to the business of living and he puts a higher priority on stability than on justice. To Jane Howell, this is less a conscious policy than an instinctive action.

> I think Basho's actions are perfectly consistent. For me he is a pretty representative—God forgive the word—artist. In the pursuit of the perfection of our craft, we attempt to retain the centre of ourselves—in order to create—at the cost of not committing ourselves to the world—not noticing the world as it really is.[19]

The concept of an artist living for, and only being responsible to, his art is not new to us. It is a corruption of Schiller's definition of the artist as outlaw, which implied a society unable to face the truth of an artist's work. The purpose of the work of art, according to Schiller, was to heal the gap between what is and what should be in society. For Basho the work itself (or the ideal) is preeminent and the members of society can be sacrificed to it. For Bond, however, the primary responsibility of all men is to one another.

> WARDLE. Don't you think that the carrying out of big-scale designs, including artistic designs, often has to be paid for in terms of human relationship?

19. Ansorge, p. 70.

BOND. No, no, no, no. I don't accept this at all. If that is so then the large-scale designs are wrong. You can't carry those through. The thing is the fact that human beings aren't totally at home in this world. . . . It's not quite right for us, if it were, then there would'nt be any evolutionary problems . . . and in that sense, human beings will always be dissatisfied about this, and the dissatisfaction means there will always be art and art in that sense will be an evolutionary experience, an evolutionary weapon if you like, but there are certain things that by now evolution has secured. These things—the lower order of animals if you like, the lower species are quite certain about. A dog, for instance, would never have abandoned its puppy in that way, in the way that Basho does.[20]

With the same ease that he adapts to the new government, Basho permits Georgina to use him as a tool in her plan to convert the city to Christianity. She is, after all, as devoted to iconography and tradition as he is and the techniques and promises of their respective religions are interchangeable. Both "protect" the people with symbols and both emphasize form over content. Indeed, Argi, the most orthodox of the Buddhists, quickly becomes the most orthodox of Christians.

> BASHO. She says you're now Christians.
> ARGI. Can I bless people? . . . And tell them they're born evil.
> BASHO. Yes.
> ARGI. Good! We've got a lot of people like that here.
> GEORGINA. Tell them they're going to help me run the city. Our's is a religion of love, that means we teach sin and—. . . .
> ARGI. Can I do faith healing?
> BASHO. Yes.
> ARGI. Hallelujah! (II, i, 39–40).

When Shogo counterattacks, Basho abandons the person of the child-Emperor as easily as he did his championship of its claims to the throne. The baby is slaughtered and

20. Wardle, "A Discussion with Edward Bond," pp. 9–10.

Georgina goes mad before the Commodore's forces retake the city. Prior to the trial at which Basho's testimony will lead to Shogo's drawing, quartering, and crucifixion (and Kiro's subsequent suicide), Shogo upsets a stack of Basho's poems in a last vain attempt to escape. The Commodore apologizes as his men prepare Shogo for execution, but Basho is not upset: "It's of no importance, I have copies" (II, iv, 53). He is right, of course. For art such as Basho's there are always adequate copies, just as Christianity is an

Roy Marsden as Shogo in Narrow Road to the Deep North
(Photo courtesy of the Northcott Theatre, Exeter; photo by Nicholas Toyne, Devon)

adequate replacement for Buddhism, and the Commodore's cannon adequately replaces Shogo's spear. It is only lost humanity that cannot be replaced.

It is fitting that Basho should preside over Shogo's death since it is to Basho that Shogo owes his way of life. Shogo was the abandoned baby by the river that Basho failed to save, and Shogo has been left with an inexplicable guilt.

> SHOGO. (*Still looking in the water.*) An odd thing happens to me sometimes. I wake up and think I've done a crime. It's the worst crime that's ever been done.
> KIRO. (*Still looking in the water.*) You mean you dream?
> SHOGO. No. I'm suddenly wide awake and there's this idea in my head. I *know* I've done it.
> KIRO. What?
> SHOGO. I don't know. But I know I've done it, and I have to hide it.
> KIRO. What sort of thing?
> SHOGO. I don't know. I just know I've done it. If I said I remember my name, I wouldn't be *sure* I did, I *might* be making a mistake—but this *is* sure. It worried me when I was young. But not now. Why should it? Nothing happens. (*Silence. They still look in the water.*)
> KIRO. It could be anything. You're always killing people.
> SHOGO. It's not that. I remember all that. But my life goes on and on like a finger reaching out to point (II, iv, 45).

The fact is that Shogo as an infant was found unworthy to live first by his parents and later by Basho. From these rejections are derived his subsequent crimes. In contrast, Kiro's parents starved rather than abandon him, and an old priest, himself a beggar, found him and raised him. From this stemmed Kiro's subsequent piety. Shogo's life is the finger and it points to the death sentence passed on him as a baby: "The upturned boat knocks against the pier" (II, iv, 55). In a discussion with Bond, Harold Hobson, theater critic of the London *Sunday Times*, argued that the really disastrous events of the play would not have occurred had Shogo not been "saved." In answer, Bond pondered the question of whether or not Shogo actually survived.

> Ah, yes, but after what trauma, after what chaos. I mean, in fact, the child [found by the historic Basho] was actually left there, probably fell into the river and drowned. So this is a play about a nonexistent child. What I am saying is that if the child does survive, then, yes, it will have been taught that the world in which it finds itself is not an uncomfortable world, but an absolute alien enemy world that it must fight, because it has had to be fighting for its life. . . . Human beings are produced into, are told that their environment is their enemy. They must fight it all the while. So, of course, human beings become vicious, wild, dangerous, and all the rest of it. In fact, you could say, Basho didn't save the child so the child grew up dead.[21]

It is the death of the soul that Shogo suffers, much as Arthur describes it in *Early Morning*. As we all are, Shogo is in turn victim and victimizer. He survived by chance in a hostile society. Therefore, when he builds his own society, he makes it "in the image of other men" (I, v, 30). The image that it follows is Basho's. It is thus an enlightened city in the sense that Shogo has learned enlightenment from Basho. That is, it subverts all human values to its own perfection.

> It has the best drains, schools, churches, water, houses, food, laws, hospitals—but most important it has a purpose: perfection. That gives the people something to do. Instead of arguing and rotting away in hovels, they work for the city, they live for it. If the city wasn't there they'd start cutting each other's throats, there'd be chaos, and that's worse than all the ancient plagues and famines (I, iv, 28–29).

Shogo justifies the legalized murder by which the city survives by believing that it eliminates chaos and, on the aver-

21. Wardle, "A Discussion with Edward Bond," pp. 10–11.

age, prolongs life. In fact, it is merely the codification of the philosophy that permitted his parents to abandon him in the first place.

> We're poor and there's no food. We have five other children and if we let this one go perhaps the others will live. Better lose one than all of them. People do it everyday (Introduction, p. 7).

Shogo's city serves another purpose for him. It excuses his survival in the eyes of the enlightened elders who condemned him. Shogo exalts them by creating an entire society in their image. This in turn justifies his survival against their wishes. As long as the city survives, Shogo's death sentence is deferred: "I won't die! The city's mine—they can't kill *me!*" (II, iv, 53). When the city is lost irrevocably, Shogo's death is assured.

Shogo's policy toward the subjects of his city is a blend of the philosophies of the characters in *Early Morning*. Like Albert, he believes erroneously that putting the people to good use for society will provide a suitable outlet for their energies. Like Arthur in his madness, Shogo believes that life, not society, is the real cause of people's suffering. Therefore, by taking control of life out of their hands, he prevents them from destroying it haphazardly. Finally, like Victoria, Shogo is capable of justifying any atrocity in the name of what he believes to be the common good.

> KIRO. But why d'you put people in prison and kill them?
> SHOGO. To prevent suffering. (*He laughs.*) It's true. It stops the chaos. That's why I have a policeman for every two streets. . . .
> KIRO. If you didn't have police there wouldn't be any crime. Any one knows that. Punishment makes crime.
> SHOGO. (*Laughs.*) No, life makes people unhappy, not my city. You think I'm evil. I'm not—I'm the lesser of two evils. People are born in a tiger's mouth. I snatch them out and some of

them get caught on the teeth—*that's* what you're blaming me for. . . .
KIRO. You've already forgotten the man in the sack.
SHOGO. Nearly. You pity him. But I'm proud of him—he was a hero. He died for the city—to protect the rule of law and order (I, iv, 29).

It is important to note that Shogo only kills in the name of the city, the perfect society that he has created in the image of others. In that sense, he is as much a victim of social morality as Len is in *Early Morning*. Both are merely administering capital punishment to rule breakers. In his infancy, Shogo was taught that killing was so advantageous to society that even he could be sacrificed. Therefore he justifies his survival to society by killing in its name. In a psychological sense, Shogo is overcompensating.

Nevertheless, Shogo has a sense of the value of life and does not kill without some provocation. Although his subjects hate him with considerable justification, he sincerely believes the society he has created is best for them. He killed the Emperor whom he overthrew while capturing the city, but he did not harm the Emperor's pregnant wife—although "luckily she died in childbirth." Nor did Shogo harm the baby, even though he recognized its potential danger to him.

I kept him in the palace, but now he's beginning to notice things and I can't keep him here any more. It's too risky. People mustn't know there's someone else who could claim my city. That would start trouble. . . . I'm sorry for him. He's done no harm. I've taken everything he was going to have. But you've got enlightenment, so perhaps you can give him something (I, iv, 24).

It is, of course, ironic that Shogo should put the baby into Basho's hands for enlightenment. It was Basho's abandonment of Shogo that led indirectly to the overthrow and death of the child's father. Although for political reasons he treats the Emperor's son more kindly than Shogo, Basho's actions will bring about the son's death just as surely as it did the father's. It is also ironic that Shogo's downfall is the direct result of two of his rare failures to follow Basho's early example of putting his own interests before human life. First, Shogo saves Kiro's life at the expense of a religious symbol, an act which sets Basho against him. Second, he spares the Emperor's son, an act that gives Basho the weapon with which to overthrow Shogo. In a sense, Basho's use of the baby to incite the subjects of the city to revolt is the second and last lesson in societal control that Basho gives Shogo: If killing is necessary to maintain society, it is impossible for a leader not to kill. After he recaptures the city, Shogo is faced with the task of identifying the Emperor's son from a whole class of identical schoolchildren. It is a difficult decision, but Shogo at last accepts Basho's lesson.

SHOGO. Which is the Emperor's son?
GEORGINA. Only Mr. Basho knows. . . .
SHOGO. (*Goes to the children.*) Which is the Emperor's son? Which of you's the strongest? Point at him! Which one wins the arguments? Which one's the subtlest? Which one's the leader? Which one d'you hate? Hands out! (*He looks at a child's hands.*) He bites his nails (*He looks at the other children's hands.*) They all bite their nails! . . . (*To a boy.*) Who was your mummy and daddy? (*To another boy.*) Were you brought up in a palace? D'you remember soldiers and lots of toys? (*To another boy.*) Have you seen me before? You remember me, don't you? Don't you? (*He shakes the boy.*) Answer when you're told! Which one of you's the Emperor's son? Please! D'you want to make me do something terrible? (*Shouts.*) Basho! Basho! Help me! Help me! Help me! (*A long complete silence.*)
All right. Let's go on. I don't know who's the Emperor's son so I kill them all. . . .
GEORGINA. He's not there, my brother took him away; they've

gone!
SHOGO. Liar!
GEORGINA. No.
SHOGO. Kill them! Kill them! Kill them! (II, iii, 50–51).)

The death of the identical schoolboys arouses more than one Bondian memory. On one level they are the baby battered to death in the park because it was never granted a human identity. On another, they are the whole faceless mass of society's children slaughtered by the forces created by society itself. "Who's the Emperor's son?", a mad Georgina asks of the dead bodies and then answers herself: "That one and that one and that one" (II, iii, 52).

The Shogo who destroys a symbol to save a man is still potentially human. The Shogo who slaughters children to eliminate a symbol is not. Law and order at last reign supreme, having finally triumphed over human compassion. Shogo sets out to build a new city, one that "will last a thousand years" (II, iii, 51). The parallel with Nazi Germany is not lost. When Kiro arrives from the Deep North to question the report of Shogo taking the city, he is told "that was last month" (II, iv, 54). The barbarians have returned. In a sense, however, Shogo's city is not lost. With the killing of the children, Shogo and the city have become perfected, fit to be handed over to the man in whose image they were created. Basho, the new Prime Minister, who once destroyed Shogo's soul, now destroys his body.

> BASHO. Now I come to the worst of all—I, Basho, saw that child, I saw it in its rags by the river, already lying in its own filth. I looked at it and went on. O god forgive me!—If I had looked in its eyes I would have seen the devil, and I would have put it in the water and held it under with these poet's hands.... (*The crowd groans.*) ... I am a poet and I would have known....
> COMMODORE. (*Shouting through a microphone.*) The head of the city has paid for his sin. The city is purged. (*The sheet*

is dropped.) Feed your eyes and rejoice!
(*Shogo's naked body is nailed to the placard. It has been hacked to pieces and loosely assembled upside down. The limbs have been nailed in roughly the right position, but the whole body is askew and the limbs don't meet the trunk. The head hangs down with the mouth wide open. The genitals are intact.*)
BASHO. (*Shouting through a microphone.*) This is your Prime Minister addressing you! Shogo is dead! The sin is broken! Let the new city live for ever! (II, iv, 56–57).

The sentence is carried out. The "upturned boat" no longer "knocks against the pier." After thirty-odd years, a child whose crime was being born pays his debt to society.

The sentence has been carried out; from Narrow Road to the Deep North (Photo courtesy of the Royal Court Theatre, S.W.1, London; photo by Donald Cooper, London)

Basho sacrifices humanity in the name of heaven. Shogo sacrifices humanity for the sake of the city. Georgina would teach humanity to sacrifice itself in the name of heaven for the sake of the city.

Initially, Georgina appears to be merely a crude caricature of Victorian fanaticism.

> Mr. Basho, before we agree to lead your city of the plains out of its ignorance, vice, mischief-making, and darkness, I require a few undertakings. . . . We will give you soldiers and guns to kill your enemies—and in return, you must love Jesus, give up bad language, foreswear cards, refuse spicey foods, abandon women, foresake drink and—*stop* singing on Sundays . . . except hymns and the authorized responses. . . . *Secondly,* you will leave the education of all children to me. In this suburb of hell they are all orphans of Jesus, and I claim them on His behalf. Hallelujah! (*She bangs her tamborine.*) (I, v, 32).

Later, when the Commodore announces plans to install English industry in Shogo's city, it appears that Bond is using Georgina as a convenient symbol for linking Christianity to the military-industrial complex. It is a common argument by anti-Imperialists that British colonists used the Church to control the lives of the natives in the countries England dominated and thereby reduce the possibilities of revolt. But however religiously fanatical she may seem, Georgina's character is far more complicated. It quickly becomes obvious that she and not the Commodore is the military, legal, and social brains behind their imperialism. In the battle for the city, she mans the artillery and urges the soldiers and the cannonballs forth with a combination of religion and patriotism: "I saw an angel hovering over it with a Union Jack!" (I, vi, 35).[22] When the city is subdued, her accomplishments are even more spectacular.

22. This particular image of Divine Right Imperialism is reminiscent of Victoria's "I never abandon God" in *Early Morning*.

> I've been running the city a week, haven't we George? I've relaid the sewers, straightened the streets, shut the "music" houses, put a curfew on for nine-thirty, and recoded the law. That was Monday. On Tuesday I shut the drinking shops and the theatres, unveiled a statue, gave a garden party, laid twelve foundation stones, and brought the curfew down to eight-thirty. I haven't time to go through the rest of the week, but I would like to mention that we now only allow people out for an hour at luncheon (II, i, 39).

Georgina's fanaticism is merely a mask for her social reform. Unlike Basho, she has no real interest in religion except as a tool with which to control people. Her philosophy is merely a paraphrase of Basho's own: "We need the devil to protect people from themselves" (II, i, 42). Her intention, like Shogo's, is to maintain law and order. Unlike Shogo, however, she is wise enough to realize that exterior oppression always leads to rebellion.

> Shogo ruled by atrocity. . . . It didn't work, because it left people free to judge him. They said: he makes us suffer and that's wrong. He calls it law and order, but we say it's crime against us—and that's why they threw spears at him. So instead of atrocity I use morality. I persuade people—in their hearts—that they are sin, and that they have evil thoughts, and that they're greedy and violent and destructive, and —more than anything else—that their bodies must be hidden, and that sex is nasty and corrupting and must be secret. When they believe all that, they do what they're told. They don't judge you—they feel guilty themselves and accept that you have the right to judge them. That's how *I* run the city: the missions and churches and bishops and magistrates and politicians and papers will tell people they are sin and must be kept in order. If sin didn't exist it would be necessary to invent it (II, i, 42).

The necessity felt by the leaders to control the people is a theme that echoes throughout the work of Edward

Bond. "The mob's sadistic, violent, vicious, cruel, anarchic," says Arthur in *Early Morning*. "I've learned that justice depends on law and order." [23] Shogo puts people in prison and kills them "to prevent suffering. . . . It stops the chaos" (I, iv, 29). In the end the dead rise up before Arthur to prove his error and for Shogo there is always the sudden spearthrower, each time with "a different face, but the eyes are always the same" (I, iv, 22). The type of coercion represented by Georgina is more subtle. Convince an oppressed man that he is evil and he will call for less freedom and more oppression. Convince his neighbors and in the name of morality they will sacrifice their own kind. In a discussion concerning the political interpretation made of his plays by audiences in Eastern Europe, Bond found no difficulty in equating rule by moral inhibition with rule by force.

> I think it is as true of this country as it would be of a Communist country. I don't think there is any real freedom in this country. Having said that I think one has to make the obvious distinction that the impositions of this country tend to be moralised; whereas in a Communist country which has had a radical break with tradition, it might be that many Russians are now moralised in the Communist system, but still they have to resort to force a lot more than we do, because, but only because, we can do it by more educated means.[24]

Georgina's leadership, no matter how enlightened, is morally bankrupt, an example of what Bond has described elsewhere as "opportunist prudentialism." [25] Basho quotes to her an old Japanese proverb: "People who raise ghosts become haunted" (II, i, 42). Georgina fears that she is corrupted morally, that her human sexual urges are sin.

23. Edward Bond, *Early Morning* (London: Calder & Willingham, 1968), xii, p. 73.
24. Wardle, "A Discussion with Edward Bond," p. 8.
25. Edward Bond, Preface to *Saved* (New York: Hill and Wang, 1965), p. 7.

Therefore, she exorcises her fears by projecting them onto others. Their shame is her relief. Georgina is another example of innocence corrupted by social morality against its wishes. Societal restrictions cause rebellion in everyone. Those who have accepted as truth society's morality, however, can only release their aggressions in support of society. Taught that society kills the weak, Shogo kills to prove that he belongs in society. Taught that sex is sinful, Georgina teaches people to feel shame over their sexual drives.

> The aggressive response of such people has been smothered by social morality, but this only increases its tension. So they try to relieve it in extrovert ways. Often they become missionaries and campaigners. They are obsessed with a need for censorship—which is only the moral justification of the peeping Tom. They find the wicked and ungodly everywhere —because these things are in themselves. Their social morality denies their need for justice, but that need is so basic it can only be struggled against by dying or going mad; otherwise it must be struggled against obsessively. In this struggle pleasure becomes guilt, and the moralizing, consorious, inhuman puritans are formed. Sometimes their aggression is hidden under strenuous gleefulness, but it is surprising how little glee is reflected in their opinions and beliefs, and how intolerant, destructive, and angry these guardians of morality can be. Their morality is angry because they are in conflict with themselves. Not merely divided, but *fighting* their own repressed need for justice with all the fear and hysteria of their original panic. Because this isn't something that is done once, in childhood or later; to go on living these people must muder themselves every day. . . . Socially moralized people must act contemptuously and angrily to all liberalism, contentment, and sexual freedom, because these are the things they are fighting in themselves.[26]

Georgina goes made because she loses the struggle against her need for justice. She has, through great personal

26. Edward Bond, Preface to *Lear* (London: Eyre Methuen, 1972), p. ix.

Narrow Road to the Deep North 149

control and tremendous energy, transferred her own phobias to her charges. When the children are murdered, Georgina must resume her old shame and the added burden of guilt for their deaths. Not surprisingly, when the restrictions of her sanity are lifted, Georgina becomes obsessed with visions of rape. The society of *Saved* increased violence by restricting it. The society of *Narrow Road* perverts sex by denying it.

> One of those priests! (*She bangs her tambourine at him.*) Out! Out! Out! O god, the devil's everywhere! Ha! Ha! (*She looks in panic over her shoulder. She turns round.*) There! There! (*She bangs her tambourine at space.*) Out! Out! Out! (*She sees Kiro again.*) There he is—running around! Out! (*She kneels and prays silently, her mouth working.*) Is he gone? Yes. (*She opens her eyes and looks at him.*) He's there! Still there! . . . Ah! He's going to rape me! I'm going to be raped! (*She shuts her eyes and prays.*) Jesus, help me! Help your little girl! He'll split me up and open me out! He's got his clothes off! I can feel him! (*She tries to move her arms.*) Ha! My arms are chained! (*She tries to move her legs.*) My legs are chained! . . . He's going to murder me! Murder before I'm raped! I shan't know what it's like! (*She prays.*) O god, spare me! I'll lead a cleaner life! My mind! Jesus-us-us-us-us! (*She tears open her dress.*) O Jesus, Jesus hears! Yes, yes! Jesus hears! Dead and no shame? Jesus hears! . . . (*Eyes shut in prayer.*) He's coming! I can hear him coming! There's something wet! (*Two soldiers come on upstage. One sees Georgina and points to her. They creep towards her.*) Coming! Coming! (*The soldiers grab her.*) At last! Now! Up! (*They jerk her to her feet. She opens her eyes and sees a soldier. She screams. She sees the other soldier and screams again. She hits them with the tambourine.*) No! No! My shame! My shame! (II, iv, 57–58).

Georgina, and Shogo, represent a very real advance in characterization for Bond. In them, he has created ambivalent villain/victims who demonstrate clearly his theory that the agents as well as the victims are affected by their crimes.

> I had sympathy with her [Georgina] as a person, because I thought that she was a person who was going to be very unhappy, because she had no understanding of herself and was so full of contradictions, and came to no understanding of herself, so that she didn't know how to live and couldn't live, but must finally crack up in some way . . . but the point about that scene [the killing of the children] is that there is sympathy in it for absolutely nearly everybody, because one sees, in a sense, everybody in that scene is a victim. Shogo, for instance, is very much a victim of what happens.[27]

While directing the first production of *Narrow Road to the Deep North,* Jane Howell noted that Kiro, the man of meditation, and Shogo, the man of action, seemed like opposite halves of the same character. Each saves the other's life. Each is attracted, almost against his will, to the other's life-style. They are happiest with one another and finally, when one dies, the other follows soon after. Moreover, both die in a fashion approved by religious ritual. The hacked-apart Shogo is crucified upside down in the manner of the Christian martyr Saint Peter. Kiro performs a Buddhist protest *hara-kiri.*

Kiro is more, however, than just Shogo's passive nature. He is the Innocent, the true seeker of enlightenment who wanders through all of Bond's plays. It is Kiro's fate to question and to seek solutions from the others. Nevertheless, it is he who eventually must answer the question of the correct relationship between men and the social order.

SHOGO. How would you run the city?
KIRO. (*Thinks for a moment.*) Some problems have no solution,

27. Wardle, "A Discussion with Edward Bond," pp. 7–8.

but it's hard to know which problems these are.
SHOGO. Another problem.
KIRO. Our Father Abbot has a puzzle from China. You have to fit eight pieces of wood into a circle. In fact, they're specially made so they can't fit. But for the last forty-eight years he's spent ten hours a day trying to make them fit—because one day they *might*. He's very holy (I, iv, 29).

Kiro watches the attempts of men to deal with one another. He sees the enlightened priest he wanted to follow, standing at the helm of a military dictatorship, preaching infanticide over the body of a man he has crucified. He sees his closest friend, the man who saved his life, slaughter men, women, and children in the name of protecting society. He sees a woman who has controlled a people's mind lose control of her own.

As Basho recites the condemnation of Shogo before the crowd, Kiro sits cross-legged reading the poems that Shogo upset in this attempt to escape, poems whose imagery suggests the impossibility of humanity surviving in society.

> A feather falls from the sky
> There are no birds here
> The nests are broken and
> The migration's over.
>
> The soil was dry
> The flower bent its petal mouth
> To drink from the soil
> The soil was still dry.
>
> . . . .
>
> I drain the cup
> At the bottom
> Flags (II, iv, 55–56).

In numb despair Kiro kills himself, seconds away from the answer to his search. As he draws his knife through his stomach, a man's voice is heard from the river.

(*Off. Distantly.*) Help! (*Pause. Nearer.*) Help! (*Pause.*) Ah! (*Silence. A man clambers up at the back of the stage. He is naked except for a loincloth. He is soaking wet and spits water.*) Didn't you hear me shout? (*He shakes water from his hair.*) I shouted help. You must have heard and you didn't come. . . . I could have drowned. (*The man is drying under his arms. In one movement Kiro lurches forward onto his back and straightens his legs. His robe is vivid red where the bowels have fallen. The man has his back to Kiro. He dries himself.*) (II, iv, 58–59).)

At their first meeting, Basho tells Kiro that you get enlightenment where you are. Bond's lesson lies in the relationship between Kiro and the man who nearly drowns as Kiro is committing suicide. The lesson is simply that men must behave humanely toward one another. If they do so, they will create a society that behaves humanely toward individuals. Kiro had no right to kill himself when the other man needed help. Men must keep their souls alive to save the souls of others. If others will not help them, they must save themselves. Some problems have no solutions, but it's hard to know which problems these are.

Narrow Road to the Deep North has much in common with Bond's earlier plays. Its targets are the same: leadership in all forms, particularly the twin pillars of society, government and religion, and the force they use to insure their continuity. The themes center around the narrowing opportunities for humanity in a society strictly regulated by a combination of force and inhibition. Even the plot is familiar in concept: An innocent young man follows a reverse Pilgrim's Progress course, searching for goodness while questioning the evil around him.

Certain elements of Bond's imagery are also familiar. Oedipal complexities continue to proliferate: Kiro withdraws from the world—first into the priesthood and then into the sacred vessel. Less obviously, Shogo attempts to force himself back into the society that rejected him as a child. These are all womb images, but they are all negative.

So, if a desire to return to the womb means a desire for a place where you just exist and are cared for and don't have to act for yourself—that's a very bad thing. In realistic terms, its tantamount to equating the womb with the coffin. It's politically dangerous.[28]

We also have the Oedipal atavism of the insane Georgina's release from sexual inhibitions and, as always, we have the images of violence based upon the Christian legend. Bond is haunted by the Slaughter of the Innocents. In *Narrow Road* this atrocity is personified in the butchering of the five schoolboys, but on a metaphorical level it also includes the destruction of Shogo, Georgina, and Kiro. Shogo's death is an obvious allusion to Christ's Crucifixion. Once again, a Supreme Power (society in the guise of Basho, Shogo's molder and spiritual father) has loaded all his followers' sins on one of his sons and executed him for them. The Resurrection figure is the Naked Man who saves himself unaided from drowning, dries himself off, and walks off to face the world again.

The structure of *Narrow Road* is a perfection of the method used in Bond's earlier plays. Like them, it progresses from action to action in the fragmented sense of actual experience rather than through cause-to-effect development. Nevertheless, because of its deliberate distancing, it does not require the extent of naturalistic detail necessary in *Saved*. Nor does it have the allegorical density of *Early Morning*. Consequently, *Narrow Road*, with its eleven brief scenes, is the shortest of all Bond's long plays, less than half the length of *Early Morning*. Occasionally, Bond supplies necessary exposition through narration. For the most part, however, he merely shows what happens.

> The essential thing for me, for instance, to explain that structure in *Narrow Road* is, you see, Shogo in complete control and all the rest of it and then the next minute someone says that was last week and it's all over, it's changed.

28. Edward Bond, letter to Richard Scharine, 2 October 1974.

You see it's like that, and the careful arguing what, what, why, why, and yes he was caught and then he went through the courts and they said this and they said chain him and dont' chain him and all the rest of it, this somehow was very interesting but not very relevant to our experience; I mean, I wanted to say, look, it's happening.[29]

Nevertheless, many critics persist in seeing in *Narrow Road's* deliberately narrative intent a radical structural change in Bond's writing, derived from either Brecht or the conventions of the Japanese Nō play. Like Brecht, Bond historifies the action by setting it in "Japan about the seventeenth, eighteenth, or nineteenth centuries," and "alienates" the audience by including such anachronisms as the microphone with which Basho addresses the crowd. Jane Howell attributes this innovation to Brechtian intentions rather than Brechtian imitation.

I think that Bond was upset about the hysterical attacks on *Saved*—particularly over the baby business. He thought that if he put the same problems into a cooler, more distant context then people might be ready to view those problems with much less immediate prejudice.[30]

The scene with the most Brechtian flavor is the consciously formal Introduction in which Basho identifies himself, states his intentions, and encounters the abandoned baby. However, this particular scene belongs as much to the tradition of the Nō play from which Brecht also drew. The Nō play, particularly the *kami* or *waki-no* (god play), sometimes opens with a prologue in which a priest describes a coming journey to the shrine of a particular god. On this journey, he frequently meets the god in disguise and does not recognize him. If one follows this interpretation, Basho

---

29. Edward Bond, quoted by Irving Wardle in, "A Discussion with Edward Bond," *Gambit,* 5, no. 17: 28–29.
30. Ansorge, p. 70.

would be the secondary or *waki* character whose primary function is to lead the audience to the abandoned baby, Shogo, who is the main or *shite* character. In light of Bond's repeatedly expressed concern over the manner in which society treats its children, this seems to be a reasonable interpretation. There is no reason to suppose, however, that Bond was slavishly imitating the Nō form or, for that matter, to presume that he consciously imitated it at all. Ronald Bryden, Bond's most adamant backer among the critics, states that *Narrow Road* never could have been written had not the World Theatre Season at the Aldwych sponsored a Nō troupe the season before.[31] Bond, however, has never admitted to having been influenced by either Nō drama or Brecht.

> BOND. People say that *Narrow Road* is Brechtian, for instance. It's somewhat Brechtian in shape and so on. *Saved,* for instance, uses the same technique, it just happens to be set in a different age. There's Brechtian tie-up there, but that's purely because the original on which it was based happened to be that. So I don't think I'm influenced by Brecht at all.
> WARDLE. About *Narrow Road.* Had you seen much of Japanese production?
> BOND. I'd never seen a Japanese play.[32]

Much of the credit for the similarity of the first production of *Narrow Road* to a Nō play belongs to its director, Jane Howell, and its designer, Hayden Griffin. Griffin deliberately exaggerated the exceptional width of the Belgrade stage by lowering the proscenium arch and putting up a narrow screen in back, thus creating a Nō-like frame for the action.[33] Miss Howell added such conventions as the substitution of dolls for the children to be slaughtered and red paper streamers for the ripped-out bowels of Kiro.[34]

31. Bryden, "Bond Goes to Japan," p. 27.
32. Wardle, "A Discussion with Edward Bond," p. 35.
33. Ansorge, "Jane Howell," p. 70.
34. Bryden, "Bond Goes to Japan," p. 27.

There can be no doubt that Bond is able to use stylistic elements for his own purposes. For example, he uses a variation of Basho's most famous haiku to both identify him and characterize him in the minds of the audience.

> Silent old pool
> Frog jump
> Kdang! (Introduction, p. 7).

In doing so he overrated his audience. A number of critics, among them Clive Barnes of the *New York Times,* commented favorably upon the "exquisite haiku" of Basho.[35] Others blamed Bond for their poorness. Jeremy Kingston berated the "unfortunate" translation of the above poem.

> To deliver these lines at the start of a play witout provoking laughter is impossible. Peter Needham, for all his dignity and measured speaking—and his graceful movements later on—could not have prevented the puzzled titter. . . . Having prepared myself with a quick study of Japanese poetry, I suggest the play be approached as though it were a haiku in another form. Let the images vibrate with one another as they do after meditating upon Basho's haiku. I give the Penguin translation.

> > Breaking the silence
> > Of an ancient pond
> > A frog jumped into water
> > A deep resonance.[36]

Within the context of Bond's play, Kingston's evaluation of Basho's opening haiku misses the point. Bond is well aware of the Penguin translation, for it can be found on the opening page of the same edition that inspired the play. Bond's

---

35. Clive Barnes, "Theater: Openly Cerebral," *New York Times,* 2 December 1969, p. 64.
36. Jeremy Kingston, "At the Theatre," *Punch* 256 (26 February 1969): 320–322.

translation of the poem is intentionally bad and intentionally funny. The pretentiousness of Basho's poetry is intended to prepare us to reject his philosophy.

> What particularly incensed me about Basho was that everybody says, oh, what a marvellous poet. I think that is absolutely phoney. I mean that is bad poetry, that's academic phoney poetry, all the things he said. But I really am only talking about his actions. He says for instance that you get enlightenment where you are and so on, and everybody says, oh, how profound! People like Basho never get enlightenment where they are because, you know, enlightenment should have come in the first scene of the play where he found the child. In an ideal society he would have picked that baby up, gone off the stage, and there would have been no necessity for a play.[37]

Narrow Road to the Deep North was the first Edward Bond play to be presented without raising irrelevant objections. It is abstract without being obscure, short, sharp, and to the point. Containing all the familiar Bond themes and characters, it excites interest on a number of levels, not the least of which is simply as a story. Rated by its author as a lesser work, *Narrow Road* was nonetheless a critical watershed in the acceptance of Bond and by 1970 audiences were looking forward with curiosity to his announced reworking of Shakespeare's *King Lear*.

---

37. Wardle, "A Discussion with Edward Bond," p. 9.

6
Madmen, You Are the Fallen! The Incidental Dramatic Works

In addition to his major plays, Bond has compiled a substantial body of incidental dramatic writings, including screenplays, adaptations of foreign works, and short plays for specific occasions. He has written or contributed to the writing of a number of films—the most notable of which are *Blow-up, Michael Kohlhaas, Laughter in the Dark, Walkabout,* and *Nicholas and Alexandra.* His first adaptation, Chekhov's *The Three Sisters,* was produced at the Royal Court; his third, *Spring Awakening,* was done for the National Theatre. The second, *Roundheads and Peakheads,* was undertaken as a practical exercise in learning the technique of Brecht and has never been produced. Plans for its presentation were once announced, but Bond never finished the script to his satisfaction and now considers it an abandoned project. Finally, the short plays, *Black Mass* (written for the Anti-Apartheid Movement) and *Passion* (produced for the Committee for Nuclear Disarmament), reflect Bond's particular obsessions and techniques far better than the other incidental works.

The Incidental Dramatic Works

Bond has not written for the screen in recent years. Indeed, he stopped as soon as it became financially feasible for him to do so. In 1971, just after Bond returned from a ten-week stint writing supplemental scenes for Franklin Shaffner's *Nicholas and Alexandra,* he reluctantly responded to questions about his filmwriting:

> I write films in order to live. I've never worked on a film script that interested me deeply—or, if it did, imagined for one moment that one could be allowed to deal with the subject properly. That's why all my serious writing is done for the theatre and it's never interfered with there.[1]

In 1974 similar questions were posed and similar answers were received:

> Don't waste readers's time by making them read about this nonsense. It's boring because the subject's boring. You can't honestly pick out my contributions to the films, they are so adulterated.[2]

Not exactly a mandate for investigation, and while the films themselves scarcely justify Bond's contempt for his participation in them, it is probably not sensible to dwell too long on them in this study. Film, as we are told repeatedly, is a director's medium, not a writer's. The study of film responsibility without ready access to unedited prints, shooting scripts, and finished screenplays is unrewarding conjecture. Furthermore, not even the original screenplays can be said truly to be representative of Bond's work. The inspiration for *Blow-up* is allotted to a short story by Julio Cortazar; the screenplay is credited to the director, Michelangelo Antonioni, and to Tonine Guerra—"English dialogue in collaboration with Edward Bond."[3] *Michael Kohlhaas*

1. Edward Bond, letter to Richard Scharine, 16 May 1971.
2. Edward Bond, letter to Richard Scharine, 2 October, 1974.
3. Michelangelo Antonioni, *Blow-up* (New York: Simon and Schuster, 1971), p. 21.

was originally a novella by Heinrich von Kleist and the film carries the credit line: "Screenplay by Edward Bond, adapted by Clement Biddle-Wood and Volker Schlöndorff." *Laughter in the Dark* came from a Vladimir Nabokov novel and James Vance Walker's *Walkabout* is a children's classic in Australia.

Nevertheless, Bond is a highly individual—as well as a highly competent—screenwriter. If none of the films with which he has been associated are wholly his, it is still inaccurate to say that Bond's contributions are unrecognizable. The kinship between those films and his plays is undeniable.

Although it undoubtedly was Bond's demonstrated affinity with London colloquial dialogue in *Saved* that influenced Antonioni—who was in London much of 1965—to select him for *Blow-up,* there are also thematic similarities between the film and Bond's later work. Particularly, the tendency for technology to abstract the relationships between individuals has been a concern of both artists. The episodic, spare story line of *Michael Kohlhaas* (1968), was well suited for Bond, who was to follow this method in almost all his plays. Its themes of the injustice that is the side effect of a self-serving social hierarchy and of the Oedipal violence that is its inevitable product are especially Bondian. The crucifixion image that visually dominates the film's final scene could be produced by no other writer.

Bond's tendency toward episodic structuring played a definite role in changing the tone in Tony Richardson's film version of Nabokov's *Laughter in the Dark.* Furthermore, the Oedipus/Lear theme of the blind man who gains insight and the film's black humor in the tradition of *Black Mass, Early Morning,* and *The Sea* are immediately recognizable for their Bondian twists.

> The beautifully simple screenplay is by Edward Bond, the English playwright who strikes me as the strongest and truest

innovator to have come up in the London theatre of the sixties. It isn't surprising that his script has a tone far from Nabokov's book. Bond is a writer, not a tracer. And secondly, the passed-over theory that a novelist is capable of an intellectual complexity not open to film directors hasn't much bearing on this particular movie. Ideas are lost here, but then ideas of great interest are gained about the way a man's vision of the knowable world is shaped.[4]

James Vance Marshall's *Walkabout* tells of two civilized children who survive a plane crash in the desert because of the kindness of an aborigine boy. Later, the aborigine dies, a victim of his misunderstanding of civilized mores. The *Walkabout* of Bond and director Nicholas Roeg uses this springboard to comment on civilization itself. The children are placed in danger by their father who has concluded, like the mad Arthur in *Early Morning*, that to kill them is to save them. The indifference of society to essentials is epitomized by a portable radio that blares rock and roll while the children hunt vainly for water. The aborigine stalking a kangaroo for food is compared to white businessmen machine gunning them for profit.

> *Walkabout*'s elements have been combined with such integrity that they hold in any analysis. See it, if you wish, as an allegory, or as a tale of adventure, or as an accidental arrangement of accidental events: it will support every thesis. James Vance Marshall's 1959 novel is well written and affecting . . . but for me, Edward Bond's screenplay is more exalted and more inward, and plunges us into deeper stillness.[5]

Even Bond's shorter filmwriting stints—such as the brilliant scene written for Laurence Olivier in *Nicholas and Alexandra*—show flashes of his talent and his obsessions.

4. Penelope Gilliatt, "Cackle in Hell," *New Yorker* 45 (24 May 1969): 121.
5. Marion Armstrong, "Terror and Beauty," *Christian Century* 88 (September 1971): 1,030.

Furthermore, many of Bond's efforts never reached the screen. Some years ago Bond and Bill Bryden wrote a filmscript of Wedekind's *Spring Awakening* that was never filmed.[6] Onstage, however, Bond's translation of the same play was commissioned by the National Theatre for performance in May 1974. Ironically, the director was Bill Bryden. Similarly, a biography of Nijinsky written by Bond to star Rudolph Nureyev in the title role and Paul Scofield as Diaghilev never reached the filming stage for producer Harry Salzburg.[7]

Given his growing acceptance as a playwright, it would seem we have seen the last of Edward Bond, the screenwriter. If this permits him to write still more for the stage, it is a good thing. One might wish that such a popular medium as film might prove more tractable to Bond's ideas, but this at the moment seems highly unlikely.

The impetus for Bond's adaptations has been educational rather than financial. In the late 1950s when Bond began to train himself as a playwright, he undertook an enormously detailed dissection of the structure of Chekhov's *The Three Sisters*. A decade later when he was searching for a more effective way of presenting his ideas, Bond began work on an adaptation of Bertolt Brecht's *The Roundheads and the Peakheads* "because it seemed the best way of getting to understand Brecht."[8]

In 1965 William Gaskill startled one critic by saying that of all the modern plays he had read, *Saved* reminded

6. The exact authorship of this filmscript seems to be in doubt. According to Bryden, "I had . . . worked closely with Edward Bond on a screenplay of *Spring Awakening*. . . . This script has never been filmed, but one day I would like to direct it since Bond's version is very good indeed" (Bill Bryden, letter to Richard Scharine, 11 August 1971). In contrast, Bond has stated: "It was *his* script. I read it for him and made a few suggestions. . . . People exaggerate!" (Edward Bond, letter to Richard Scharine, 8 January 1974).
7. Marina Warner, "One Distraction Only: Bond Honoured," *Vogue* (London) 126, no. 13 (1 October 1969): 34. Christopher Hampton, among others, also wrote a script for the aborted project.
8. Bond, letter, 16 May 1971.

The Incidental Dramatic Works 163

him most strongly of Chekhov: "It doesn't make any moral statements. Though it is, of course, an immensely moral play." [9] It was a comparison that went unappreciated by many. They were still more startled when Gaskill commissioned Bond to do an adaptation of *The Three Sisters* a year and a half later. In 1971 Gaskill commented upon both the comparison and the commission.

> I can't now remember why I called Bond the most Chekhovian of modern playwrights but I think it may be connected with the theme of optimism in a despairing situation and the relation between the two. . . . I knew from conversations that Edward had spent a certain period of his life visiting all plays on in London and studying their craftsmanship. He had also done a very careful analysis of *Three Sisters*. When I decided to do the play, it was obvious that I should turn to him for a new version.[10]

The obviousness of the choice was clear only to a few. At the time, Bond was only known as a creator of working-class milieu. Still, Gaskill might have recalled that similar doubts were expressed when Ann Jellicoe was commissioned by the English Stage Company to translate *The Seagull* in 1964. Subsequently, however, the authoress of *Sport of My Mad Mother* and *The Knack* produced a straightforward chronicle-play in *Shelley* and the seeming incongruity was quickly forgotten. Within a year, Bond, too, had moved dramatically beyond the streets of South London.

The Three Sisters opened at the Royal Court on 18 April, 1967, and was instrumental in dispelling the myth that Edward Bond was merely a tape recorder with questionable morals.

> The word *revival* literally means "alive again." . . . Of course, Chekhov is modern anyway, in the sad sense that his plays

---

9. William Gaskill, quoted by Hilary Spurling in "A Difference of Opinion," *Spectator* 215 (12 November 1965): 619.
10. William Gaskill, letter to Richard Scharine, 19 March 1971.

are the products of a society without faith. . . . Aimless, unable to come to terms with death, that's modern. Living again, that's revival. A living-again production of a marvellous aimless play, one of the best, and the credit, of course, goes to William Gaskill and specifically to Edward Bond who (with Richard Cottrell's expert help) wrote this new version of *Three Sisters*.[11]

Most reviewers of the production, including such ardent enemies of *Saved* as J. C. Trewin of the *Illustrated London News*, generally found favor with the adaptation. Bond's text might possibly have been accorded the adaptor's highest honor and been ignored completely had not the English Stage Company included it in the "eighteen-penny programme." A study of the Royal Court text reveals no startling new interpretations. As might have been expected of Bond, the translation is spare and unaffected. Gaskill emphasized the theatrical craftsmanship of Bond's version.

He understood one basic thing about translating which is to use fewer words than the original. It is often the attempt to translate every single detail and nuance of the original which makes translations so stiff. As someone pointed out when Irina in some version says, "It is not within my power," in Bond's version she just says, "I can't."[12]

Both text and production aimed for, and largely achieved, the impression of a universal rather than a particularized story, an intention that critic David Benedictus greeted with mixed feelings.

There are moments, but only a very few, when the revival becomes less kiss of life than an assault (when, for instance, Chebutykin sings: "Tarara-boom-d-ay, I changed my socks today") but in the main the atmosphere is fresh and ostenta-

11. David Benedictus, "Saved Again," *Plays and Players* 14, no. 9 (June 1967): 43.
12. Gaskill, letter, 19 March 1971.

The Incidental Dramatic Works 165

tiously realistic. . . . How pleasant to be able to use the word "realistic" without implying squalor. Thus the Prozorov household is an instantly recognizable one. . . . Just like home. Anyone's home. And all the tensions so carefully explored, wrapped in the formal movements of a symphony. Wonderful craft, wonderfully rendered into modern English. Yet nothing is for nothing and the price paid at the Royal Court is Russianness. It is a most unRussian production.[13]

It is more relevant to this study to ask what effect Chekhov had upon Bond, rather than what effect Bond had on Chekhov. The only answer one could make with certainty is the influence was definitely not structural.

I think I started by writing a three-acter—one would have done—but I soon discovered that I couldn't tell the truth in that long-winded sort of way any more. It didn't relate to my experience at all, which was much more a series of sudden reverses and changes. And I felt it was important not only to know what was happening in the room I might happen to be in, but also what was happening in that room over there, that house down the road. So that in order to say something useful about experience now, one has to keep track of all those things. . . . I think that's what my structure does.[14]

Bond and Chekhov are most similar in the honesty of their reflection of life's experience. It is doubtless this honesty, given the changing pattern of our lives, that also accounts for the greatly dissimilar structure of their plays. Thematically, as Gaskill has indicated, there are similarities. Bond's plays, like Chekhov's, do not contain moral statements; they *are* moral statements.

Roundheads and Peakheads properly does not belong to this study since Bond never completed the project and it

13. Benedictus, "Saved Again," p. 43.
14. Edward Bond, as quoted by Roger Hudson, Catherine Itzin, and Simon Trussler in "Drama and the Dialectics of Violence," *Theatre Quarterly* (January–March 1972): 11.

was never subsequently published or produced. The story of its creation, however, is useful for its insight into Bond's method of work. Keith Hack, most recently a director for the Royal Shakespeare Company at Stratford-on-Avon, served as Bond's translator while still a Cambridge student.

> I rang up Bond with the idea. I knew through friends that he was interested in Brecht. At the time I was in my last year at Cambridge and he happened to live just five miles away. He would pick me up in Cambridge most afternoons and I suppose we spent four or five hours a day working on the play. We worked on it for five to six months on and off. From Bond's point of view it was a way of learning to understand how Brecht worked. From mine, it was a chance to see how Bond worked. I worked for two years with the Ensemble as an asistant director and speak great German and had done a number of translations. . . . I was interested in *Roundheads,* but thought that it needed considerable adaptation to make it playable. I wanted the best playwright possible to work on it with me, hence Bond. As you know the play is based on *Measure for Measure*—which I was directing at the time and one that fascinates both of us. Bond was also particularly interested in what Brecht made of a Shakespeare play (he was writing his *Lear* at that time—in the mornings). I was the linguist. First we made a very literal translation where Bond insisted that every nuance of the text be rendered. Then we decided to do our own version of the play—really a new play, loosely based on the Brecht play but modernized and set in England, with many new scenes and a total shift of emphasis. This was to be a comment on the Brecht version —a sort of a criticism of his play. We wrote the first draft of this version and some of the scenes reached second draft stage. I then had to go away for a month and by the time I returned, we had both lost interest in this version (there is no point in writing a criticism of a Brecht play nobody knows). So he then spent three months doing a more faithful translation and adaptation, setting the play in Enoch Powell's England.[15]

15. Keith Hack, letter to Richard Scharine, 11 October, 1971.

The Incidental Dramatic Works 167

Bond's interest in the relationship between *Roundheads and Peakheads* and Shakespeare's play extended to his doing a program note for Hack's Cambridge production of *Measure for Measure* that was later reprinted in *Gambit* magazine. In it he not only does an analysis of the play that is instantly recognizable as Bondian, but also points the way toward his future interpretations of the Brecht play and of his own *Lear*.

> I think Shakespeare set out seriously to justify the behaviour of the Duke, and to try to understand the Duke's political problem of reconciling, "Morality and mercy...," but that in writing the play he saw that the problem was artificial and the Duke was a fool. That is, as an artist he sided with the child and the oppressed, and that like all artists he opposed human justice against law and order. Angelo is a lying, self-deceiving fraud, the constable a buffoon, the Duke a face-saving, hypocritical bumbler, and the saintly Isabella a vicious sex hysteric. That is a total arraignment of conventional authority and the morality used to explain and excuse it.[16]

Bond sees *Measure for Measure* as a failure because Shakespeare recognized while writing it that the Duke's attempt to control sexual conduct is inherently immoral. Shakespeare, therefore, was forced midway to turn his play into a farce. *King Lear,* which immediately followed, was his attempt to write the same story on a morally and politically viable level. Following this parallel, it seems likely that Bond's adaptation of *Roundheads and Peakheads* was a means of preparing himself for his own treatment of the Lear legend.

Bond's most recent translation, Wedekind's *Spring Awakening*, reveals more about changes in theatrical attitudes than it does about Bond's techniques. At the time the Lord Chamberlain was busily hunting for loopholes in the

16. Edward Bond, "The Duke in *Measure for Measure*," *Gambit* 5, no. 17: 43.

Royal Court's presentation of *Saved,* he was fresh from having banned a proposed National Theatre production of an earlier translation of *Spring Awakening.* Less than a decade later, the most consistent critical quibble over the National Theatre's presentation of Wedekind's landmark sexual drama concerned the wisdom of fighting a battle already long won.

Although neither Bond nor Wedekind are as controversial as they were in 1965, their mutual compatibility is as strong as ever. Indeed, Wedekind's story of youth suffering sexual repression under those in authority resulting in butchery and suicide, and with a sole escapee into a more natural existence, could easily pass as a Bond scenario—although his treatment would doubtless be less obvious. Stylistically, too, there are similarities, as Jeremy Kingston noted in *Punch:*

> The succession of sharp scenes has no real equivalent in this country till you come to the plays of Edward Bond—the apt choice, therefore, to make this new translation of the uncut text.[17]

Benedict Nightingale of the *New Statesman* pointed out the typically Bondian method of achieving sharp mood changes by changing the tone of the dialogue.

> With the lively assistance of Edward Bond's translation . . . the words, which have been leaping like trout, become grounded and arid as these venerable gentlemen discuss the subject of most burning concern to them: whether to open the courtroom window.[18]

Adverse critical comment was not lacking, of course, but even that which touched on Bond was mostly aimed at the original play. For example, Kenneth Hurren bemoaned "the

17. Jeremy Kingston, "Childhood's End," *Punch* 261 (12 June 1974): 1,021.
18. Benedict Nightingale, "Overdue Awakening," *New Statesman* (7 June 1974), p. 810.

woefulness of the caricatures provided by Wedekind and the translator, Edward Bond,"[19] and *The Stage and Television Today* commented upon the "fault" of too much respect for the original by the translator: "This apart, Mr. Bond has handled the play with clarity, taste, sympathy, and interest-holding excitement."[20]

Of considerably more relevance to a study of Bond's work are the two short plays he wrote on the specific requests of two different humanitarian groups. *Black Mass* was written for the Anti-Apartheid Movement and was first presented at the Lyceum Theater on the Sharpeville Massacre Tenth Anniversary Commemoration Evening, 22 March 1970. *Passion* was commissioned by the CND for their Festival of Life held on Easter Sunday, 11 April 1971.

Black Mass is set at a High Church altar in Vereeniging, South Africa. It is 22 March 1960, early in the afternoon of the day when hundreds of black men, women, and children will be shot down in the streets by government troops for having protested the country's racial policies. The prime minister kneels to take communion from the priest, but his mind is on the ungrateful Kaffirs whose unmoving presence in the streets is giving the government a bad name abroad. An inspector enters to tell the prime minister that reinforcements have been brought up. After he leaves, the service is interrupted again by the sound of massed gunfire. The inspector brings news of the massacre and the prime minister and the priest go with him to congratulate the "victors." In their absence, Christ climbs down from the cross and poisons the communion wine. When the mass reaches Christ's Blood, the prime minister falls dead. The inspector traces Christ back to the cross by following a trail of tears. As he is about to make the arrest, however, the priest intervenes. After a stern lecture, Christ is banished from the

19. Kenneth Hurren, "On the Hallmarks of Failure," *Spectator* 232 (8 June 1974): 712.
20. L. G. S., "National *Spring Awakening*,' *The Stage and Television Today* (6 June 1974), p. 18.

Church and his place on the cross is filled in a more satisfactory fashion.

Those gathered for the play's initial performance must have been aware that its target was far broader than the particular atrocity of a single African afternoon. The incident was, of course, a blatant example of the ruling-class's repression of the people. Bond's addition to that interpretation was to show that he saw no recognizable difference between a government that ordered murder and a church that condoned it. Both were societal institutions more devoted to their own survival than to the humanity they were originally formed to serve. Their essential sameness is emphasized by the mutually advantageous replacement on the cross of a Christ in open revolt against the Church by one of the soldiers who earlier took part in the massacre.

The title of the play is a double entendre of the type Bond likes. A "black mass" evokes the images of both a Christ ritually sacrificing himself for black people and a ritual commitment to the Anti-Christ. Both interpretations could easily find support.

The play begins with the prime minister making a confession that he profanes by planning new sins even as he kneels:

> Almighty god judge of all men we acknowledge and bewail our manifold sins and wickednesses which we—and now there's that crowd of Kaffirs down the road—from time to time most grievously have committed by thought word and deed—just stuck there—we do earnestly repent and are heartily sorry for these our misdoings the remembrance of them is grievous unto us the burden of them intolerable have mercy upon us—you'd think they'd have the decency to go, they get pleasure out of causing trouble and giving me a bad name abroad—padre, yes, have mercy upon us—and what can I do, they tie my hands and stand in front of the gun and when I squeeze the trigger it's my fault because they're aggressive enough to get hit, I must make a note of

that for the cabinet meeting (he writes in a little notebook)—
did I say we acknowledge and bewail our manifold—note
how I'm on my knees, I wish they could see that abroad, I'm
not ashamed to pray for guidance, how else could I be sure
I was doing the right thing? [21]

Rules and religion uphold one another in Bond's view. Georgina sees the angel with a Union Jack hovering over the cannonball in *Narrow Road,* but in *Black Mass* the Church supplies were tangible support to the government.

> INSPECTOR. (*He goes to the altar, where the Priest is making ritual gestures.*) Could I disturb you for a moment, padre? (*He takes rifles from under the altar.*) Could you say a prayer for the boys while you're at it, padre?
> PRIEST. I'm always praying for the boys.
> INSPECTOR. Thank you padre. We'll do you a good turn some day, man (49–50).

The crime of Sharpeville resulted, suggests Bond, from the failure of societal institutions to recognize that they were dealing with human beings. The Blacks butchered at Sharpeville are merely Pam's baby multiplied many times, his identity still unrecognized and his needs still ignored. Bond describes this mass "slaughter of the innocents" in terms of an athletic match, a subtle attack on both the inhumanity of the act and the equally great inhumanity of those who see warfare in terms of glory rather than the reality of death and suffering.

> INSPECTOR. There's no fun in shooting at people nowadays. Too many rules in the game. It doesn't really qualify as a sport any more—though, mind you, the lads still try to play in the spirit of the old amateurs, even if they've turned professional. But it can't hold a candle to wildfowling. You've shot one man and you've shot them all. Still, they put up a show.

21. Edward Bond, *Black Mass, Gambit* 5, no. 17: 48–49. Subsequent references to this play will be noted in the text.

PRIME MINISTER. What was the final score?
INSPECTOR. 69–0. They certainly didn't let the opposition walk over them. The lads really put their backs into the training. There *were* a few they could have brought off if they'd been on the ball. They set them up, but they couldn't follow it through. Still they showed real style and you can't ask fairer than that. They've gone off to the shower. Might be as well if you had a word with them, sir. After all, they won. They're good lads and I don't doubt for one moment they're their own hardest critics. I watched their faces and you could see how when one of them missed he knew he'd let the team down. The lady folk have prepared some beer and sandwiches and a few party dainties—perhaps you'd care to join us, padre?
PRIEST. Later on, I'd like that.
PRIME MINISTER. We'll just give them a pat on the head now, while they're hosing down. They like to see the board going round straight after that the whistle—show them you take an interest (51).

Given government's general disregard of Christian principles, there is nothing surprising in the failure of the inspector to recognize Christ even when he has traced the tear stains on the carpet to the cross. Nor is it surprising that he finds the priest's proposed prayer for guidance illegal under the Conspiracy Act. What shocks is the realization that the priest sincerely believes that while the state's action against the people may be sanctioned, Christ's acts against the state may not.

(*To Christ*.) You've heard, I've been able to spare you some of the public disgrace. But now I must ask you to collect your things and go immediately. I can't risk your contaminating the young people we have here. I'm very disappointed in you. Oh, I'm not thinking of myself and all the wasted effort I've thrown away—but you've let yourself down. It's too late to say it now, but you weren't without promise—and you've thrown all that away. You'll regret it in a few years and you'll look back on this and see we were right. I hope by then you'll have learned something. You'll never make anything of yourself if you go on the way you've started. I shall say no more. (*Christ comes down from the cross and starts to leave. He stops when the Priest talks again.*) God knows what your family will think of this. You've got a good family and they gave you a start in life many others would envy—and you've let them down, too. I shan't go on. Please leave quietly. It's too late for explanations and apologies. It's past amends. There is some conduct that's too underhand to be put right. I've finished now. (*Christ leans against the cross in boredom.*) Why didn't you say if something was troubling you? You know you could always turn to me. I'm not a hard man, I'm fairly reasonable and open—I think I can say that. There's nothing more to be said. The whole thing is best left in silence. In fact I'm too upset to speak. (*Christ hangs one arm over the horizontal bar of the cross.*) I'd give you another chance if I thought it would help. But there's no point. I have to remember the others in my charge. It's not fair on others to allow someone like you to continue to be in a respectable institution like this. Go, and I hope you find somewhere where you can fit in. Have I made myself clear? (*Christ goes.*) (54–55).

Black Mass is Bond's shortest play. It has only six characters, three of which are nonspeaking, and less than a hundred speeches. Yet, it contains the usual Bond images and themes: the slaughter of the Innocents (this time offstage); the Crucifixion and the Resurrection; and, of course, a condemnation of the strictures of society as enforced by the dual abstractions of god and government. Even the ending, with society firmly in power and humanity on the outside, is familiar. What is new is the comic context. Black humor is present in all of Bond's plays, but it always tends to underline rather than lighten the horror of his dramatic vision. *Black Mass*, an exception, proves that Bond can present his ideas with a light touch, but prefers not to protect his audience from the pain he believes that they should feel. The light touch is still evident in his next short play, *Passion*, but the pain once again dominates.

Passion, according to the play's director, Bill Bryden

(now of the Royal Lyceum Theatre Company of Edinburgh), was written by Bond with both location and date in mind.

> It was a particular event for a particular environment (Alexandra Park race course in London) on a particular day. C.N.D. for some reason gave the play to the Brighton Combination—a politically active group strongly connected with C.N.D. However, the group felt that for various reasons, although they liked the play, they could not do it justice, so William Gaskill . . . decided that like the previous Bond plays this should be an English Stage Company production. I was Bill's assistant during that time and he asked me to direct it, quite simply because my response to the work was strongest of all the Court Directors. I had been Associate Director on the first production of *Early Morning*. . . . We rehearsed *Passion* at the race course in extreme cold but since the company was, as you so correctly described, "Court stalwarts," including Nigel Hawthorn [Albert and Disraeli in *Early Morning* and the Commodore in *Narrow Road*], Roddy Maud-Roxby [Tusenbach in *Three Sisters*,] and Susan Engel, rehearsals, most of which were attended by the author, were most exciting. We used the large grandstand as the stage, the large crowd of about 4,000 stood on the tarmac looking up, the audience being on the racetrack itself. Christ and Buddha entered along the track, through the crowd, and onto the stage. Microphones were used through the whole play as at the following of a public political event.[22]

Passion consists of four scenes with an introduction and transitions being provided by a narrator. An old woman, whose son was killed in the war, goes to the queen to have him resurrected. The prime minister carries this message in to the queen and, after three days of well-bred conversation and playing with their yo-yos, they decide to call in a magician (who can play with two yo-yos at once) to help them solve their problem. He suggests that they tell the old woman her son is being turned into bronze to serve as

22. Bryden, letter, 11 August 1971.

a monument to the war dead. At the front of the monument there are two buttons: the first is designed to unveil the monument; the second is a rocket bomb (with a bang twice as loud as anyone else's) aimed at the enemy. The queen sets off the bomb, and, as soon as she can get her finger unstuck from the switch, she unveils the monument. It is a plain cross, containing a crucified pig. The old woman at first does not recognize her son, then concludes that the changes are probably a result of his military training. Before she can comment further, the magician of the enemy (who can play with *three* yo-yos at once) sends his bomb that is even bigger than the queen's. They wander through a wilderness of dust where they come upon a limping Christ, aided by Buddha, on his way to be crucified. He finds the pig on the cross ahead of him and leaves in despair. Meanwhile, the magician discovers a way to make a bomb out of dust and the rulers exit, leaving only the old woman holding her dead son who had been exhumed by the bomb blast. The dead soldier speaks the elegy that ends the play.

Edward Bond embodies all of his usual themes in *Passion*. Only one, the ability of our advanced technology to multiply the aggression caused by our socialized morality, is brought to the stage for the first time. It is, however, a concept that has haunted his thinking for some time.

> Well, as a society we are destroying ourselves through violence. All people say is, we must do something about these violent people, let's hit them harder. Or, look at those wicked Russians, we must make bigger bombs. Russell before the last war said that society could never survive another war, but in fact society did, so people keep thinking it wouldn't actually destroy us next time. But it could and will. . . . A competitive society must destroy itself. There is no alternative, because this is the whole dialectic of violence—I threaten you, you threaten me, and finally you have to carry out your threats, otherwise there is no credence behind them. And also because aggression creates fear and this leads to more violence and

this has an escalation of its own. So that if society goes on as it's going on now, it will destroy itself. Not will it, could it, might it—it *will*.[23]

The society of *Passion* does not completely destroy itself, but it will continue until it does. Meanwhile Bond catalogues his theses: the inhumanity of the leadership role; the destruction and corruption of its children by society; and the ambivalence over what should be man's relationship to his society. They are expressed through the usual images (the Crucifixion and the Resurrection) and a familiar conclusion is presented.

Bond establishes the queen's inhumanity by the simple but ingenious device of having her respond to all communication in a manner suggesting an IBM computer.

> Ideal weather for bowling/swimming/running/jumping/giving a garden party/getting crowned/getting married/making your will/taking in lodgers/lifting up your heart/counting your blessings/or departing this life. Select the word or phrase of your choice and delete the others as appropriate. . . . And how is your wife/mistress/mother/boyfriend/dog/aunt/son/pet alligator/lady love/ fancy man/little bit on the side/the old other/your Saturday night grunt-and-grind? Take appropriate action as already indicated.[24]

Therefore, the blandness with which she sends off the giant bomb is predictable. She has no concern about her subjects; she is merely doing as she is programmed. Oddly enough, the bomb that destroys her nation also turns the prime minister into a multiple-choice-spouting machine. The queen's immediate and accurate reaction is that he is mad, an evaluation that recalls Victoria's inability to see that

---

23. Bond, as quoted by Hudson, *et al.*, "Drama and the Dialectics of Violence," p. 9.
24. Edward Bond, *Passion, Plays and Players* 18, no. 9 (June 1971): 66. Subsequent references to this play will be noted in the text.

Arthur's insane plot to murder his army is only a reflection of her own actions.

The queen's madness is also reflected in the magician, whose blind worship of technological advancements in aggression is the means by which Bond develops the theme already mentioned. The technological irresponsibility of the scientist is to put the blame for both the bomb and the slaughter of an innocent on a more personal level. By way of polite inquiry, the queen asks the magician if he has a family.

> I did have but they left me. I don't know why. All except my son—he was one and a half and too little to walk, but he's gone, too, now. I had to go out one day to give a lecture to my students. I left him playing happily on the mat in front of the fire and I gave him a box of matches, a loaded machine gun, several large plastic bags, and an open razor to amuse himself with. When I came back from the lecture—which was called Science and the Responsible Citizen and which by the way was a great success—I found the little chap had had an accident. Robin or William or Charles, or whatever it was I'd christened him, was dead. But one feels that being so clumsy he would not have grown up to be a scientist anyway. (ii, 67).

The magician's son is another in the vast graveyard of Bond children to be denied an identity. Just as representative of these accusing ghosts, however, is the old woman's dead son. Wooed into the army and prepared for the battle by lies, his shot-away face symbolizes his loss of identity. Even more arresting are the corrupting changes in his humanity as embodied by the changes in his physiognomy.

> (*The wind has died down to a low, sinister howl. The queen presses the button and the white sheet falls. There is a full-size cross and on it is nailed and bound a crucified pig. A soldier's helmet is nailed over its head. . . . The queen, pm, and magician salute. The National Anthem is played in the Elgar version*).

OLD WOMAN. That doesn't look very like my son. But then I haven't seen him naked since he was a child. I don't recognize his hands, but of course they've made him into a soldier and taught him to hold a rifle so his hands are bound to be changed. And now I look I do see my son's face—and his mouth—and his eyes. He was such a quiet, kind, inward boy. He seemed to suffer such a lot and I could never really help him. Yes, I know him now. That's him. I can see the old suffering in his face. My poor child! (iii, 68).

The crucified pig is not literally the old woman's son, of course, but in recognizing its suffering she comes to understand that of her son. Both have had the irreplaceable gift of life and both have been slaughtered to further the aims of their societal structures. By seeing his pain in something else, the old woman—who had previously seen her son primarily as a means of support—now understands him as a human being. She comes to realize, as the dead soldier says in his elegy, "that a pig is a form of a lamb" (iv, 69).

In the wilderness that results from the bomb-caused holocaust, Christ confronts the problem faced by all Bond heroes and the sympathetic members of his audience as well. Even when God appears on earth to sacrifice himself and end men's suffering, he cannot because men are too busy crucifying themselves.

How can I suffer for men when they suffer so much, what are my sufferings compared to theirs? How can one innocent die for the guilty when so many innocents are corrupted and killed? This is a hell worse than anything my father could imagine (iv, 68).

On another level, we must repeat Christ's question with him. If Bond's pessimism about the human condition is justified, and he supports it well, how are *we* to act? Len continues to try, Arthur abandons society completely, and Kiro commits suicide. Buddha, like Arthur, suggests finding another world, but to Christ, this is a physical and moral impossibility.

But where? This is our place. There was to be love and kindness and good sense here. There was to be peace. How can we leave this wilderness to its misery and hate? (iv, 68).

All the alternatives seem frustrating and unsatisfactory. If Christ or Buddha has another answer, we are prevented from hearing it by the discovery that the magician can make a bomb out of dust. In the resulting nationalistic revitalization, the old woman finds the body of her son.

NARRATOR. It had been blown out of its grave. She lifted him up by the shoulders and rested him against her and as she did so he seemed to speak. It was only gas escaping from his decaying belly and passing out through his teeth, but he seemed to say this. . . .

A Dead Soldier's Thoughts: :
My tanks set fire to corn
My bullets stripped trees
I made where I was a grave
And walked and laughed in it
Once in a little quiet
I watched a singing bird
Build a nest
In the cardboard boxes we used to put bodies in

My flares blind stars
My guns shatter thunder
I ravaged more than plagues and famine
My bayonet was sharp
Whetted on blood and cries of unpitied men
I crippled to make men happy
Built prisons to set them free
The simpleton drooling in a bath chair inherited under my will
I am the father of millions of orphans

I am dead
The bird sang when blood ran out of my arms
It sings still

> I lie in my grave and it has the sky
> If I could rise now on wings and fly
> I would sing
> I would sing
>
> Madman, peace!
> You who bend iron but are afraid of grass
> Peace!
> The dust on my wings shines in the sun
> I have learned to sing in winter and dance in my shroud
> I have learned that a pig is a form of lamb
> And power is impotence
> Madmen, you are the fallen! (iv, 69).

The dead soldier has given us Bond's answer and, however ingenious it may seem to be, we must follow it if we are to survive as a species. We must live in the way for which we were evolved, biologically, and in protection of one another rather than in competition.

To date, Bond's incidental work has been a sizeable proportion of his creative output. In the long run, his film scripting is important only in that it made economically possible the writing of his plays. The adaptations are academically more important, if less accessible, because they provide the means by which Bond develops himself as a playwright. Finally, the short plays represent, perhaps, Bond's most successful attempt at unifying theme and structure. Bond is a writer of great intensity and his longer plays are often as exhausting as they are convincing. *Passion*, with its narrator and its use of titles before each scene and the dead soldier's elegy, also takes Bond further into Brechtian methods than he had before ventured. Bond has promised still another short play to be presented with *Black Mass* and *Passion*, the entire trilogy tentatively to be labeled *The Cross Plays*.[25] Considering his mastery of the medium, it would be a shame if it were the last.

25. Bryden, letter, 11 August 1971.

7
Lear:
"Suffer the Little Children"

BOND. Well, I am writing a play about King Lear.
HOBSON. Somebody else has done that.
BOND. Who's that?
HOBSON. Shakespeare.
BOND. Oh, yes.[1]

When Edward Bond first revealed in an interview that he was writing a play based upon Shakespeare's *King Lear,* he displayed a renewed capacity for raising the eyebrows and ire of English intellectuals, Never one to mollify his contemporaries or his critics, Bond once insisted on the absence of a dramatic tradition in England for the last three hundred years.[2] Shakespeare, falling outside this time period, had presumably been excluded from the evaluation. With

---

1. Edward Bond and Harold Hobson, quoted by Irving Wardle in "A Discussion with Edward Bond," *Gambit* 5, no. 17: 24.
2. Irving Wardle, "The Wrong Quarrel over the Wrong Play," *New Society* 56 (25 November 1965): 27.

Playbill jacket for Lear
(Permission for use of jacket design from the Royal Court Theatre, S.W.1, London; drawing by Yves Simard)

the new announcement, however, Bond watchers took heart. Their hero had not gone Establishment yet.

Bond's real target was not Shakespeare or his play, but the fact that modern audiences cannot see *King Lear* with a Tudor sensibility. Therefore, he initially proposed to recreate the play so that contemporary viewers might experience the impact felt by *King Lear's* original audiences.

> I very much object to the worshipping of that play by the academic theatre, which I dislike very much because I think it is a totally dishonest experience. "Oh, yes, you know, this marvellous man suffering" and all the rest of it. I think that at the time it would have been a completely, totally different experience to see Lear reacting in the Tudor set up and I think he would have meant so much more on more different things. Now, I think it's an invitation to be artistically lazy to say, "Oh, how marvellous[ly] sensitive we are and this marvellous artistic experience we're having, understanding this play," and all the rest of it. It's nice and comfortable. You don't have to question yourself, or change your society. He's a Renaissance figure and he doesn't impinge on our society as much as he should. So that I would like to rewrite the play to try and make it more relevant.[3]

The first production of *Lear*, originally scheduled for April 1971, failed to materialize, but the Easter performance of *Passion* whetted rather than dampened critical curiosity. William Gaskill delayed the opening of *Lear* until 29 September while he and the cast (including Harry Andrews in the title role) polished the production. They might well have saved themselves the trouble. The critical reaction to Bond's work was predictable.

Gregory Dark, whose position as Gaskill's assistant director disqualifies him for objective comment, believes that "*Lear* is the finest and most important play to have been premiered at the Royal Court." It is his probably accurate

3. Wardle, "A Discussion with Edward Bond," p. 24.

opinion that the critics simply did not understand the play, but were reluctant to admit it.

> We searched for a few intelligent remarks for our front-of-house quoteboards, but these were not all that forthcoming. On the whole, we felt that the critics were scared of giving an outright condemnation—they had been caught out that way with *Saved*—but obviously did not like the play, so they chose a middle road which satisfied nobody, and really meant nothing.[4]

Predictably, magazines and out-of-town newspapers, whose later deadlines gave them more time for reflection, were more perceptive in their reviews than were the dailies. Nevertheless, for every one like Kenneth Hurren of *The Spectator* who called *Lear* "an achievement that could stand comparison with the late Shakespeare at his most monumental,"[5] four others qualified their praise with reservations concerning Bond's lack of an objective correlative[6] (Nicholas de Johgh in *The Guardian*), or his inaccurate psychology (Benedict Nightingale in the *New Statesman*), or his political naiveté (Charles Marowitz in *The New York Times*) or, finally, and most cuttingly, social irrelevance[7] (John Weightman in *Encounter*).

Having salvaged their academic and aesthetic pride, all seemingly concurred with the conclusion drawn by *Plays and Players*'s John Holmstrom: "I take it we are all agreed, we shattered ones who have seen Bond's *Lear,* that it is an imposing and disturbing piece of work."[8] Frank Marcus of the London *Sunday Telegraph* called *Lear* "the most cour-

---

4. Gregory Dark, "Production Casebook, no. 5: Edward Bond's *Lear* at the Royal Court," *Theatre Quarterly* 2 (January–March 1972): 22, 31.

5. Kenneth Hurren, "Lord Mansfield's Advice to Judges," *Plays and Players* 19, no. 4 (January 1972): 20.

6. Nicholas de Johgh, "Bond's *Lear*," Guardian, 9 October 1971, p. 29.

7. John Weightman, "Stage Politics," *Encounter* 37 (December 1971): 31.

8. John Holmstrom, "Royal Court *Lear*," *Plays and Players* 19, no. 2 (November 1971): 42.

ageous play" of 1971,[9] and Michael Billington of *The Guardian* categorized it as "the sort of play that gets failure a good name." [10] Marowitz suggested that perhaps the diminutive size of the Royal Court stage lessened its effectiveness.

> There is an inescapable magnitude about Bond's *Lear*. The play is enhanced by the parallels which underlie its every invention. It is studded with sharp theatrical images, and cries out for the full-scale, epic production it is bound to get on the Continent.[11]

Finally, Benedict Nightingale, who had felt himself being driven to facetiousness by the unrelieved horror of the early acts, praised *Lear's* accumulating power.

> I must admit that the more the seats around me emptied, the more the play impressed me, albeit against many of my instincts and much of my judgment. It undeniably has something, this untidy moral melodrama, with its odd mixture of the idiomatic and the rhetorical, of *Saved* and *The White Devil*; its Shakespearian ghosts, Brechtian soldiery, and scurvily Bondish politicians. . . . The play's horrors, then, have their perhaps overemphatic place in plot and theme: they also, you feel, reflect authentic pain and anger. . . . Yet another horror, you say; but not one that quite eradicates the impression of human nobility, briefly and precariously achieved. One could not call this journey into Bond's mind a totally dispiriting one.[12]

Critical opinions being so diverse and so contradictory, it may well be too soon to rate *Lear*. None of Bond's longer

9. Frank Marcus, "Once Again, the See-sawing Fluctuations of Fortune," *Plays and Players* 19, no. 4 (January 1972): 22.
10. Michael Billington, "First, a Personal Note," *Plays and Players* 19, no. 4 (January 1972): 18.
11. Charles Marowitz, "A Modern *Lear* Amid Political Evil," *New York Times*, 24 October 1971, sec. 2, p. 5.
12. Benedict Nightingale, "Bond in a Cage," *New Statesman* 82 (8 October 1971): 485.

plays have been well eccepted in their first production and all have received a much more intelligent press in revival. Gregory Dark, whose eulogistic evaluation of *Lear* was quoted earlier, remarked in almost the same breath on the difficulties suffered by the cast and technicians "in getting onto the wave-length of the play." [13] It may well be, as William Gaskill has said of *Early Morning*, "you have to live with it."

In his Preface to *Lear*, Edward Bond has called the eighty speaking parts of the play "one role showing the character of a society." Structurally, the play is divided into three acts and eighteen scenes:

> Act One shows a world dominated by myth. Act Two shows the clash between myth and reality, between superstitious men and the autonomous world. Act Three shows a resolution of this, in the world we prove real by dying in it.[14]

ACT I

Scene 1: Lear, the king, is building a wall to keep out his enemies, North and Cornwall. He and his Court are inspecting the wall when they discover the body of a workman who was killed in a construction accident. Lear accuses the worker who caused the fatal accident of being allied to the local farmers who sabotage the wall at night and insists that he be court-martialed and executed immediately. Bodice, Lear's eldest daughter, interferes on behalf of the worker, challenging her father's authority. She and her sister Fontanelle announce they are going to marry North and Cornwall, respectively, and have the wall pulled down. The sisters order Lear to free the worker, whom Lear himself then shoots, and then leave to join their future husbands.

Scene 2: Lear stands on a saluting platform with War-

13. Dark, "Casebook no. 5," p. 22.
14. Edward Bond, Preface to *Lear* (London: Eyre Methuen, 1972), p. 14.

rington (his chief administrator), the Old Councilor, and a Bishop reviewing his army as it marches by on the parade ground. Lear "smells victory" as Warrington tells him he has received letters from each of the daughters asking him to betray Lear and the other sister.

Scene 3: Lear's daughters meet with North and Cornwall in war council. In asides, Bodice and Fontanelle describe their sexual disappointment in their husbands. Each plans to destroy the other, have her husband murdered, marry Warrington, and run the country.

Scene 4: The daughter's armies are victorious and Warrington is taken prisoner, but their schemes to murder their husbands fail. Warrington, his tongue previously removed, is beaten as the sisters watch, Bodice calmly knitting, and Fontanelle leaping about in excitement. Bodice deafens Warrington with her knitting needles.

Scene 5: Lear, retreating deep into the woods, is abandoned by the Old Councilor. He finds a plate of half-eaten bread. Warrington, whose bread it was, is about to attack Lear when the Boy who left the bread for Warrington frightens him away. The Boy takes Lear into his home.

Scene 6: The Boy and his pregnant wife (Cordelia) feed Lear, who is delirious and speaking in riddles. The Boy, who used to work with his father as a grave digger, describes his peaceful, pastoral life. As Lear sleeps, the Boy and Cordelia argue over whether or not to protect him. Warrington tries unsuccessfully to stab Lear, then hides in the well.

Scene 7: The next afternoon at the house of the Grave Digger's Boy, Lear awakes from a long, restful sleep. The Carpenter, who is in love with Cordelia and does odd jobs for her, arrives to mend the door and bring a cradle he has made for the expected child. The Boy offers to let Lear stay and look after the pigs, but while the Boy is down in the well trying to find out why the water is dirty, Cordelia tells Lear to leave. Warrington is discovered dead in the well. Soldiers arrive searching for Lear. They kill the Boy and the pigs. Some of the soldiers take Lear away as the others rape Cordelia. The Carpenter appears and kills the soldiers.

ACT II

Scene 1: Lear is put on trial by his daughters and their husbands. The judge, appointed by Lear because he was corrupt, is instructed to convict Lear. Fontanelle and the Old Councilor testify against him, but Lear refuses to acknowledge either the court or his daughters. Bodice gives Lear a mirror in which he sees "not the king" but "a cage of bars with an animal in it." North and Cornwall intervene and Lear's sentence is commuted to imprisonment. Undaunted, Bodice and Fontanelle discuss how to deal with the agitators in the villages led by Cordelia.

Scene 2: Lear is thrown into his cell where the ghost of the Grave Digger's Boy appears to him. At Lear's request, he brings the apparitions of Bodice and Fontanelle who come to Lear in the form of children. Fontanelle sits on his knee and Bodice puts on her mother's dress. When Ben, a young orderly, brings Lear his food, the girls realize they're in a prison. Three soldiers come in to make a routine search of the cell and the girls go. An old orderly collects Lear's uneaten food. The Ghost and Lear comfort one another and the Ghost asks Lear if he can stay with him.

Scene 3: Cordelia and some rebel soldiers wait for the Carpenter to arrive. They have skirmished with government scouts and one of their men was badly wounded. The captured scouts are executed, except for the one who is interrogated. He asks to join the rebels, but Cordelia has him shot because he doesn't hate enough to be trusted. They depart, leaving their wounded comrade behind to count the stars and die.

Scene 4: At the headquarters of Lear's daughters, Bodice and Fontanelle find that their power is weakening. The peasants are getting stronger and their husbands have tried

Lear

to desert. They sign Lear's death warrant and put their husbands under arrest.

Scene 5: Lear and a group of other prisoners, all of whom are blindfolded and chained together, are being led along a country road. Their guards have lost their way. The Carpenter and his rebel soldiers capture the convoy, but do not free the prisoners. They merely add Fontanelle to the end of the line and Lear, who does not recognize her, pleads to find "his boy" whom he once did a "very great wrong."

Scene 6: Lear, Fontanelle (whom Lear still does not recognize), and the other prisoners are back in their cell. The guerrillas are in power, but there is still chaos in the kingdom and prisoners are being shot. The Ghost, now thinner and weaker, appears to Lear and is embraced as his son. Fontanelle pleads for help from the unhearing Lear. She is shot on the order of the Carpenter. Lear watches the autopsy performed on Fontanelle and is astonished by the purity of her organs and viscera. Bodice, now a prisoner, argues with the Carpenter for her freedom. The soldiers bayonet her, and the prison doctor uses one of his new inventions to blind Lear by hygienically extracting his eyeballs. The Ghost comforts Lear and leads him away.

Scene 7: Lear, begging in an open field near the wall, encounters a farmer and his family who have had their property and possessions confiscated by the government. The farmer is going to work on the wall, and his son is going into the army. They can only hope that he won't die. Lear is filled with pity for them and wishes he could do something to save them from their suffering.

ACT III

Scene 1: The house of the Grave Digger's Boy is now inhabited by Thomas, his pregnant wife (Susan), and John. They care for the blind Lear. A deserter from the wall that Cordelia continues to build comes to Lear for help. He is hidden from the soldiers who arrive looking for him. Ben, the young orderly who fed Lear in prison, also comes begging for sanctuary. Lear, despite protests from Susan, refuses to send anyone away.

Scene 2: Strangers gather at the house of the Grave Digger's Boy to hear Lear speak. After the speech, soldiers arrive to arrest Ben and the other deserter. The Old Councilor, now in Cordelia's pay, comes to ask Lear to stop speaking in public. The Ghost, already in an advanced state of deterioration, advises Lear to send the people away, but he feels he can't abandon Lear.

Scene 3: Lear talks to the Ghost in the woods, trying to decide what to do. The Ghost weeps because he knew how to live, because he is dead, and because he is dying again. Cordelia comes to ask Lear to stop speaking what men wish to hear. He refuses and she announces that he must go on trial. The suffering Ghost watches his former wife, wishing that she would recognize him or at least remember him. The pigs go mad and attack him. The Ghost dies in Lear's arms.

Scene 4: Susan leads Lear to the base of the wall and leaves at his request. Lear climbs painfully to the top of the wall and starts digging it up. The Farmer's son, now a junior officer, enters and shoots Lear who dies on the wall.

Lear is the latest in a lengthening line of Bond Innocents. He is also the first character in Bond's plays to reach the level of a tragic hero. Protected by his position on the throne, Lear is not "born" to the society that he, in fact, helped to create until he is usurped from power as an old man. In his old age, he suffers the physical and emotional battering that results in the moral death of most children before they can ever reach biological adulthood. Despite these torments, Lear gains in his understanding of humanity. He matures morally and, although he suffers setbacks, he learns basic truths about men and their social institutions. Lear learns how to live; that is, he becomes a morally healthy human being. This state of moral maturity de-

Lear

mands a course of action that conflicts with the limits set by society, and Lear is killed. He achieves a state of understanding after great suffering and acts according to that understanding. Lear's death is inevitable and he knowingly brings it upon himself, banishing pity and fear in a classic catharsis. Lear's passage from the destructiveness of his prenatal power to moral maturity and tragic stature is the spine of the play.

At the outset of the play, Lear is an autocrat who demands and has always received total subservience. Born to power, his position has allowed him to remain as totally self-centered as a child. Because he combines moral immaturity and great power, Lear is capable of great, if unintentional, evil. His primary purpose in life has been the building of a great wall to keep his people safe from the enemies outside their borders.

> I started this wall when I was young. I stopped my enemies in the field, but there were always more of them. How could we ever be free: So I built this wall to keep our enemies out. My people will live behind this wall when I'm dead. You may be governed by fools but you'll always live in peace. My wall will make you free.[15]

The wall is the dominant image of *Lear*. Like Stonehenge in *Early Morning* and the sacred vessel in *Narrow Road*, it is a symbol of those social institutions such as government and religion that are created to help men and end by enslaving them. Dramatically, however, it is an improvement on the earlier works in that it provides a continual visual embodiment of the social oppression that creates the atmosphere in all Bond's plays.

> The king was mad. He took all the men from this village. But I hid. They'd worked with their hands all their lives but

---

15. Edward Bond, *Lear* (London: Eyre Methuen, 1972): I, i, 3–4. Subsequent references to this play will be noted in the text.

when they started on the wall their hands bled for a week. . . . There was a disease . . . "Wall death." Their feet used to swell with the mud. The stink of it even when you were asleep! Living in a grave! . . . We used to dig his wall up at nights, when they were working near here (I, vii, 25–26).

The Grave Digger's Boy's description of the wall workers as "living in a grave" recalls the dead soldier's use of the identical phrase to define warfare in *Passion*. The workers become ill on the wall and rebel against it because the mentally healthy always protest against work that gives them no personal satisfaction and from which they feel alienated. According to psychologist Wilhelm Reich, this is proof of their mental health. Reich also believed that physical and mental health were closely related and that to curb one was to endanger the other.[16]

The wall symbolizes the great crime of Lear's moral immaturity. To Edward Bond, Lear is a renaissance figure who stands for the shift from man's being responsible to himself to his being responsible to a central government. This is a crime because concentration of power acts primarily to perpetuate itself. People are responsible to government, but government is not really responsible to the people. That those in power sincerely believe that they are acting for the people's good is beside the point. In *Narrow Road*, Shogo easily excuses the atrocities of his administration: "People are born in a tiger's mouth. I snatch them out and some of them get caught on the teeth—*that's* what you're blaming me for."[17] It is symptomatic of Lear's moral blindness (itself on obvious Oedipal allusion) that he sees himself as the savior of his subjects at the same moment that he murders one of them.

---

16. M. B. Zweig, "Wilhelm Reich's Theory: Ethical Implications," *American Imago* 28, no. 3 (Fall 1971): : 280.

17. Edward Bond, *Narrow Road to the Deep North* (New York: Hill and Wang, 1968): I, iv, 29.

> My enemies will not destroy my work! I gave my life to
> these people. I've seen armies on their hands and knees in
> blood, insane women feeding dead children at their empty
> breasts, dying men spitting blood at me with their last breath,
> our brave young men in tears—. But I could bear all this!
> When I'm dead my people will live in freedom and peace
> and remember my name, no—venerate it! . . . They are my
> sheep and if one of them is lost I'd take fire to hell to bring
> him out. I loved and cared for my children, and now you've
> sold them to their enemies! (*He shoots Third Worker, and his
> body slumps forwards on the post in a low bow.*) There's
> no more time, it's too late to learn anything (I, i, 7).

Another way to define Lear's centralization of power is to call it nationalism, an abstraction that is abhorrent to Bond as any other. If a man is regarded first as a national, he loses his rights and his identity as an individual. Loss of identity (for example, Pam's baby in *Saved*, the schoolchildren in *Narrow Road*, the blacks in *Black Mass*) is the sure sign of a Bond victim. Lear can kill the worker without conscience because he sees him in terms of national aims rather than as an individual. His death will make the others work faster and the wall will be finished more quickly. As Bond has pointed out, violence is licensed by our society as long as it is for national rather than personal objectives. Lear is aware that such policies make him hated. He has been hateful; therefore not to hate him would be in Brechtian terms an exception to the rule, and government must act according to rules, not exceptions. Nevertheless, he does not resent the hatred that he accepts as proof that he is acting in the nation's best interest. "Men of vision," says the prime minister in *Black Mass*, "are bound to be misunderstood in their own time and being misunderstood is part of the privilege of being a man of vision." [18]

Lear's victims extend beyond the common people. His concerns are national, but since he is the head of the nation,

18. Edward Bond, *Black Mass*, *Gambit* 5, no. 17: 48.

they are also personal. Since Lear is acting for the people, any methods he uses to insure that he will continue to act in the name of the people are acceptable. Power protects itself with this rationalization and the lesson it teaches is that power is the only protection. Lear's daughters learn this lesson and are corrupted by it. They fear, with justification, that Lear would turn on them if they disputed him. So they move to strip him of his power. When they have done so, they condemn him to death. This does not make them basically inhuman any more than their attempted prevention of the worker's execution proves that they are good. Both acts are intended to neutralize Lear and consolidate their own position. Lear is to blame for his daughter's acts against him and against one another. Evil is not inherent biologically in Lear's daughters. They are the victims of the social morality he has taught them. This is the real lesson Lear learns at Fontanelle's autopsy.

LEAR. Is that my daughter . . .? (*Points.*) That's . . .?
FOURTH PRISONER. The stomach.
LEAR. (*Points.*) That?
FOURTH PRISONER. The lungs. You can see how she died. The bullet track goes through the lady's lungs.
LEAR. But where is the. . . . She was cruel and angry and hard. . . .
FOURTH PRISONER. (*Points.*) The womb.
LEAR. So much blood and bits and pieces packed in with all that care. Where is the . . . where . . . ?
FOURTH PRISONER. What is the question?
LEAR. Where is the beast? The blood is as still as a lake. Where . . . ? Where . . . ?
FOURTH PDISONER. (*To Soldier O.*) What's the man asking (*No response.*)
LEAR. She sleeps inside like a lion and a lamb and a child. The things are so beautiful. I am astonished. I have never seen anything so beautiful. If I had known she was so beautiful. . . . Her body was made by the hand of a child, so sure and nothing unclean. . . . If I had known this beauty and

patience and care, how I would have loved her. (*The Ghost starts to cry but remains perfectly still.*) Did I make this—and destroy it? (II, vi, 59).

Bodice and Fontanelle's concept of morality reflects the society that formed them. Therefore, it reflects their father. The judge who condemns Lear at the trial was originally appointed by Lear because he was a corrupt judge. There is more truth than irony in Bodice's assessment of her spies as "the only moral institution in this country" (II, iv, 46). In a nation where betrayal is the rule, a spy is by definition the epitome of morality.

In Edward Bond's view, the socially moralized person is one who accepts the assumption of societal institutions that men are naturally bad and must be severely restricted by legal or moral force if they are not to destroy themselves or others. It is a familiar way of accounting for men's social aggressions and self-destructive tendencies, and has received academic support from Freud's theory of an antisocial, amoral unconscious and a biologically given Death Instinct and fundamental masochism (published in *Beyond the Pleasure Principle*). Bond frequently points this out whether or not this ideology is believed is irrelevant, since society does, in fact, operate in this manner. By so doing Bond believes society creates among its members a sense of repression, that results in rebellion among those who recognize the source of their oppression and unmotivated and unpatterned acts of aggression among those who do not. Both rebellion and aggression justify society's hypothesis and are thus used to excuse continuing or increasing restrictions. The Bondian theory that violence is cultural rather than inherent receives strong support from anthropologists such as Alexander Alland, Jr., in *The Human Imperative*. That it proceeds from frustration rather than freedom is amply reasoned in Desmond Morris's *The Human Zoo*.

According to psychologist Wilhelm Reich, men exist at three psychological levels within a restrictive society: (1)

The morally and emotionally mature individual follows his biological instincts to a course of action that is best for himself and best for others. He is an enlightened hedonist who realizes that contributing to the good of others is to his own ultimate benefit. An honest acceptance of, and action in support of, his instincts invariably places him in political revolt against society. (2) The individual repressed by societal institutions has the same healthy biological instincts as the rebel, but not realizing the source of his frustrations, he is indiscriminantly aggressive. He does not really believe the morality of societal institutions, but he accepts the reality of their power over him and cannot conceive of an existence without them. These are the characters Bond wrote about in *Saved*. When they are temporarily released from institutional control, their frustrations can explode as they do in the stoning of the baby. (3) The corrupted Innocent, the acceptor of society's morality also has the aggressiveness born of the restriction of the basic biological urges. Therefore, he must struggle against them obsessively or sublimate them into such socially approved occupations as policeman, soldier, censor, missionary, or politician. In any case, the socially moralized individual is dangerous, not only because he extends the repression that formed him, but because he, too, can explode into orgiastic violence if the stress of the situation penetrates his social armor.[19] Bond illustrates this release of atavistic fury and identifies its source in Fontanelle's progression from interested spectator to hysterical participant in the beating of Warrington.

> FONTANELLE. Use the boot! (*Soldier A kicks him.*) Jump on him! (*She pushes Soldier A.*) Jump on his head!
> SOLDIER A. Lay off, lady, lay off! 'Oo's killin' 'im, me or you?
> BODICE. (*Knits.*) One plain, two pearl, one plain.
> FONTANELLE. Throw him up and drop him. I want to hear him drop.

19. Zweig, p. 279.

SOLDIER A. Thas's a bit 'eavy, yer need proper gear t' drop 'em—
FONTANELLE. Do something! Don't let him get away with it. O Christ, why did I cut his tongue out? I want to hear him scream!
SOLDIER A. (*Jerks Warrington's head up.*) Look at 'is eyes, Miss. Thas's boney-fidey sufferin'.
FONTANELLE. O yes, tears and blood. I wish my father was here. I wish he could see him. Look at his hands! Look at them going! What's he praying or clutching? Smash his hands! (*Soldier A and Fontanelle jump on Warrington's hands.*) Kill his hands! Kill his feet! Jump on it—all of it! He can't hit us now. Look at his hands like boiling crabs! Kill it! Kill all of it! Kill him inside! Make him dead! Father! Father! I want to sit on his lungs!
BODICE. (*Knits.*) Plain, pearl, plain. She was just the same at school.
FONTANELLE. I've always wanted to sit on a man's lungs. Let me. Give me his lungs. . . . Look at his mouth! He wants to say something. I'd die to listen. O why did I cut his tongue out? (I, iv, 14–15).

In theory, Lear should take pride in his daughters' ability to assimilate the lessons he has unwittingly taught. However, like most people who believe in societal institutions, he sincerely intended to preserve rather than destroy his children's innocence. Like Dickens's Christmas Past, the Ghost of the Grave Digger's Boy brings to the imprisoned Lear the shades of his daughters at the moment when, as children, they chose the death of the soul over the life of the humane. In the cell they form a tableau like that of Blake's *Job and his Daughters*. It is a winter morning after a battle and Lear has brought the dead soldiers in coffins on carts to be buried in the churchyard.

LEAR. (*Bodice gets into the dress, comes down to him. He points at her.*) Take it off!
BODICE. No.

LEAR. Take it off. Your mother's dress!
BODICE. She's dead! She gave it to me!
LEAR. (*Pointing.*) Take it off!
BODICE. No!
LEAR. Yes, or you will always wear it! (*He pulls her to him.*) Bodice! My poor child, you might as well have worn her shroud. (*Bodice cries against him. . . .*)
BODICE. Listen. (*She stands.*)
LEAR. Where are you going?
BODICE. Mother's dead. I must serve tea. They're ringing the bell.
LEAR. Stay here.
FONTANELLE. They're waiting. There's a long line behind the coffins. They're standing so still!
LEAR. Stay here and they can't begin. We can stay here together! (II, ii, 39, 41).

The incident of Bodice and her mother's dress is purely Freudian, reminiscent of the Oedipal conflicts formed in all of Bond's plays but seen for the first time from the father's viewpoint. To wear the mother's dress is to replace her in the affections of the father. The mother, however, is dead and to replace her is also to "die" (in a Bondian sense, to lose one's humanity). Fontanelle's decision to accept her father's world is also expressed in a striking metaphor: she leaves him to officiate at a mass funeral.

Although the compatability of Lear's daughters with their society seems unquestionable, the socially moralized can never be completely happy. They must struggle incessantly to prevent their being undermined by their own basic instincts. This "armoring," according to Reich, prevents their emotional maturity and, among other things, makes their sex lives unsatisfactory.

FONTANELLE. (*Aside.*) I'm bitterly disappointed in my husband. How dare he! A civil servant wrote his letters and an actor posed for his photographs. When he gets on top of me I'm so angry I have to count to ten. That's long enough. Then

I wait till he's asleep and work myself off. I'm not making do with that for long. . . .
BODICE. (*Aside.*) I'm not disappointed in my husband. I expected nothing. There is some satisfaction in listening to him squeak on top of me while he tries to get his little paddle in. I lie still and tell myself while he whines, you'll pay for this, my lad. He sees me smiling and contented and thinks it's my virility. Virility! It'd be easier to get blood out of a stone, and far more probable (I, iii, 10).

Bodice and Fontanelle, like Georgina in *Narrow Road,* foster their own repressions upon their subjects only to discover like her that "people who raise ghosts become haunted." Scarred by her father's use of power, Bodice believed that she would be free of fear when that power was hers. Once in a position of leadership, however, she finds that controlling requires an even greater restraint than being controlled.

War. Power. . . . I'm forced to sit at this desk, work with my sister, walk beside my husband. They say decide this and that, but I don't decide anything. My decisions are forced on me. I change people's lives and things get done—it's like a mountain moving forward, but not because I tell it to. I started to pull the wall down, and I had to stop that—the men are needed here. (*She taps the map with the finger tips of one hand.*) And now I must move them here and here . . . because the map's my straightjacket and that's all I can do. I'm trapped. (*Off, a clock strikes rapidly. Silence. She thinks about her life, but not reflectively. She is trying to understand what has happened to her.*) I hated being a girl, but at least I was happy sometimes . . . they didn't humiliate me then. I was almost free! I made so many plans, one day I'd be my own master! Now I have all the power . . . and I'm a slave. Worse! (II, iv, 48–49).

The rebellion that they started is continued by those even more repressed than they. Bodice and Fontanelle are defeated, captured, and, finally, executed in the same cell in which they imprisoned their father—never realizing that they have been entrapped in it ever since they chose to follow their father's principles as children.

When Lear is overthrown, he is propelled into the society he created like a baby being born. Like a baby he is punished, pummeled, and seeks only the protection that is a child's right. However, the mere fact of his being overthrown does not teach Lear moral maturity. In his insane ravings, both at the house of the Grave Digger's Boy and at his trial, he will recognize and express the human condition under the society he has created. However, Lear will not realize his own complicity in this condition until the shades of his daughters visit him in his prison. There, too, he will learn from the ghost of the Grave Digger's Boy the necessity of compassion for one's fellow man. In his second imprisonment, Lear will learn at Fontanelle's autopsy that mankind is not inherently evil, and will be blinded immediately thereafter, a symbolic representation of insight. Upon his release from prison, Lear will meet the Norfolk farmer and his family on the way to the wall and realize that his guilt extends even to the social institutions that he has created, which will live on after him. Lear will again seek protection in the house of the Grave Digger's Boy in the Golden Age that his nationalizing policies destroyed, only to find that the Golden Age no longer exists. In an age where every individual is answerable to the state, there is no refuge for individuals. Depending upon the state's degree of corruption, all men are equally safe or in danger. Himself given momentary immunity by his notoriety, Lear tries to protect others and finds that he is helpless. Political innocence in a political age is immoral. Moral maturity will eventually force Lear to act against the entire system, represented in this case by his wall.

Unexposed to the society he has created until he is old, Lear retains a baby's egocentricity. That is, he expects to be protected in the way that all animals except man protect their young. After his defeat, however, his followers, epitomized by the Old Councilor, desert him in the woods. There, he is sheltered by the Grave Digger's Boy and his wife. The Boy is representative of the Golden Age that Lear destroyed through his centralization policies. He has two fields, some pigs, and a well that he dug himself. It is important to note, however, that Lear doesn't yet recognize the Boy's significance or realize that he himself has made the Boy's lifestyle impossible. Lear sees the Boy's house (another of Bond's womb images) only as a place in which he is protected. Therefore, when Cordelia tries to make him leave, his reaction is typically self-centered.

> He asked me to stay! No, I won't go! . . . He said I could stay. He won't break his word. I'm too old to look after myself. I can't live in ditches and barns and beg for scraps and hire myself to peasants! No, I won't be at everyone's call! My daughters sent you! *You* go! It's you who're destroying this place! We must get rid of you! (I, vii, 27).

It is also important to note that while Lear and Cordelia both believe that they could be happy in isolation, the Grave Digger's Boy does not. He is a fluke, able to live in a natural manner only because he has hidden from the authorities and, necessarily, the rest of humanity as well. As a morally healthy individual, the Grave Digger's Boy instinctively recognizes his obligation to his fellow man. Cordelia can see this urge, but cannot understand it.

> You make me happy—my father said I'd be unhappy here, but I'm not, you've made me so happy—why can't I make you happy? Look at the way you brought that man here! The first one you find! Why? I'm so afraid something will happen (I, vi, 21).

Cordelia forms an interesting parallel with Lear. Her father, who was a priest, taught her everything. Therefore, she has a socially moralized background. Cordelia is happy in her husband's way of life, but her training has instilled in her the need to formalize and protect it. In the words of the Boy, "she'd like to put a fence round us and shut everyone else out" (I, vii, 26). Cordelia believes that men are essentially evil and a threat to her peaceful existence. She is a wall builder. As is inevitable in the existing society, the soldiers come and both Cordelia and Lear lose their Eden. It is instructive that the primary wish of Lear, whose position until recently protected his innocence, is to return again to the house hidden in the woods. Cordelia, on the other hand, creates a government by which she intends to control a new Golden Age from the top. It, like Lear's wall, is intended to protect the people and, like Lear, she will permit no dissent against it.

> You were here when they killed my husband. I watched them kill him. I covered my face with my hands, but my fingers opened so I watched. I watched them rape me, and John kill them, and my child miscarry. I didn't miss anything. I watched and I said we won't be at the mercy of brutes anymore, we'll live a new life and help one another. The government's creating that new life—you must stop speaking against us (III, iii, 83).

The deposed Lear is still desirous of regaining the power he lost ("I can't sleep on my own since I lost my army"), but more and more he is beginning to understand the true nature of the social order he has created that has overthrown him. Like his Shakespearian counterpart, he expresses this truth most effectively through insane ravings whose allegorical import he himself does not understand.

> It is night. My daughters empty their prisons and feed the men to the dead in their graveyards. The wolf crawls away in terror and hides with the rats. Hup, prince! Hup, rebel! Do tricks for human flesh! When the dead have eaten they go home to their pits and sleep (I, vi, 20).

It is a parable redolent of the cannibalism of *Early Morning*. A restrictive society destroys the human instincts of its subjects so that they may better serve society. Be they enforcers or outlaws, society rewards those who extend its influence in a manner that only increases their inhumanity. In comparison, the natural predators of the animal world seem timid and high-principled. According to Reich, the authoritarian society *can not* coexist with the morally healthy individual. The measure of moral health is rebellion against dehumanizing authoritarianism. The socially moralized individual becomes so frantic at the prospect of being forced to face either his basic instincts or the hatred, sadism, and infantalism their repression has produced that he will wreck all attempts to change society even for the better.[20]

At his trial Lear can smell on the steps the blood of all the prisoners who were convicted in the corrupt court he created. He still does not understand, however, that he himself is the architect of his prison. He denies that Bodice and Fontanelle are his children, even though their every action is a product of his own. Bodice tries to force him to self-recognition by showing him a mirror and, in the most eloquent of his mad metaphors, he identifies his own reflection as that of an animal in a cage.

>LEAR. (*He stares down at the mirror.*) No, that's not the king. . . . This is a little cage of bars with an animal in it. (*Peers closer.*) No, no, that's not the king! (*Suddenly gestures violently. The Usher takes the mirror.*) Who shut that animal in that cage? Let it out. Have you seen its face behind the bars? There's a poor animal with blood on its head and tears running down its face. Who did that to it? Is it a bird or a horse? It's lying in the dust and its wings are broken. Who broke its wings? Who cut off its hands so that it can't shake the bars? It's pressing its snout on the glass. Who shut that animal in a glass cage? O God, there's no pity in this world. You let it lick the blood from its hair in the corner

20. Zweig, pp. 279–280.

of a cage with nowhere to hide from its tormentors. No shadow, no hole! Let that animal out of its cage! (*He takes the mirror and shows it round.*) Look! Look! Have pity. Look at its claws trying to open the cage. It's dragging its broken body over the floor. You are cruel! Cruel! Look at it lying in its corner! It's shocked and cut and shaking and licking the blood on its sides. (*Usher again takes the mirror from Lear.*) No, no! Where are they taking it now! Not out of my sight! What will they do to it? O God, give it to me! Let me hold it and stroke it and wipe its blood! (*Bodice takes the mirror from the Usher.*) No!
BODICE. I'll polish it every day and see it's not cracked.
LEAR. Then kill it. Kill it. Kill it. Don't let her torment it. I can't live with that sffering in the world (II, i, 35).

The caged animal is the primary image of the second act. Its dominance ends, as does Lear's madness, after Lear is blinded. The animal is Lear himself and, as he implies by showing the mirror around, all other members of the society that he created. Society is the cage and the restrictions of social institutions are the bars. Those entrapped by society feel a natural urge to struggle against its restrictions ("shake the bars") but an acceptance of the morality of society makes resistance impossible. It "cuts off the hands" of the animal by teaching it that it must be caged. Lear variously sees the animal as a man, a bird, and a pig. Bond established the importance of the bird and the pig in his mythology with *Passion*. The bird represents ultimate harmony with its environment and a caged bird implies the opposite. Once again Bond has turned to William Blake for his inspiration: "A Robin Redbreast in a cage/Puts all Heaven in a Rage." The pig in *Passion* has a double significance, representing the reality of suffering on all levels of life and the dehumanization of a man resulting from their society-induced actions. Lear would free the animal and comfort it (and the authoritarian society he has created), but Bodice vows to polish the mirror and prevent its being cracked (to continue society in Lear's image). Under such conditions, Lear believes that the animal would be better off dead. Like Arthur during his *mad* period in *Early Morning*, he believes that if man requires a restrictive law-and-order society to survive, death must be a blessing to him.

Back in his cell, Lear raves about the necessity to free the animal before it destroys the earth. He is calmed only when the Ghost brings him his daughters as children (in an innocent, premoralized state). The children realize that they are in a prison (society), but Lear tells them that if they are patient, it will pass away.

> I know it will end. Everything passes, even the waste. The fools will be silent. We won't chain ourselves to the dead, or send our children to school in the graveyard. The torturers and ministers and priests will lose their office. And we'll pass each other in the street without shuddering at what we've done to each other (II, ii, 39–40).

When his daughters were children, Lear believed he could work through the system to build a society that would protect them from evil. To build that society, he himself perpetuated evil. When they leave him to take their place in his society, Lear recognizes for the first time that he is responsible for the caging of the animal and faints from the horror of what he has done.

> Listen! The animal's scratching! There's blood in its mouth. The muzzle's bleeding. It's trying to dig. It's found someone! (*He falls unconscious on his sack.*) (II, ii, 41).

Lear's recognition of his responsibility in the spiritual death of his daughters is his first real step in his journey from fancy to moral maturity. At the same time, in consoling the Grave Digger's Boy, Lear discovers in compassion a way of living with his guilt.

> GHOST. I'm afraid. Let me stay with you, keep me here, please.

LEAR. Yes, yes, poor boy. Lie down by me. Here. I'll hold you. We'll help each other. Cry while I sleep, and I'll cry and watch you while you sleep. We'll take turns. The sound of the human voice will comfort us (II, ii, 42).

Like Arthur in *Early Morning*, the Grave Digger's Boy dies twice: first he is shot by soldiers and, second, in an unmistakable Bondian parallel, he is gored to death by frightened pigs. To a large extent, the Grave Digger's Boy functions as Lear's alter ego. He first appears, as he does in subsequent scenes, when Lear needs aid to retain his humanity or to understand his duties as a human being. On the farm, he shows Lear the way life should be and was before Lear's civilization. It is instructive that the Boy does not return as a ghost until Lear is unnerved by his vision of the caged animal and calls for help in his cell. The Ghost, who is representative of the prenationalistic Golden Age, has always been free and cannot see the animal. Nevertheless, he gives Lear compassion and generates it in the old man. As Lear increases in moral maturity, the body of the Ghost deteriorates. At the moment when Lear completely understands his life and the action he must take, the Ghost dies a second time. As happens with such Bond alter egos as Shogo and Kiro in *Narrow Road*, Lear himself dies soon afterward.

Cordelia's revolution against Lear's daughters is successful, but it does not reform. Evacuated from his prison during the civil war, Lear soon returns to share the cell with his family. They are executed, but Lear's suffering is not yet over. Although Cordelia will not execute Lear, whom she knew at the farm of the Grave Digger's Boy, her new husband and consort, the Carpenter, had no objection to his being made "politically ineffective." The prison medical officer, himself a former political prisoner, supplies the method.

FOURTH PRISONER. (*Fourth Prisoner comes downstage with a heap of equipment. The Ghost stands and watches silently. Lear is immobile. He is completely withdrawn.*) Right. (*He goes to Lear.*) Good morning. Time for your drive. Into your coat. (*Lear is put into a straitjacket. He doesn't help in any way.*) Cross your arms and hold your regalia. Now the buttons. This nasty wind gets in everywhere. You've been inside too long to trust yourself to fresh air. (*Lear is seated on a chair.*) Get settled down. (*His legs are strapped to the chair legs.*) And last your crown. (*A square frame is lowered over his head and face. Fourth Prisoner steps back. Then Lear speaks.*)
LEAR. You've turned me into a king again.
FOURTH PRISONER. (*Produces a tool.*) Here's a device I perfected on dogs for removing human eyes.
LEAR. No, no. You mustn't touch my eyes. I must have my eyes!
FOURTH PRISONER. With this device you extract the eye undamaged and then it can be put to good use. It's based on a scouting gadget I had as a boy. . . . Understand, this isn't an instrument of torture, but a scientific device. See how it clips the lid back to leave it unmarked.
LEAR. No—no!
FOURTH PRISONER. Nice and steady. (*He removes one of Lear's eyes.*)
LEAR. Aahh!
FOURTH PRISONER. Note how the eye passes into the lower chamber and is received into a soothing solution of formaldehyde crystals. One more, please. (*He removes Lear's other eye.*)
LEAR. Aaahhh!
FOURTH PRISONER. (*Sprays an aerosol into Lear's eye sockets.*) That will assist the formation of scab and discourage flies. (*To Soldiers.*) Clean this up with a bucket and mop (II, vi, 62–63).

As with almost every extremely graphic or violent scene in Bond's plays, the blinding in *Lear* has roused controversy concerning its taste and its centrality to the play. However, Bond's images of horror are never extraneous or merely sensational. It is necessary that Lear be absolutely dependant on others in the third act. Second, the scene shows a continuation of the image of the bloody caged animal on the upper level of society. It illustrates Bodice's realization that she is a prisoner of the power she wields. Immobilized by straitjacket, operating chair, and extracting helmet, Lear feels that he has been turned into a king again. Third, it continues on a more personal level a theme begun in *Passion:* the horribly destructive potential of our advanced technology in the hands of those no longer motivated by humane distinctions. The scene is obviously intended to evoke comparisons with Nazi concentration camp experimentations. Unlike the prison doctor, the Nazi physicians, the creators of the atomic bomb, and countless less publicized scientists, Bond sees no difference between an instrument of torture and a scientific device when those who benefit from it are abstractions (science and society) and those who are harmed are human beings, or, for that matter, dogs. Finally, the blinding of Lear coincides with the beginning of his understanding and, as Bond reminds us, "blindness is a dramatic metaphor for insight, that is why Gloucester, Oedipus, and Tiresias are blind." [21]

The blind Lear is released from his cell, and with the Ghost as his guide, goes to the house in the woods. With his freedom comes finally the recognition that he is not only the murderer of his daughters, but the scourge of the entire nation. In the open fields near the wall, Lear meets a family who built a home on the cleared land after he was deposed. Now, Cordelia is rebuilding the wall and the farmer and his wife must go to the wall work camp and their son to the army. Lear is horrified and tells them to run away.

I am the King! I kneel by this wall. How many lives have I

21. Bond, Preface to *Lear*, p. 13.

Lear

ended here? Go away. Go anywhere. Go far away. Run. I will not move till you go! . . . They feed you and clothe you—is that why you can't see? All life seeks its safety. A wolf, a fox, a horse—they'd run away, they're sane. Why d'you run to meet your butchers? Why? . . . Men destroy themselves and say it's their duty? It's not possible! How can they be so abused? (II, vii, 66–67).

The farmer and his son stare at Lear in astonishment and then go their separate ways to the work camp and to the army, respectively. When Lear was in power, the people were still emotionally healthy. Drafted to work on the wall, they ran away and hid or dug up at night the work they had been forced to do in the day. Now, however, the society that Lear created has been perfected. Cordelia's subjects are socially moralized and go to their consumption by the social order without questioning. Given our earlier definition of the socially moralized individual, it is fitting that it should be the Farmer's son who kills Lear when he tries to act against society.

A period of time passes and Lear burrows more or less happily into the womblike house of the Grave Digger's Boy. There he is cared for by Thomas, Susan (his pregnant wife), and their friend, John. He becomes guru to those who are disenchanted with the new regime and offers sanctuary (although he himself is totally dependant) to all those who flee from its power. When the others try to explain to him the stupidity of open defiance by the powerless, his reaction is the same as when Cordelia tried to make him leave the house years earlier.

LEAR. Where else can he go? *You* go if you're afraid!
THOMAS. How can you be so obstinate, how can you be such a fool?
BEN. (*To Lear.*) Yeh, you ain' some prisoner no one's ever 'eard of, they can't mess you about.
LEAR. No, you musn't say that. I'm not a king. I have no

power. But you can stay. You're doing no harm. Now I'm hungry, take me inside. I'll write to Cordelia again. She means well, she only needs someone to make her see sense. Take me in. I came here when I was cold and hungry and afraid. I wasn't turnd away, and I won't turn anyone away. They can eat my food while it lasts and when it's gone they can go if they like, but I won't send anyone away. That's how I'll end my life. I'll be shut up in a grave soon, and till then this door is open. (*He smiles.*) (II, i, 73–74).

According to Edward Bond, the only reason Lear says he isn't the king is because he's God Almighty, untouchable to temporal oppression.[22] Lear has built another wall of protection, this time composed of the people who are kind to him. He is attempting a personal return to the Golden Age and is trying to live a nonviolent life in a violent age. Lear believes that he can eventually convince Cordelia to change her ways through reason. In reality, his preaching and his acts of magnanimity have only made his protectors vulnerable. Cordelia may be scrupulous about creating a martyr, but a few peasants will not be missed. Lear is immoral because he endangers others without doing anything to remove the source of that danger. One of Lear's beneficiaries' remarks pointedly about him: "Thas's all very well. But yer never seen 'is sort on the wall. . . . We 'ave t' act fly" (III, i, 74).

Although the parallel between Thomas and the Grave Digger's Boy extends past their home and their similar relationships with Lear to their pregnant wives being loved by a friend named John (this is also the Carpenter's name), Thomas is not like the Grave Digger's Boy. Thomas recognizes that no one can be free while the possibility for oppression exists.

> I want you to send Ben back to the wall. . . . Hundreds of people come to hear you now. The government can't let this

22. Dark, p. 23.

go on, and they could crush us like that! We need support.
We must infiltrate the camps. . . . We talk to people but we
don't really help them. We shouldn't let them come here if
that's all we can do. It's dangerous to tell the truth, truth
without power is always dangerous. And we should fight!
Freedom's not an idea, it's a passion! If you haven't got it
you fight like a fish out of water fighting for air! (III, ii, 75–76).

Unlike Thomas, the Grave Digger's Boy was a political
Innocent. When he was alive, he believed, as Lear does at
this stage, that the desire to live humanely was sufficient, as
indeed it was before Lear created the present society. When
he is killed, the Boy learns the fallacy of this belief. Since he
is dead, however, he cannot continue to mature as Lear
does, he can only decay. Therefore, the Boy's moral maturity travels a path parallel to Lear's but in the opposite
direction. By the time Lear reaches the state of only desiring
to live humanely, the position of the Boy when we first met
him, the Ghost of the Boy wishes only to be hidden and
protected. Lear must reject the advice of the Grave Digger's
Boy and move beyond his own moral infancy if he is to
become emotionally mature and uncorrupted. At the same
time, the ghost must continue to decay, to move backward
beyond birth, to die a second and final time.

> GHOST. The pigs! I'm torn! They gored me! Help me, help
> me! I'll die!
> LEAR. (*Holds him.*) I can't.
> GHOST. Lear! Hold me!
> LEAR. No, too late! It's far too late! You were killed long
> ago! You must die! I love you, I'll always remember you,
> but I can't help you. Die, for your own sake, die!
> GHOST. O Lear, I am dead! (*The Ghost's head falls back. It is
> dead. It drops at Lear's feet. The calls and pig squeals stop.*)
> (III, iii, 86).

Lear wants to be both free and nonpolitical, an impossible desire in the age he has created. To believe that men should be free and to do nothing to aid them is to support their jailers. To give men hope, as Lear does, and to allow their position to remain hopeless, is to become a social institution.

Inevitably, the soldiers of Cordelia come, even as the soldiers of Bodice and Fontanelle came and the soldiers of Lear must have come before them. They arrest those to whom Lear has given sanctuary and order Lear to curb his political activities. He reasons, but society determines what is reasonable and power determines what is society. Lear is powerless.

> SMALL MAN. (*Soldiers P and Q start to take the Small Man out.*) No—stop them!
> LEAR. There's nothing I can do! The government's mad. The law's mad.
> SMALL MAN. (*Throws himself at Lear.*) Then why did yer let me come 'ere? O God, I know I'm bad sometimes and I don't deserve to—O God, please!
> LEAR. There's nothing I can do!
> SMALL MAN. Then I should a stayed an' be shot like a dog. I lived like a dog, what did it matter? It'd be finished now. Why've I suffered all this? (*The Small Man is taken out crying. The Officer, Old Councillor, Ben, and Soldiers go with him. . . . Lear sits. Thomas, John, and Susan go into the house.*)
> LEAR. What can I do? I left my prison, pulled it down, broke the key, and still I'm a prisoner. I hit my head against a wall all the time. There's a wall everywhere. I'm buried alive in a wall. Does this suffering and misery last for ever? Do we work to build ruins, waste all these lives to make a desert no one could live in? There's no one to explain it to me, no one I can go to for justice. I'm old, I should know how to live by now, but I know nothing, I can do nothing, I am nothing (III, ii, 79–80).

Edward Bond has repeatedly said that, given man's experience with his universe, his own plays are almost naively

Lear   213

optimistic. They assume that life is of supreme importance, a belief given only lip service by our society that sacrifices life constantly to its competitive commercialism. If one accepts as fact that life (freedom to live in the way that man was biologically evolved to do) is a First Precept for men, a requirement that admits no compromise or qualifying clause, and that the maintenance of social order depends upon the prevention of life, the issue becomes refreshingly clear. Men must struggle against the social order, not because there is hope of winning, but because acceptance is death. The morally honest man must revolt or commit suicide.

Police force, political power, and morality being on the side of society, those who struggle against it have only one weapon: humanity. Lear is a blind, old man unable to enforce his own will even within his isolated shack, yet he is not "politically ineffective." The people listen to Lear because he tells them that they have an inherent right to live. Cordelia knows this, but like Basho, Shogo, and Georgina before her, she believes that the people must be protected against themselves by government. Government requires allegiance. Allegiance implies the yielding to government of the right to determine life and death, an act counter to man's basic instincts.

> CORDELIA. Yes, you sound like the voice of my conscience. But if you listened to everything your conscience told you, you'd go mad. You'd never get anything done—and there's a lot to do, some of it very hard. . . .
> LEAR. I didn't go out of my way to make trouble. But I will not be quiet when people come here. And if you stop them —that would be easy!—they'll know I'm here or was here *once*! I've suffered so much, I made all the mistakes in the world, and I pay for each of them. I cannot be forgotten. I am in their minds. To kill me you must kill them all. Yes, that's who I am. Listen, Cordelia. You have two enemies, lies *and* the truth. You sacrifice truth to destroy lies, and you sacrifice life to destroy death. It isn't sane. You squeeze a

stone till your hand bleeds and call that a miracle. I'm old, but I'm weak and clumsy as a child, too heavy for my legs. But I've learned this, and you must learn it or you'll die. Listen, Cordelia. If a God had made the world, might would always be right, that would be so wise, we'd be spared so much suffering. But we made the world—out of our smallness and weakness. Our lives are awkward and fragile and we have only one thing to keep us sane: pity, and the man without pity is mad. . . .
CORDELIA. In this situation a good government acts strongly. I knew you wouldn't cooperate, but I wanted to come and tell you this before we put you on trial: we'll make the society you only dream of.
LEAR. It's strange that you should have me killed, Cordelia, but it's obvious you would. How simple! Your Law always does more harm than crime, and your morality is a form of violence (III, iii, 83–85).

Lear is stronger than Cordelia because he can tell the truth. The truth will be believed and, while one person wants to hear, Lear will tell it. Lear can be executed but humanity cannot be destroyed as long as memory of it remains. To be human is to have compassion for life. Cordelia's society is inhuman because it kills to maintain power. Therefore, it can maintain control only by threatening to increase the killing. The holes in the protective walls are stuffed with bodies.

Cordelia has made her decision. Lear must cease speaking or die. He chooses the latter, but he goes beyond that choice to make his death a political act. As a character Lear is tragic because he achieves his potential by transgressing society's limits and pays for it with his life. As a social being, Lear is heroic because he dies striking at the symbol of oppression. He is shot while attempting to tear down the wall.

In *Lear,* Bond answers the question many of those familiar with his work have asked. It is a question faced by the revolutionary idealist in every age. In the chaos that followed World War I in Germany, Ernst Toller raised it in *Eine Jugend in Deutchland:*

> I wondered what becomes of the man who seeks to intervene in the world's destiny—that is, who resorts to political action—if he wishes to see a morally irreproachable ideal brought to realization through the struggle of the masses. Was Max Weber right when he said that, if we wished never to resist evil with violence, we would have to live like Francis of Assissi? Must he who takes action always be guilty—always? Or, if he doesn't wish to be guilty, must he go under?[23]

Edward Bond has answered that we must take action, even violent action, against social repression if we are to survive as a species. It may not be immediately successful, but the alternative is certain death. Lear manages just five shovelfuls of earth before he is killed, but as they are being quickly and orderly marched away, one of the workers looks back. Humanity will continue to exist as long as one person remembers its existence.

> I have not answered many of the questions I have raised, but I have tried to explain things that often go unnoticed but which must be put right if anything is to work for us. . . . Finally, I have not tried to say what the future should be like, because that is a mistake. If your plan of the future is too rigid you start to coerce people to fit into it. We do not need a plan of the future, we need a *method* of change.[24]

Because of its revolutions and counterrevolutions that change but do not reform, *Lear* bears a structural resemblance to *Early Morning* and, of course, the Bond themes remain consistent from play to play. It is more interesting to compare *Lear* with its Shakespearian namesake and inspiration.

23. Ernst Toller, quoted by Nicholas Hern in "The Theatre of Ernst Toller," *Theatre Quarterly* 2 (January–March 1972): 76.
24. Bond, Preface to *Lear,* p. 13.

In the chapter on Bond's shorter works, I have already speculated on the relationship between his unpublished adaptation of *Roundheads and Peakheads* and Shakespeare's *Measure For Measure,* the source for the Brecht play. Bond believes that *Measure For Measure* was an unsuccessful attempt to resolve the conflict between Christian morality, Tudor law, and justice, an effort that Shakespeare abandoned midway and finally turned into a farce. Shakespeare then began to rewrite the play, deliberately setting it in a pre-Christian and prelegal era, and the final result was *King Lear.*

The most immediate change Bond made in Shakespeare's play was to eliminate the opening scene.

> But the thing is I'm afraid that we use the play in the wrong way; as a society we use the play in a wrong way. And it's for that reason I would like to rewrite it so that we now have to use the play for ourselves, for our society, for our time, for our problems. . . . The thing I wanted to do was, because everyone says that this man abdicated his power, you see, he's given up his authority, law and order, and a bit more of this, you see, and this seems to be all wrong. So I begin at the Revolution.[25]

Bond cannot agree with either the traditional or the Kott-Beckettian method of producing *King Lear.* The first uses the political and moral framework of the play merely as an excuse to depict some set-piece scenes showing man's enobling by suffering. The second shows suffering to be a matter of unfathomable chance. In either, Lear is often explained as having caused his own torments by abandoning his rightful responsibility to the state and delegating his authority unwisely.

To Bond, whether Lear gave up his control over society or had it wrested from him is beside the point. The fact is that Lear is a Renaissance man. He created the society

25. Wardle, "A Discussion with Edward Bond," pp. 24–25.

under which he suffers and what he suffers is no different
from what many others suffered under him. In his old age,
Lear discovers the society he created by being immersed
in it. His problem then becomes finding a way to live in it.

> The astonishing thing about Lear is that you see that all his
> life he lived a very protected life, he is king. Then he dis-
> covers himself without power and suddenly realizes the world
> isn't there for his benefit, everybody's looking for what he
> wants. He's got to come to some sort of terms with that
> world that he lives in. For me the fascinating thing is, I'm
> sorry if it goes back to this child thing again, in fact he's
> rather like a child growing up and learning to live, but the
> astonishing thing and the disturbing thing is that you see
> him do it as an old man. The astonishing thing about the
> play is that you see an old man behaving like a child, asking
> the childish questions, asking for the security of the child
> and not finding it.[26]

The Grave Digger's Boy is Bond's Fool. Like his Shakespearian counterpart, however, he can only point out
obliquely where Lear went wrong. He cannot solve Lear's
problems nor change his own fate.

> Well, it's quite complex for Lear, because he recognizes that
> this person did live in a workable society, did have everything
> he needed—a field where nobody troubled him, food, water.
> Admittedly, his wife has been trained by a priest somewhere
> and she's worried, but Lear can't any longer live and operate
> in that way at all, though he can only rid himself of it with
> a great deal of nostalgia because it must have been a way
> of life with a great deal of beauty and happiness about it.
> So all societies must resign themselves to the loss of their
> golden ages, I suppose. Anyway, Lear has this clear vision of
> a golden age, which his own political activities have helped
> to destroy—his insistence on building his wall to defend his
> kingdom—but he has also to recognize that its loss is irrevoc-

26. Wardle, "A Discussion with Edward Bond," p. 25.

able. It doesn't mean accepting compromises or not fighting for what is important, but that there are great dangers in romanticizing and clinging to the impossible. Some things are dead—but they die with difficulty.[27]

Bodice, Fontanelle, and the wife of the Grave Digger's Boy, Cordelia, are also parallels to Shakespeare's characters. Bond sees Shakespear's Cordelia as an extension of *Measure For Measure*'s Isabella, whom he calls "a vicious sex hysteric." [28] Shakespeare's Cordelia is evil because she is most like her father. Under the conditions, her most humane action would be to give the old man the reassurance he apparently needs. Cordelia, however, values her abstract honor more than her father's needs. Bond's Cordelia, too, most resembles the old king. She works within his system with the same conviction that she is the saviour of her people. Like Lear, she kills more in her altruism than do the others in their hedonism. Like Bodice and Fontanelle, Goneril and Regan are their father's victims as well as aggressors.

> One of the very important things in the play was to redefine the relationship between Cordelia and Lear. I don't want to make this seem easy or slick, but Cordelia in Shapespeare's play is an absolute menace. I mean, she's a very dangerous type of person, and I thought that the other daughters, though I'm not excusing them, were very unfairly treated and misunderstood. What I wanted Lear to do was to recognize that they *were* his daughters—they had been formed by his activity, they were children of his state, and he was totally responsible for them.[29]

27. Edward Bond, as quoted by Roger Hudson, Catherine Itzin, and Simon Trussler in "Drama and the Dialectics of Violence," *Theatre Quarterly* 2 (January–March 1972): 8.
28. Edward Bond, "The Duke in *Measure For Measure*," *Gambit* 5, no. 17: 43.
29. Bond, as quoted by Hudson, *et al.*, "Drama and the Dialectics of Violence," p. 8.

Certain other characters seem to exist in relation to Shakespeare's play. Thomas, for example, is like Albany in that he is more important to the future of the society than to the action of Gloucester and Edmund. The number two man in Lear's administration, Warrington, like Edmund, is coveted by both of Lear's daughters. Nevertheless, they turn against him easily enough when he remains loyal to Lear. The scene in which he is deafened by Bodice parallels the blinding of Gloucester, as does, of course, the blinding of Lear himself. Warrington, unlike Gloucester before him, does not necessarily gain in understanding. At the house of the Grave Digger's Boy, Warrington tries to kill Lear—not for revenge or because of some gain in existential understanding—but for a crust of bread.

The Old Councilor resembles Shakespeare's Oswald, but more than that he is a parody of Lear himself. Unlike Lear, however, he remains a "baby" because he is able to rationalize himself into adapting to each successive regime and thus is never exposed to the oppressions of society.[30]

Finally, Lear himself is social in Bond's play, rather than personal.

> I wanted to explain that Lear was responsible, but that it was very important that he could not get out of his problems simply by suffering the consequences, or by endurance and resignation. He had to live through the consequences and struggle with them.[31]

In *Lear*, Bond has achieved his best blend of fantasy and realism. Bond's plays have always moved forward on an intellectual level, yet the strength of his earliest plays lay in the reality of their social background. Therefore, the anachronisms and the primarily symbolic scenes have not always meshed well with their context. For example, in

30. Dark, p. 22.
31. Bond, as quoted by Hudson, *et al.*, "Drama and the Dialectics of Violence," p. 9.

the baby stoning scene in *Saved*, the literal representation of the slaughter of innocence that is the major theme of the play, is so strong a theatrical image that it sometimes blinds the audience to the play's message. In *Lear*, Bond's opening scene establishes the play as a timeless allegory by introducing modern workmen engaged in building a prehistoric wall. The conventions of the play are immediately evident and such subsequent anachronisms as the automatic eyeremover and the aerosol astringent are easier to accept.

In his dialogue, Bond again captures neatly the differences in class and locale. All members of the government and anyone who is ever a regular resident at the house of the Grave Digger's Boy (a significant combination) speak unaccented establishment English. The soldiers and the workers on the wall under Lear have Cockney accents and their counterparts under Cordelia speak a Suffolk/Cambridgeshire dialect.

Possibly because of these contrasts, the dialogue seems to lack the natural rhythms that enlivened *Saved*. Lear alone is given lines with rhetorical power and poetic ambivalence. The most striking of these take the form of elaborate metaphors and thematic parables, such as Lear's sermon to the discontented citizens in the third act.

> A man woke up one morning and found he'd lost his voice. So he went to look for it, and when he came to the wood there was the bird who'd stolen it. It was singing beautifully and the man said, "Now I sing so beautifully I shall be rich and famous." He put the bird in a cage and said, "'When I open my mouth wide you must sing." Then he went to the king and said, "I will sing your majesty's praises." But when he opened his mouth the bird could only groan and cry because it was in a cage, and the king had the man whipped. The man took the bird home, but his family couldn't stand the bird's groaning and crying and they left him. So in the end the man took the bird back to the wood and let it out

of the cage. But the man believed the king had treated him unjustly and he kept saying to himself, "The king's a fool," and as the bird still had the man's voice it kept singing this all over the wood and soon the other birds learned it. The next time the king went hunting he was surprised to hear all th birds singing, "The king's a fool." He caught the bird who'd started it and pulled out its feathers, broke its wings, and nailed it to a branch as a warning to all the other birds. The forest was silent. And just as the bird had the man's voice, the man now had the bird's pain. He ran round silently waving his head and stamping his feet, and he was locked up for the rest of his life in a cage (III, ii, 74–75).

The parable of the man, the bird, and the cage is as much a definition of the society of *Lear* as Arthur's dream about the mill defines the society of *Early Morning*. Taken as a whole, it illustrates the right of all creatures to life and freedom. It also shows that the responsibility of living creatures is the same to one another as to themselves, for in the end the oppressor suffers the same fate as the oppressed. He who must hold the cage door shut is as entrapped as his prisoner.

Without altering his concerns, Edward Bond appears to have taken a step forward in Lear. Technically, he has found new ways of presenting his themes. He relies less overtly upon Oedipal and Christian images, although the house and well and the crucified bird and resurrected ghost indicate that he has lost none of his mastery. Bond continues to be obsessed with the causes and nature of violence in our society, but seems to find answers that satisfy him in the social and political ideas of psychologist Wilhelm Reich. As a hero, Lear is an advance on earlier Bond protagonists. Scopey, Len, and Kiro do not understand what manipulates them. Arthur comes to see his society clearly and passes beyond it. Lear travels the greatest dramatic distance of any Bond character. Beginning as an oppressor of men, he comes to understand what he has done, and takes action to change it. For the first time, too, we see positive evidence that the Innocent character has passed his vision on to others within society. *Lear* is an effective illustration of Bond's that the product of greater understanding is greater optimism. It is this path that is followed until the production of *The Sea*.

8
The Sea:
"You Must Change the World"

Edward Bond has been an advisory editor to *Theatre Quarterly* since it first was published in January 1971. One of the new magazine's initial promises was a production casebook of Bond's next play, *Lear*, at the Royal Court. A feature of that casebook (which appeared in the January-March 1972 issue) was an interview with Bond taken in August 1971. This interview ended with the tantalizing question: "Can you say anything about your next play [after *Lear*]?"

I really don't know very much about it. It's just called *Two Storms*. I know its background—the sea. When I was quite young I was taken to a photographer's shop which overlooked the sea, and I thought that was very curious—the idea of cameras in this room, quite high up, and this sea at the back. And then I heard about somebody who had been drowned after a ship had sunk, and he was found washed up, dead, lying on the beach. And he'd been trying to get his jumper off over his head so that he could swim better—his head

Playbill jacket for The Sea
(Permission for use of jacket design from the Royal Court Theatre, S.W.1, London; drawing by Yves Simard)

The Sea

was covered by this jumper, and his hands were stretched upwards, still caught in the thing, and he'd drowned like that. I just couldn't sit down after I'd heard it, it seemed to me so extraordinary, that he'd pulled this hood thing over his head trying to escape. And I'd been thinking about writing a play around those two images for years. Now I'm going to.[1]

Retitled *The Sea,* Bond's new play opened at the Royal Court Theater under the direction of William Gaskill on 22 May 1973. The working title and the photography shop were casualties of the play's development period, but Bond's other early images survived intact.

Scene One: Willy Carson scrambles ashore on a storm-wracked coastal beach, searching for help for his friend, Colin Bentham, who went down when their sailboat overturned. He finds only a drunken old man, Evens, and the draper, Hatch. The latter is the coastguard, but he screams at Willy and refuses to help him.

Scene Two: At Hatch's shop, Mrs. Rafi, the village's dominant social leader, bullies the draper while she selects curtain material and gloves. Her rather repressed companion, Mrs. Tilehouse, attends her. Mrs. Rafi calls in the passing Willy Carson and invites him for lunch. Colin was engaged to her niece, Rose. After they leave, Hatch meets in back with the other coasguards—young Billy Hollarcut and the two older men, Carter and Thompson. Hatch has convinced them that Carson, Evens, and the storms at sea are part of a plot to invade from outer space.

Scene Three: As Mrs. Rafi suggested, Willy has gone to Evens's hut on the beach to find out where Colin's body will be washed up. Hatch and Hollarcut follow him there and shout abuse at Willy and Evens from a distance. Evens

1. Edward Bond, as quoted by Roger Hudson, Catherine Itzin, and Simon Trussler in "Drama and the Dialectics of Violence," *Theatre Quarterly* 2 (January–March 1972): 7.

says they are mad, but ignores them. He talks to Willy of the vagaries of the tide and of his distrust of people and society. Hollarcut remains on guard and, even though a reasonably friendly banter exists between them, Evens is unable to shake his faith in Hatch.

Scene Four: In Mrs. Rafi's drawing room, the Ladies Coastguard Auxiliary is rehearsing a production of *Orpheus and Eurydice.* Despite her grief, Rose is present. Mrs. Rafi, as director, star, and balladeer, dominates this farcical rehearsal. Among those in the cast are Rose as Eurydice, Mafanwy Price as Cerberus, the three-headed dog, and the local vicar as Pluto. Willy serves as audience until the rehearsal is ended by the sound of harbor guns. The guns also fired when the boat overturned and Colin was drowned.

Scene Five: Hollarcut, Thompson, and Carter meet in the draper's shop to hear Hatch explain the invasion procedures of the extraterrestial visitors. Mrs. Rafi enters the shop, having learned that Hatch refused to help Willy on the beach. In reprisal, she sends back the 162 yards of curtain material she had ordered—an action she has employed arbitrarily many times before. Hatch, ruined financially, pleads with Mrs. Rafi as she drives out Thompson and Carter. Hatch begins to madly hack the cloth into the lengths Mrs. Rafi ordered. When she and Mrs. Tilehouse return, a scuffle ensues in which Mrs. Rafi is cut by Hatch's scissors. Mrs. Tilehouse faints and Hatch escapes. Carter helps Mrs. Tilehouse home and Mrs. Rafi goes for the constable. Hollarcut sneaks back into the shop, hunting for Hatch.

Scene Six: At the beach Rose and Willy search for Colin's body. They speak of their mutual love of Colin and of those who come to stare at grief. Rose feels she can not face living, but Willy tells her that living is the only thing worth facing. They find Colin's body, his jumper pulled up over his head. Rose goes to get Evens. Hatch comes on, trailing Willy (who hides), and finds the body.

Thinking it is Willy, he stabs it, and is horrified when water spurts out instead of blood.

Scene Seven: Colin's funeral is held on the cliff from which his ashes are to be scattered to the sea. There is a piano, a procession, prayers, and hymns highlighted by a

Scene Seven from The Sea
(Photo courtesy of the Royal Court Theatre, S.W.1, London; photo by John Haynes)

duel in descant between Mrs. Tilehouse and Mrs. Rafi. The Vicar's sermon revealing that the battery is silent in Colin's honor is interrupted by the guns firing. Mrs. Rafi, holding the urn in her hands while she gives a dramatic recitation, becomes irritated at Mrs. Tilehouse's noisy search for smelling salts. The ensuing argument is terminated by the wild entrance of Hatch and Hollarcut. A wild ash-flinging melee follows that ends when Hatch confronts Willy, whom he thought he had killed. Hatch is taken to jail and Hollarcut sullenly agrees to work out his penance. Mrs. Rafi tells Willy of her fear of growing old, revealing that she is as trapped by her dominating position as those under her. She tells Rose to go away with Willy. Rose hesitates, then decides for life.

Scene Eight: Hollarcut is again on guard at Evens's shack, having learned nothing from Hatch's madness. Willy and Evens discuss whether to live means to kill. Evens says that the instinct to live is always stronger, in the last analysis, than destruction. He worries only that society will dehumanize men for its own purposes. Evens tells Willy he must change the world. Rose comes and the two young people leave the village.

The Sea is about death and resurrection. It begins with a young man drowning and his friend making it to shore. It ends with the young man's fiancé and the friend leaving the village, perhaps with changing the world as their mission. Colin drowns. Willy does not. Hatch stabs Colin's dead body when it washes up on the strand, thinking it is Willy asleep. On the day of Colin's funeral, Rose agrees to go away with Willy.

Life and death are sometimes a matter of chance, but one must choose life always. Willy loved his friend. He tried to get others to help and he kept going back into the water himself until he was exhausted. Yet Willy does not let Colin's death ruin his own life. Rose is horrified by the knife attack upon Colin's body, but Willy is not: "How can you descrate dust?" [2] Willy falls in love with Rose. His guilt over surviving when Colin died might have prevented

2. Edward Bond, *The Sea* (London: Methuen & Co., Ltd., 1973), vi, p. 46. Subsequent references to this play will be noted in the text.

it, but it does not. Rose's love for Colin might have made her stay in the village forever or to throw away her life in some other fashion, but it does not.

The death of Colin on his way to Rose and the rebirth of love, now between Willy and Rose are only the framing events of the play, but the theme of death and resurrection asserts itself throughout. The play's two central images are the sea and the village. The sea represents nature. It is turbulent, unstrictured, and uncontrollable. The main currents can be discerned, but luck and chance affect individual instances. The village represents society and has been deliberately placed on the isolated East Coast of England in the year 1907. The class system is rigidly structured and, dramatically important, highly visible. It is a time before the victory of the House of Commons over the House of Lords extended political power to the lowly born and before the folly of World War I goaded them into using it. The village is small enough so that the classes are readily seen in interaction. The sea kills—that is natural—but it is also a symbol of rebirth. The village constricts and manipulates, preventing growth.

Death and resurrection are inseparably joined. *The Sea* begins the way *Narrow Road* ends. As one man dies, another rises up out of the water, first calling for help, and then saving himself by his own efforts. It is as if Bond had taken the lone figure used to symbolize the author's optimism at the end of other plays and demanded of him that he justify that optimism. The action of *The Sea* is partly Willy's attempt to come to terms with his resurrection and partly Bond's attempt to show the effect of society upon individual humanity.

To understand the resurrected Willy, we must deal with the dead Colin who appears in the play only as a dead body and as an urn of ashes, but whose spirit is felt throughout.

He'll be washed up where the coast turns in. . . . If he goes past that point you've lost him. He should come in. He's hanging round out there now. He could see us if he wasn't dead (iii, 13–14).

Why did Colin die instead of Willy? He was the better sailor of the two, handsome, a hero, etc. To some extent his death must be ascribed to chance. When Willy is sent to Evens to find out where Colin's body will wash up, the old man answers with what is clearly a metaphor for life.

Don't believe what they say: I don't understand the water. I know the main currents, but luck and chance come into it. It doesn't matter how clear the main currents are, you have to live through the details (iii, 14).

Nevertheless, there is another reason more typical of Bond's viewpoint. Colin is the victim of a rigidity that springs both from his position in society and from his recognition that society is, in itself, unnatural. In the one event of his life central to the play, his love for Rose, he was successful. Yet, given the nature of his society, Colin could not be sure that even his success in love was justified.

You were brought up together. Your aunt wanted you to marry. Everyone knew you would. It was too easy. He was afraid one day you'd meet another man—perhaps even a weaker man—and then he'd lose you (vi, 42).

Rose thinks of Colin as a fire that burns in the sea because she remembers how the fires they built on the beach as children reflected on both his face and the moving waves. But in the version of *Orpheus and Eurydice* that Mrs. Rafi is staging for the Ladies Coastguard Auxiliary fund, the white light shining in the water is the reflection of Narcissus, so concerned with his image during life that he is condemned to haunt the River Styx after death. Colin wanted

The Sea

to take Rose away from the narrow restrictions of the village. At the same time he feared to lose her to someone not bound by those restrictions—a loss that to Colin would include both love and sense of self. As Willy says: "a hero must be afraid of weaker men" (vi, 42).

In the end it is the natural force of the sea that destroys Colin. He drowns while unsuccessfully trying to remove his jersey so that he can swim. Symbolically, he is resurrected by being washed up onto the beach even as Willy and Rose are beginning to understand one another and the world around them.

(The jersey is pulled up over the head and the arms, which are lifted up and bent at the elbows in the act of removing the jersey—so the jersey forms a hood covering the head, neck, shoulders, arms, and hands) (vi, 40).

It is a classic figure of Bondian iconography—a crucifixion figure who is simultaneously a resurrection image. As in other Bond plays, however, it is not the resurrection of the dead man's body that is important. It is the rebirth of the love he represented. Once his love is reborn between Rose and Willy, Colin has no further purpose. The jersey in which Colin drowns while trying to remove it represents the societal shell of which he was unable to free himself, the symbol that completes the crucifixion image. Willy, not so encumbered, makes it to shore and wins the love of Rose.

Bond gets considerable humor out of the rehearsal of the play produced by Mrs. Rafi for the auxiliary, but even it has its thematic significance. The story of *Orpheus and Eurydice* is an archetype of death and resurrection. When Eurydice dies, her husband, the great musician, Orpheus, is so in despair that he goes down into the Underworld to get her back. Bond's account, however, differs from some other versions of the legend. Bullfinch's rendition, for example, has Orpheus so charming Pluto and his wife,

Persephone, with his singing and lute playing that they agree to allow Eurydice to return to the upper world. Their only qualification was that Orpheus go ahead of Eurydice and not look back at her until they had both reached the surface—a rule that, of course, Orpheus violated. In Bond's version, Eurydice was coveted by Pluto while still on earth and was brought down in the Underworld to be his wife. Moreover, Eurydice (who is played by Rose) has no intention of returning to the surface.

> I am queen of this dark place. My heart burns with a new cold fire. Your love, your fear, your hope—what are they to me now? Dust scattered over the sea. . . . Go back (iv, 26).

The rehearsal ends before we are shown the climax of this drama, but its implications are interesting: (1) No matter what changes are wrought on the legend, Eurydice can not satisfactorily return to Orpheus. (2) Bond's Eurydice has a new love that is both desirable to her and is willing to fight for her. (3) Eurydice's description, as delivered by Rose, of her past relationship with Orpheus as "dust scattered over the sea" is an accurate forecast of what will happen to Colin's ashes in a later scene. (4) Eurydice's new love is associated with the act of passing over flowing waters—in this case, the River Styx that is also associated with death. (5) The only element of Orpheus and Eurydice's relationship to survive is their love that in Eurydice's case has been transferred to another. (6) Nevertheless, Orpheus does try to rejoin Eurydice physically.

Bond's account of the legend may then be taken as a *roman à clef* for the remainder of the play by substituting Colin, Rose, and Willy for Orpheus, Eurydice, and Pluto. One of a pair of lovers dies, but their love survives. That love attaches itself to a new lover who is associated both with death and with flowing waters. The lover tries to return physically to his loved one, but death makes this

The Sea

impossible. He is left to become merely "dust scattered over the sea."

If the love of Rose and Willy represents resurrection, these characters are themselves resurrections, respectively, of Mrs. Rafi and Evens. Mrs. Rafi is a familiar Bond character type—the personification of society. She rules law, labor, acquaintance, and clergy by decree, evincing subtlety only when she knows that it will wound. She is a supreme bully and if she occasionally appears to be less of a monster than Queen Victoria in *Early Morning*, it is only because the play's realistic format and comic tone do not make it possible. The consequences of Mrs. Rafi's indiscriminate application of social pressures, particularly as they relate to the social moralization of Hatch and his subsequent Oedipal violence, will be discussed later in the chapter. For the moment we are concerned with a characteristic of Mrs. Rafi that is new to a Bond villain.

Mrs. Rafi is aware that what she does is bullying and is even more aware of the life-limiting strictures of the society that she dominates. Victoria never sees herself as being anything but correct, and—since as society she sets the rules—technically she can not be. Shogo in *Narrow Road to the Deep North* has flashes of intuition that tell him that he has committed a crime, but those flashes have nothing to do with his actual atrocities. Indeed, the play's true villain is the poet-priest, Basho, and Shogo is only a socially moralized victim. Lear recognizes the inhumanity of the society he has created, but only after he is no longer wielding power in it. Like an actress aware of her image, Mrs. Rafi does only what is expected of her, realizing even as she does it that she is only a societal icon.

> I've always been a forceful woman. I was brought up to be. People expect my class to shout at them. Bully them. They're disappointed if you don't. It gives them something to gossip about in their bars. When they turn you into an eccentric, it's their form of admiration. Sometimes I think I'm like a

lighthouse in their world. I give them a sense of order and security. My glares mark out a channel to the safe harbour (vii, 56).

Mrs. Rafi is the village's substitute for Stonehenge, a surrogate priestess who relieves the people of their fear of hell by bringing it to them on earth. Prince Albert says of Victoria that her true calling was to be a prison governess. Mrs. Rafi believes she should have been a Catholic abbess: "I'd have terrified the nuns. They'd have loved it. Like living next door to the devil" (vii, 57). She did not, however, create her situation. She is guilty only of lacking the courage to deny it. The village is socially moralized and is, therefore, morally unhealthy. They believe that they should be controlled, and demand to be controlled, for it relieves them of the responsibility for their actions. But an actor's image can show no tarnish and a dictator's strength cannot weaken. George Orwell has written of an incident in which, while serving as a colonial administrator in India, he had to shoot a native's elephant—not because he thought the elephant was dangerous, but because his authority as an administrator would be lost if the other natives thought him sensitive to their individual problems. The oppressor is as trapped as the oppressed. The leader is also the scapegoat. Mrs. Rafi is aware that the village's tolerance of her will last only as long as she can dominate it.

> I'll grow old and shout at them from a wheel chair. That's what they're waiting for. They get their own back for all the years I bullied them. They wheel you where they like. "Take me there." "You went there yesterday. We want to go the other way." "Take me down to the beach. I want to see the sea." "You don't want to se the sea. You saw the sea yesterday. The wind's bad for your head. If you misbehave and catch a cold we'll shut you in bed. You'll stay there for good this time." Subtle. . . . You give up shouting. You close your eyes and the tears dribble down your ugly old face

The Sea

and you can't even wipe it clean—they won't give you your hanky. "Don't let her have it. She gets into a tizzy and tears it to shreds." There you are: old, ugly, whimpering, dirty, pushed about on wheels and threatened (vii, 57).

In explaining why he considers *Lear* an optimistic play, Edward Bond has said:

> Lear is old by then, but most of the play's audiences will be younger. It might seem to them that the truth is always ground for pessimism when it is discovered, but one soon comes to see it as an opportunity.[3]

Mrs. Rafi is locked into her way of life and for her there is no escape. Rose is young, however, and Mrs. Rafi is determined to help her avoid the same fate.

> Go away, Rose. Don't stay in the town and marry the solicitor or doctor or parson. You can't breathe here. . . . Colin would have taken you away. He'd never settle down in this ditch. Oh no. But they've got him now. He's up on these cliffs for ever. A ghost haunting the sea. . . . You take her, Willy (vii, 57–58).

In the end it is possible to be sympathetic towards Mrs. Rafi, but difficult to forgive her entirely. She is the knowing victim of what she recognized to be a lie from the first. The village is her Vietnam—a lie that she has accepted, perpetrated, and—most disgracefully—and made others victims to. This fact, more than her aunt's advice, will be the cause of Rose leaving the village.

> It was different for Aunt Louise. Perhaps you couldn't do much then. No, I don't believe it. She's such a coward. Haven't you noticed? It's safer to stay in the garden and shout over the wall. Don't feel sorry for her. She's a bully and only the weak ones like being bullied. The town's full of her cripples (vii, 58).

3. Edward Bond, Preface to *Lear* (London: Eyre Methuen, 1972), p. 13.

Rose is what Mrs. Rafi was and Mrs. Rafi is what Rose could become, a truism that director William Gaskill underlined in *The Sea's* original production by having the two characters assume the same position and the same physical relationships to Willy in their *scene six* and *seven* confessions to him on the beach.[4] When Rose leaves the village and breaks the pattern, Mrs. Rafi is symbolically reborn.

There is an affinity between Mrs. Rafi and the old tramp, Evens. It is natural, of course, that it would be to Evens that Mrs. Rafi would send Willy to find out where Colin's body would wash up. However, the townswomen are shocked when she also invites Evens to the funeral. Furthermore, after the funeral, it is Evens whom she asks to help her choose a niche for Colin's urn. Both are essentially outside the village's mentality, a factor that Gaskill emphasized in Colin's cliffside funeral scene by placing them on opposite sides of the stage, both separate from the tight-knit little group of mourners in the middle.

Evens is the latest in a long line of Bond recluses who are willingly or unwillingly isolated from society. Alen in *The Pope's Wedding* forms the obvious point of comparison and, through Alen, we are also reminded of Harry in *Saved* who is alone even within his own family. Both Lear and the Grave Digger's Boy also belong to this group during the time when they believe that it is possible to live painlessly apart from society.

Like Alen, Evens is old and lives in a shack well outside the village. Because of this deviation both become the butt of their societies' fears and hatred, the charges in each case ranging from treason to abnormal sexual appetites. Alen was rumored to have signaled the Germans from his shack during the war and to have been Pat's real father. Hatch believes that Evens is the earthly liaison for the invaders from outer space and the young girl, Jilly, has other, perhaps less exotic, fears:

4. Jeremy Kingston, "Theatre," *Punch* 260 (30 May 1973): 774.

The Sea

> Oh, is that what he looks like? Oh dear. You must let me stand by you. I feel quite afraid. How silly. Are those stories true? . . . The girls say that if you go by his hut at night— (vii, 47).

Later, when Evens tries to help Jilly with Colin's ashes, she screams and faints.

Unlike Alen, however, Evens has moved away from the village by choice. Both his decision to move and his choice of an exile are evidence of moral health. The village corrupts, so Evens goes to live by the sea, which is natural and regenerative. Notwithstanding, as we shall see later, it is an act that arrests the disease. It does not cure it.

Evens sees the dangers of society as the product of commercial competitiveness rather than social structure: "They hate each other. Force. Make. Use. Push. Burn. Sell. For what? A heap of rubbish" (ii 14). The society that Evens sees as the future extension of his own is so dehumanized as to make it impossible for mankind to survive in it biologically.

> We sit here and the world changes. When your life's over everything will be changed or have started to change. Our brains won't be big enough. They'll plug into bigger brains. They'll get rid of this body. It's too liable to get ill and break. They'll transplant the essential things into a better container. An unbreakable glass bottle on steel stilts. Men will look at each other's viscera as they pass in the streets. There'll be no more grass. Why? What's it for? (viii, 64).

Evens's vision of the future is initially reminiscent of H. G. Wells. It becomes more chilling when we realize that he is speaking of today. Yesterday's science fiction has become our reality—complete with computers, parking lots, and organ transplants. Nonetheless, the problem does not lie with advanced technology, but in our perceptions of technology. Our society has made competition, particularly commercial competition, its most prominent attribute. The commercial competition cycle is a familiar one: (1) The economy demands that we produce more goods so that more people will be put to work making these goods. (2) The economy also demands that the money the people receive for making these goods be spent to buy those goods. (3) Technology is the most efficient way of producing the goods, therefore the people must adapt themselves to technology. Because human beings are not technocratic, it follows that this adaptation is being made at a cost to the human physical, intellectual, and emotional stability. There are limitations to which this adaptation can continue and still allow human beings to remain human. Furthermore, whether human beings benefit from either the goods or their making is a secondary matter. The health of the economy is synonymous with the health of the nation: "What's good for General Motors is good for America." Unfortunately for the economy, material needs—like human beings—also have limitations. Beyond a certain point, the acquisition of manufactured goods runs afoul of the law of diminishing desires. To some extent, this can be countered by replacing present material goods—hence, planned obsolescence. To some extent, it can be countered by creating a desire for goods that are not necessary—hence, advertising. These measures only postpone the inevitable. The society based upon economic competition requires, Bond says, a "final solution."

> We evolved in a biosphere but we live in what is more and more becoming a technosphere. We do not fit into it very well and so it activates our biological defences, one of which is aggression. Our environment is changing so rapidly that we cannot wait for biological solutions to evolve. So we should either change our technosphere or use technology to change human nature. But change in our society is really decided on urgent commercial imperatives so nothing is done to solve our main problem. . . . Alternatively, governments

could begin to use technology to enforce socialized morality. That is by using drugs, selection, conditioning, genetics, and so on, they could manufacture people who would fit into society.[5]

It is this society that Bond fears, and Evens sees: "You can see why the draper's afraid. Not of things from space, of us. We're becoming the strange visitors to this world" (viii, 64).

As it is with Mrs. Rafi, Evens's separation from society is indicative of his understanding of it. Where she chose to dominate society, however, he chose to withdraw from it. While Evens's reasoning seems the clearer and his courage the greater, it is still not the action in which Bond believes. The heroes in all Bond plays opt in and attempt to change society rather than to escape it. Although this change is never achieved, the character himself is usually morally victorious and, as a result of his efforts, some indication is given that the fight will be carried on. Only Scopey in *The Pope's Wedding* and Kiro in *Narrow Road* are unequivocally defeated and only the former play ends in total pessimism. Len continues to struggle against the growing apathy of the household in *Saved*. Arthur transcends even "heaven" in *Early Morning*. Christ leaves the cross to poison the communion wine in *Black Mass* and refuses to abandon the world even when He finds the cross occupied by a pig in *Passion*. Lear tries to dig up the wall he began. In *The Sea* the battle must be continued. Like Lear, Evens is old, but unlike Lear, he does not choose to fight. Like Mrs. Rafi, Evens has made his compromise and must find another to do what must be done.

> I'm a wreck rotting on the beach. Past help. That's why I live here out of people's way. It wouldn't help *them* if they

5. Bond, Preface to *Lear*, p. 12.

lived here. We all have to end differently. Don't trust the wise fool too much. What he knows matters and you die without it. But he never knows enough. . . . Go away. You won't find any more answers here. Go away and find them. Don't give up hope. That's always silly. The truth's waiting for you, it's very patient, and you'll find it. Remember, I've told you these things so that you won't despair. But you must still change the world (viii, 65).

Change the world. It need not be the way it is. Mankind's total thrust seems to be toward his own self-destruction, but if we accept this as law, we write our own death sentences—the ultimately foolish act. In the Preface to *Saved*, Bond said that religion must be based on what it is possible for men to believe. The lowest common denominator of that belief is that life as man was biologically evolved to live it is better than the corrupted existence that is the legacy of modern society. How can we change the world? In Bond's short story, *Christ Wanders and Waits*, Christ is condemned to walk on earth until men are no longer miserable. For thousands of years he wanders through hatred, famine, war, and plague asking two questions: "How can men stop being miserable and where can I find a happy man?" At the point when he feels unable to continue, he chances upon a worm who can speak. The worm answers the first question: "Love one another." Jesus then asks the second question.

> The worm said, "The earth is my house yet you walk on it and use it as your own. I don't complain about it, friend, and when you die I welcome you into my house. We are very close together and I would like to help you. But how can I tell you where to find a happy man? Still, I will do what I can. You are very tired. Sit here and I will go round the world for you, preaching this new philosophy to every man I meet. And then I will tell him I am christ and ask him if he is happy—and when I come back I will tell you if I have been able to find such a man."

The Sea

So the little worm set out to crawl round the earth and Jesus sat down and waited.[6]

How do we change the world? No one ever said it was easy.

Nonetheless, if a character does exist among the Bond gallery of Innocents who is capable of changing the world, it is Evens's symbolic descendant, Willy. He is young, physically vigorous, and will have in Rose a partner who understands the nature of the problem almost as well as he does. Rose and Willy leaving the village may well be intended by Bond as representatives of the search for counter-cultures and alternative politics in which he finds a healthy resistance to technological competition and socialized morality. Furthermore, Willy has been explicitly tutored in what to expect from the world by Evens. Most important, however, is his natural instinct to search and to survive. It is Willy who saves himself from the sea by his own efforts and who articulates Bondian optimism long before its source is explained to him by Evens. While they rest in their search on the beach for Colin's body, Rose, absorbed in her grief, can find no reason for living. Willy realizes intuitively that life comes before reason and, if reason denies life, then it is reason that must be ignored.

ROSE. I can't bear to lose him. I don't think I can live without him.
WILLY. I think that love can be a terrible disaster. And hope is sometimes pride and ambition. When I'm lost in darkness I'll shut my eyes and feel my way forward, grope like an animal, not be guided by some distant light.
ROSE. How can you escape from yourself, or what's happened to you, or the future? It's a silly question. It's better out here where he died. At home there's so much to do. And it's all done on time. How can I escape from *that*? People coming and going. Why? What does it matter to them?

6. Edward Bond, *Christ Wanders and Waits*, a short story published with *The Pope's Wedding* (London: Eyre Methuen, 1971), p. 111.

WILLY. If you look at life closely it is unbearable. What people suffer, what they do to each other, how they hate themselves, anything good is cut down and trodden on, the innocent and the victims are like dogs digging rats from a hole, or an owl starving to death in a city. It is all unbearable but that is where you have to find your strength. Where else is there? (vi, 43–44).

Social morality is the second major theme of *The Sea*. Its symbol is the village and it may also represent the choosing of death over resurrection. Every inhabitant of the village is to some extent socially moralized, although the most obvious case is Hatch, the draper. He believes that what he has to fear are invaders from outer space. Significantly, he believes Evens to be their agent. The system is right and decent. Therefore, anyone who deliberately places himself outside of it is suspect. Even the old man's decision to live near the sea is taken as evidence. Hatch is a coastguard. He must watch the sea at night for signs of ships in distress. The sea is unpredictable in a way that the village is not. It does not always operate according to the rules. Therefore, when unforseen storms occur, it is probably because the invaders can control the sea.

> Oh, we know how to handle you, Evens. This isn't your sort of sea. This is real sea where you drown. It's not governed by your fancy, twisted laws of gravity. You'll find out. (*Yells back to Hollarcut.*) They're afraid of our sea, Billy. They're not immune to wetness. It soaks in and melts their insides. You watch: they're terrorized of it (iii, 13).

It is Hatch who is terrorized of the sea, of course. It is because Willy Carson came out of the sea that Hatch has identified him as an alien agent. After all, Willy is an outsider and he survived the sea, while Colin Bentham, a native of the village, did not. Furthermore, when Willy came out of the sea, Evens was waiting for him on the beach. Finally, there is the army battery that began its practice just as

The Sea

Willy went back in the water to look for Colin. Individuals may be fooled but our leaders can be trusted to recognize the extraterrestial danger.

There are, Hatch realizes, those within the village proper who are alien agents. He can recognize them because of their deviations in his two major preoccupations: business and sex.

> You soon spot them behind this counter. You get a fair indication from the way they pay their bill. That shows if they respect our way of life, or if they're just out to make trouble by running people into debt (v, 30).

Further, the aliens are unalterably opposed to the sacrament of marriage and what Hatch deems to be its major purpose —the production of Christian soldiers to do battle for Saint George and England against outside invaders. That, in itself, was sufficient to doom Colin who, about to marry a "nice, well-brought up member of the gentry," was certain to provide offspring.

On the other hand, salacious and provocative sex is the space travelers' chief weapon. From a civilization more advanced than ours, they do not suffer from what Hatch considers to be the foremost of human weaknesses, a sexual appetite. It is instructive to note that when Hatch breaks down under financial pressure, he accuses his oppressors of sexual deviance.

> You know they come in here and whisper, ask for intimiate garments. Could I try this on, Hatch. Then they're off to the fitting room before you can stop them and leave the curtain open. All the intimate things. Wriggling into this and that. Is it too tight, Mr. Hatch? Is this gusset in order? . . . There's the worst. Leaves the curtain open and turns the mirror —brazen!—so you can see the darkness underneath (v, 38).

Hatch was head scholar in his Bible class. Like *Lear*'s Cordelia, who was the daughter of a priest, he tries to put up fences to separate the bad from the good, not realizing that the fences are evil in themselves. One of his most tightly walled up concepts is that of sex, which can never cohabit with good unless it be for the purpose of legitimate motherhood and for the benefit of the nation. According to sociologist-psychiatrist Wilhelm Reich, this highly restricted view of sex is typical of both the pathological individual and the pathological society.

> The pathological behavior of the average mass individual shows clearly the traits with which the individual patient has made us familiar: general sexual inhibition; the compulsive character of the moral demands; the inability to conceive of the compatibility of sexual gratification and achievement in work; the peculiar belief that the sexuality of children and adolescents is a pathological aberration; the inability to think of any form of sexuality than lifelong monogamy; the lack of confidence in one's own strength and judgment, with a consequent longing for an omniscient, guiding father-figure, etc.[7]

Hatch believes that the village is endangered from outer space because he is insecure and he is unable to admit the source of his insecurity—his arbitrary control from above. He is socially moralized, however, and therefore saw the vulnerability of the village as stemming from lack of leadership. He is uneasy because of control. Thus he desires more and better control. Hatch's social, economic, and spiritual values are derived from the higher stratas of his own society. His escape from the semi serfdom in which Hollarcut, Carter, and Thompson are trapped depends literally upon Mrs. Rafi's whims. She is the authority figure who determines his progression, regardless of his individual merit. Hatch believes, indeed has been taught from birth, that Mrs. Rafi has that right. Even when her refusal to

---

7. Wilhelm Reich, *The Sexual Revolution* (New York: Farrar, Straus, and Giroux, 1969), p. 3.

The Sea

take delivery of the curtain velvet he has purchased for her ruins Hatch financially, he does not contest her privilege. He can only assume that it is because the aliens, in the form of Willy, have deceived her.

> You will take the material, Mrs. Rafi? This whole shop's tied up in it. The little I've put by—not much, there's no big buyers, here. I couldn't set up in the larger towns. No capital. But I've worked hard, much of it against the grain. . . . D'you want me to crawl, Mrs. Rafi? Feel the stuff, m'am. Really, an educated person of your taste can't resist a product as beautiful as—(*crying*) but oh the pity of it is you don't see the whole community's threatened by that swine, yes swine, bastard, the welfare and livelihood of this whole town! He's tricked you. Only I spotted him. Well I've warned the coastguards. We don't let anyone land here now. They'll drown. I'll kick them under with my boot (v, 33).

In *Narrow Road* Georgina teaches the people to police themselves, to turn the aggressions resulting from their restrictions upon those who try to evade the restrictions or upon those who, being different, might try to evade the restrictions. A scapegoat—be it Jew, nigger, hippie, or pig—can be a useful political diversion, but once given it cannot be safely taken away. Unlike Georgina, Mrs. Rafi does not provide a safety valve for her victims. Hatch requires a scapegoat, both to relieve his tensions and as a means of advancement. More imaginative than the others in his substrata, Hatch aspires to rise in his society. To do so, he must anticipate society's will. He must identify and act against the enemies of society, which he knows from his own unhappiness *must* exist. For this act, Mrs. Rafi punishes him—not for having attacked another human being, but for judging wrongly and for having presumed to judge. Hatch's attack upon Willy and his war against the space aliens is equivalent to Len and Joyce eating the man who pushed ahead of them in the cinema queue. Society, Bond says, pointing to bombed foreign cities and untouched home slums, condones inhumanity, but only to further its own ends.

The aliens are, of course, the projection of Hatch's own fears. Does his business totter because of ruling class caprice? The invaders need slaves to produce goods for their planet. Are his emotions so armored that he can find no satisfaction in either lover or work? The space travelers have "come t'corrupt our manhood." Is it possible to gain respect without financial security? The aliens try to bribe him with notes left in the jam and messages written on steamy windows. Most important of all, is Hatch entrapped by his society? The aliens offer him an alternative, and it is that alternative that Hatch must suppress. "The living haunt the dead," says Arthur in *Early Morning*, by reminding them of their lost humanity. Death in the Bondian sense is acceptance of inhumanity as man's natural condition. Hatch knows no other existence than that of the village. All his conditioning teaches him that it is the best of all possible worlds and yet he is not happy. If there is another way of life, then his sacrifice of his humanity has been unnecessary. A socially moralized man can not face this recognition. Therefore he must make any other way of life his enemy. When Hatch stabs Colin's drowned body and water spurts out instead of blood, his greatest fear is underlined. What if in the alien world it is not necessary to die?

> No blood. Only water. How do I know he's dead? Surely, surely! (*Stabs.*) There, that's hard enough. Hack his throat. Cut it! Tear it! Rip it! Slash it! (*Stops stabbing. Rambles on quickly to himself.*) Still no blood! Who would have thought of this? Surely they die? Why come here, why do anything, if you're not afraid of death? Yes. Their world's dying and they'll die if they stay—they know, they know! Of course they die! (vi, 45–46).

When Hatch cuts Mrs. Rafi with his shears, it is an act of Oedipal violence—the repressed son, driven to a crossroads by an attempt to save his father, striking out at his father. Hatch, like *Narrow Road*'s Shogo, is an Oedipus figure. Each is left to "die" by his society in order to serve society's needs. Each thinks to appease society by killing others. Each is punished for killing without society's approval. The death of the son at the hands of the father parallels the corruption by society of its children. The Massacre of the Innocents parallels the Crucifixion. The only difference between Christ and Oedipus, Bond would say, is that God was a more efficient murderer than Laius.

Hatch is the logical product of a society headed by Mrs. Rafi, even as Lear's society logically produces his daughters and Cordelia. Mrs. Rafi believes she is dominant only because people want "a sense of order and security." However, when the price of security is the corruption of humanity, the effect upon the next generation is to institutionalize corruption. Hatch sees Martians behind every wave. The harbor guns practice because the Germans are preparing to invade. Who is the more mad? Imperialism is as much an extension of Mrs. Rafi as is Hatch. If we must kill in defense of our way of life, isn't the next rational step to kill those who might be a threat before they can act?

> Lenin thinks, for example, that he can use violence for specific ends. He does not understand that he will produce Stalin, and indeed must produce a Stalin because he has created this atmosphere of violence and somebody will finally have to take this thing over and control it. And the only way you can do this is by using more violence.[8]

8. John Hall, "Edward Bond," Manchester *Guardian*, 29 September 1971, p. 10. Three years later, Bond, concerned that his choice of examples might limit understanding, attempted to clarify his earlier statement: "but it takes you back to the central problem of our species, is there a rational and non-dehumanizing force, and if not how can we cope with irrational force?—I mean as an aid to change, not as a reactionary force defending the status quo. The problem is fundamental because we're a social species and private answers are not adequate to public questions." (Edward Bond, letter to Richard Scharine, 2 October 1974.)

Hatch's allies in his war of the worlds are the other coastguards—Hollarcut, Carter and Thompson. If they appear less eager than he to do battle, they are no less socially moralized. Carter and Thompson, at least, do not suffer Hatch's pain because they lack both his imagination and his ambition. It has never occurred to them, as it has to Hatch, that they might either rise within their society or leave it. Therefore, they are less tortured by frustration and ambiguous guilt. Hatch's appeal to them is straightforwardly patriotic. They must help their society to help itself. The true extent of their social morality can be measured by the speed with which they turn on Hatch when they discover that society in the form of Mrs. Rafi disapproves of their antialien activities. Thompson meekly permits Mrs. Rafi to lead him away by the ear while Mrs. Tilehouse energetically tans his behind with her umbrella. Carter accepts his scolding like an abashed schoolboy and attempts to prove his contrition by twice trying to capture Hatch, the second time (at Colin's funeral) successfully.

Hollarcut is another and far more interesting case. He is reminiscent of the gangs in *The Pope's Wedding* and *Saved*, and most especially of Len in *Early Morning*. That is, he is not intelligent, but he does sense that a discrepancy exists between what is and what should be. He possesses a certain cunning that protects him from being completely duped by either Hatch's reasoning or Mrs. Rafi's traditional authority. He is insightful, even though he does not understand the implications of his insight. Finally, he alone among the coastguards remains loyal to Hatch.

Hollarcut is Hatch's most faithful supporter in his battle against the extraterrestrial beings. He reinforces the commitment of the other coastguards in group meetings. He is Hatch's eyes, shadowing Evens and Willy. He alone does not desert when Mrs. Rafi exposes Hatch and he concerns himself with the draper's well-being after the others have left. Hollarcut is with Hatch when he storms Colin's funeral

The Sea

and even after the draper is locked up, Hollarcut continues his surveillance of Evens. Yet he understands both that Hatch is mad and that Evens is not a space invader's agent.

If Willy and Rose are resurrections of Evens and Mrs. Rafi, Billy Hollarcut is certainly a resurrection of Hatch. As with the others, it is tempting to find this development optimistic. Hollarcut's continued harassment of Evens indicates that he does not yet understand the nature of his problem. Unlike Hatch, however, he recognizes that it comes from within his society rather than beyond. He feels a need to rebel and that is healthy. This need is directed partly toward very real human oppressors and partly in behalf of loyalty to Hatch, a human being as opposed to an abstraction, and this, too, is healthy. He may, of course, give in to the pressures of his society and beat Evens to death with his club, but Evens seems to think this unlikely. His youth and his general good nature are in his favor. Most important of all, Hatch has given Hollarcut a sense of himself as a person of value. It is an asset that he will not easily yield.

> HOLLARCUT. He allus treat me right. Who else talked t' me 'cept t' say goo here, fetch that, yoo en't got this in yoo, yoo can't doo that? He on't ashamed t' talk t' me, or listen. He on't used me like that ol' bitch an' the rest on yer. He wanted me with him. . . . I count in the end. Yoo may not like it but mostly I'm like yoo an' I count. He knew that. That on't so mad. Thas's all I'll say for today.
> EVENS. All right, Billy. But don't do mad things. Drop your stick on the ground.
> HOLLARCUT. Mr. Hollarcut. . . . No. I'll howd on to en now I got en. That remind yoo I'm here. . . .
> WILLY. Morning, Billy. I see Mrs. Rafi's got you digging in her garden.
> HOLLARCUT. Mr. Hollarcut. . . . I'll tell you something you ought a know, boy. I dig for her—(*he lays the side of his index finger against the side of his nose and looks crafty*)— but will anything grow? (viii, 60–61).

The closer association a character has with Mrs. Rafi, the more farcical the treatment by Bond. The vicar, for example, is a foolish, sentimental, and ridiculous soul, who would seem more likely to be found in a play by Brian Rix than in one by Edward Bond. Still, his spiritual leadership is dispensed or dispensed with by the pressure of Mrs. Rafi's thumb. In that, he proves a worthy successor to the bishop who blesses Lear's armies and the priest in *Black Mass* who feels safer when Christ is replaced on the cross by a fascist trooper. Organized religion, Bond says, is concerned with its own preservation within society rather than the work of Christ.

A better example of what Rose describes as her aunt's "cripples" is Jessica Tilehouse, Mrs. Rafi's companion. She exists in a state of subdued, but almost constant rebellion against Mrs. Rafi: making suggestions at the draper's shop and during the play rehearsal; delaying the hymns at Colin's funeral with her elaborate descant; and fussily searching through her bag for smelling salts during Mrs. Rafi's dramatic declamation. Those rebellions are petty and are, as much as anything, a childish attempt on Mrs. Tilehouse's part to get Mrs. Rafi's attention and to force from her an admission of Mrs. Tilehouse's basic worth. She has assumed without question that Mrs. Rafi has the right to make that determination, as good an example of socialized morality as Hatch's creation of outer-space invaders. Mrs. Rafi recognizes Mrs. Tilehouse's motives and continually and openly humiliates her while consciously withholding her approval: ordering her to walk home when she invites Willy to lunch, "Pony can't manage three"; adding to her drama duties as program seller and assistant to the stage carpenter by assigning her the task of simulating the River Styx by crawling under the stage with a water basin; and loudly chastising her in front of the rest of the mourners for being a distraction at the funeral. Still, Mrs. Tilehouse returns for more punishment in a vain hope of approval. Her combined resentment and ambition is best expressed as she is being revived after fainting when Hatch goes mad.

    CARTER. Mrs. Tilehouse, m'am.
    MRS. TILEHOUSE. (*Jumping to her feet.*) Help! I am about to be attacked by a large man.
    CARTER. Mrs. Rafi tol' me t' say—
    MRS. TILEHOUSE. Louise is dead! What were her last words? She apologised to me for it all! I forgive her! I hold no grudge, however justified— (v, 39).

If Jessica's chances of recognition are nonexistant, her hopes of revenge are just as futile. Mrs. Rafi has anticipated her again. When she becomes too old to control Mrs. Tilehouse, Mrs. Rafi plans to have her pensioned off: "She is one of those ladies who are meant to die alone in a small room." It is an unfeeling epitaph, but a fitting one.

The Sea, a comedy performed in a relatively realistic setting—an English coastal village about the year 1907—is the first Bond play with a recognizable, if not immediate, locale since *Saved.* Although none of his plays lack moments of incisive satire, *The Sea* also maintains a comic tone over a longer period than any previous work. Bond's two shorter plays, *Black Mass* and *Passion,* are also comedies, but they were first seen in the context of two highly serious events—the Commemoration of the Tenth Anniversary of the Sharpesville Massacre and the Committee for Nuclear Disarmament Festival of Life, respectively. Therefore, the audience presumed serious intent. Moreover, both plays were brief and neither imposed a realistic plot between idea and audience. *The Sea,* on the other hand, stands alone. It is Bond's most conventionally plotted play and the first to have a conventionally happy ending.

The Sea represents a refinement in Bond's structural style. Bond has always insisted, and his plays have amply proved, that his writing is not loosely episodic but rather is very tightly constructed along intellectual lines. The problem has been throughout, especially in *Early Morning*, that if one failed to grasp Bond's idea, he was left with a number of marvelous scenes that didn't add up to a play. *The Sea*, on the other hand, poses no such problem. While the full richness of the play can in no way be tapped by following only the "boy-meets-girl" plot, it does provide a highly visible lifeline in relation to which the significance of other secenes and characters can be more readily understood.

Bond has also developed in his control of mood. One of his strengths has always been the evocation of atmosphere and many of his best effects have been the result of contrasting the tones of consecutive scenes—effects that have sometimes been dissipated by the change of scene itself. For example, *Narrow Road*, Bond's shortest "full-length" play, contains eleven scenes. *Early Morning* contains twenty-one. *The Sea*, however, manages with only eight scenes because Bond is able to sharply change moods within the scene. There is, for instance, the side-splitting rehearsal of *Orpheus and Eurydice* at Mrs. Rafi's house that is interrupted by the firing of the harbor battery. The sound of the guns, which also fired the night Colin drowned, has as definite an effect on the scene's mood as the sound of the mine lift cable snapping does in *The Cherry Orchard*. Even more impressive is the clifftop funeral scene that passes from comedy of manners (the funeral service and Mrs. Rafi's recitation) to knockabout farce (the pelting of Hatch with Colin's ashes) to confessional self-insight (Mrs. Rafi's monologue and Willy's proposal to Rose) without ever taking a false step.

The question has been asked as to why Bond this time chose to make a comedy the vehicle of his ideas. To begin with, it may be a false question. Bond has said that he writes as a way of coping with problems that bother him. *Narrow Road* was written in two-and-a-half days after the chance reading of a 300-year-old travel narrative. The two images that culminated in *The Sea* germinated for years. Artists do not always choose their media. If the choice of comedy was deliberate, however, it was an excellent one. Jane Howell has speculated that the deliberately nonrealistic temper of *Early Morning* and *Narrow Road* were attempts to present the conditions and ideas of *Saved* without inciting the emotional antagonism of the earlier play. Comedy is an intellectual medium, demanding detachment, and, as such widely diverse literati as Ben Jonson and George Bernard Shaw could attest, is thus an excellent means of dispensing ideas. Furthermore, two of Bond's most didactic plays, *Black Mass* and *Passion*, were highly praised in their comic form. In *The Sea*, Evens decides that "without tragedy no one can laugh" (viii, 64). Bond shows us, not for the first time, that it is sometimes easier to accept tragedy if we can laugh.

The Sea also shows a certain progression in Bond's handling of character. Mrs. Rafi is the linear descendant of Victoria, Georgina, and the queen in *Passion*. Unlike them, however, she is a complete human being with fears, disappointments, and self-knowledge. In her, Bond has combined the sharply observed reality of his earlier plays with the psychological/sociological truth of his nonrealistic works.

Willy is the latest in Bond's continually evolving line of Innocents. He begins with an instinctive understanding of the nature of Man and develops an intellectual understanding. *The Sea* also shows us the failed Innocent, the man who was broken under society's strain. Hatch is an improvement on earlier members of this species in that we come to understand his development by seeing in the form of Mrs. Rafi the pressures that have molded him. In contrast, Shogo's shaping influences occurred during his childhood and the development of the Grave Digger's Boy can only be understood if he is considered as Lear's *doppelgänger*. *The Sea* provides an instructive look at Society's daily corrosion factor.

Finally, in *The Sea* Bond has permitted himself for the

first time a *raisonneur*. Evens is not a hero. He cannot surmount that obstacle that he sees so clearly, but he can, at least, articulate the optimism that Bond has always seen as the focus of his work.

> I believe in the rat. What's the worst thing you can imagine? The universe is lived in by things that kill and this has gone on for all time. Sometimes the universe is crowded with killing things. Or at any rate there are great pools of them in space. Perhaps that's so now. At other times it falls out that they've killed everything off, including each other, of course, and the universe is almost deserted. But not quite Somewhere on a star a rat will hide under a stone. It will look out on the broken desert and from time to time it will scatter out to feed on the debris, A shambolling, lollaping great rat—like a fat woman with shopping bags running for a bus. Then it scuttles back to its nest and breeds. Because rats build nests. I believe in that. And in time it will change into things that fly and swim and crawl and run. And one day it will change into the rat catcher. I believe in the rat because he has the seeds of the rat catcher in him. I believe in the rat catcher. I believe in sand and stone and water because the wind stirs them into a dirty sea and it gives birth to living things. I believe the universe lives. It teems with life. Men take themselves to be very strong and cunning. But who can kill space or time or dust? They destroy everything but they only make the materials of life. All destruction is finally petty and in the end life laughs at death. . . . I also believe in the wise rat catcher. He can bear to live in the minutes as well as the years and he understands the voice of the thing he is going to kill. Suffering is a universal language and everything that has a voice is human (viii, 63–64).

Bond entitles his play *The Sea* because it is the symbol of both death and rebirth—the killer who "makes the materials of life." It is fitting concept upon which to build a future.

9
The Edward Bond View of Life: A Summary of Themes and Techniques

Edward Bond was born in 1934. He has had produced just six long plays, the first of which was presented less than a dozen years ago. Normally, an academic review of a writer's accomplishments, no matter how successful he may have been (and Bond has been a commercial failure), at this stage of his career would be presumptuous in the extreme. However, Bond is unique among English playwrights in that he has a world view, an evaluation of human potential and the conditions that obstruct it, that has remained consistent from his earliest work to his most recent. This viewpoint is the controlling factor in his plays and he presents it with such conviction and power that, although many have attempted to dispute, ridicule, and refute it, it cannot be ignored. Acceptance of this viewpoint, and the willingness to take social action that this acceptance implies, has become more and more inseparable from the acceptance of the plays themselves. It is to be expected that this trend will endure and that, although Bond will continue to pursue a wide range of theatrical techniques, his themes will remain essentially the same.

The dominant concern of Edward Bond is the relationship between society and its subjects. He believes that society destroys its children in a number of ways. Primarily, they are not allowed to function in the way for which they were evolved. Designed to live biologically, human beings are forced to live technologically. That is, they are treated as parts of a commercially competitive cycle. Society measures its success in terms of its Gross National Product rather than the mental, moral, or spiritual health of its citizens. In order to produce these goods, men must work at jobs and under conditions for which the human being is physiologically and psychologically unsuited. His reward for this dehumanizing labor is a share of the consumer goods that he has produced. Indeed, he must consume an ever-increasing amount of these goods if the commercially competitive cycle is to continue. Leaving aside the fact that the amount of raw materials on the earth is finite and that nature must eventually end this cycle, it is true that very few of these products fit any inherent physical, mental, or emotional needs of the human being. Therefore, as John Kenneth Galbraith has observed in *The New Industrial State,* society devotes a vast amount of effort to creating a desire for new consumer goods among its citizens. Thus far, this method has been reasonably successful. However, Bond believes that society will eventually be forced to more drastic methods.

> Forgetting whether or not it's a good thing that we live in a technological society—and I don't think it is—we have to ask whether a government will have enough knowledge to be able to manufacture the human beings it wants. It might be that it will *have* to start developing, genetically, people who are stupid—or stupified. Even now, most of capitalist society

A Summary of Themes and Techniques

is a process for manufacturing consumer drugs—because nobody would want these extraordinary things they consume like mad if they were living a natural life. Right: so you spend all your life as a slave, producing tranquillizers to make slavery bearable—yes? . . . It might happen in a few years time that governments will be trying to make people take drugs.[1]

It is a prospect explored chillingly many years ago by Aldous Huxley in *Brave New World*, but for the moment it is still largely speculation. What society has already done is sufficiently alarming.

Society's destruction of its subjects can be quite subtle. One of the dehumanizing factors of industrialization is that the worker no longer has a personal relationship with his work. He bears no responsibility for the total end-product and the quality of the end-product itself has no immediate bearing on the quality of his life. Even the part of the product for which the worker is responsible requires automatism from him rather than skill. Whatever their other shortcomings, the farmhands of *The Pope's Wedding* feel a pride in their tools, in the tractor that Ron oils and the scythe that Lorry shines. The cricket match that absorbs their interest is dependant upon their clearing of the field and their team is weakened because Bill's presence is required by the farm animals. In short, their individual effort accounts for something. In contrast, the work in *Saved* has no more identity than the city itself with its "miles and miles of long straight streets that always look the same"[2] and the relationship of human beings to their recreation is symbolized by the distorted television picture that no one knows how to adjust properly. The workers that Lear assigns

---

1. Edward Bond, as quoted by Roger Hudson, Catherine Itzin, and Simon Trussler in "Drama and the Dialectics of Violence," *Theatre Quarterly*, 2 (January–March 1972): 9.
2. Bond, as quoted by Hudson, et al., "Drama and the Dialectics of Violence," p. 8.

to the nonfulfilling chore of building the wall find the hands with which they have worked all their lives immediately begin to bleed from the effort. Their feet swell from the mud during the day and during the night they rebel by digging up what they have built. When Lear himself tries to tear down the wall at the close of the play, the shovel that he finds there has no edge because "no one cares for it."[3] According to psychologist Wilhelm Reich, illness and rebellion are the natural reactions to unfulfilling work.

In Bond's view, the question of dehumanization is based on more than just the incompatibility of biological man and technological society. It begins with the onset of tribalism and is inherent in all social institutions. Man's original relationship with his environment was one to one. He had to live in harmony with it or die and, since the environment itself was often upredictable, his margin for error was distressingly thin. In order to take full advantage of times of plenty and to protect themselves against times of famine, men formed loosely organized societal groups. Within these groups leaders evolved naturally. Those who contributed most to the welfare of the group's members gradually assumed more responsibility for group affairs. This was natural because "the whole structure [was] held together by the negative biological response to deprivation and threat."[4] With that increased responsibility, the leaders received more privileges and more control over their fellow tribesmen. In times when nonconformity could be disastrous to the community's safety, these controls and privileges were justified. Injustice set in when the controls were continued beyond the period of crisis and when the privileges were designated to others (for example, inherited by a son from his father) regardless of merit. In other words, controls and privileges became unjust when they became social institutions.

3. Edward Bond, *Lear* (London: Eyre Methuen, 1972), III, iv, p. 87.
4. Edward Bond, Preface to *Lear*, p. 7.

A Summary of Themes and Techniques

Once developed, social institutions tend to perpetuate themselves. On one level, they can do this because they already possess the power. In this manner, Shogo rules the city in *Narrow Road* despite his subjects' resentment because of the efficiency of his army. The force that the leader is able to bring to bear on the individual citizen insures that the "rules of society" will be obeyed. This method, however, has certain disadvantages. All forms of control that force men to behave unnaturally breed resentment. This is as true of the economic sanctions of the industrial state as it is of the military sanctions of the police state. In the case of a military dictator, a highly visible point of focus is provided for that resentment. Shogo must guard himself constantly against assassination attempts and, because he can never relax his iron control, he is as much a prisoner of his dictatorship as his subjects. Furthermore, the dictates of a police state need only be followed as long as the police are in sight. Just as an economically competitive state creates a citizenry that demands pay for any action, a state based on force creates a citizenry for whom nothing unseen is immoral. Thus, the untended baby in the park can be stoned to death because there is "no one around. . . . Might as well enjoy ourselves. . . . Yer don't get a chance like this everyday." [5]

A more effective method of institutional perpetuation, as Georgina demonstrates in *Narrow Road*, is social morality. That is, men must be convinced that they are inherently evil and require the enforcement of law and order by societal institutions for their own protection. It is because she is socially moralized that June in *The Pope's Wedding* can believe that the streets of her town are dirty because "people are pigs" [6] rather than because living in towns causes

---

5. Edward Bond, *Saved* (New York: Hill and Wang, 1955): vi, 55. All subsequent references to this play will be noted in the text.
6. Edward Bond, *The Pope's Wedding, Plays and Players* 16, no. 7 (April 1969): vii, 43. All subsequent references to this play will be noted in the text.

dirt to collect. It makes it possible for Fred to rationalize that the baby was killed because "the bloody police don't do their job," the choice of moral action no longer being an individual responsibility. In *Lear,* the farmer and his son who give up their land and go to work on the wall and in the army, respectively, even though they know it will probably mean their deaths, are socially moralized because they accept the promise that their government has the right to demand their lives. The most extreme case of social morality is Shogo, who himself rules by force rather than morality. Society, in the form of his parents and Basho, told him categorically that he had no right to live by abandoning him as a baby. His death was required, on the one hand, for the economic welfare of society and, on the other, by the will of heaven. Shogo accepts this verdict and feels guilt for having survived. Therefore, he builds a city in which any or all lives may be sacrificed for the good of society, the perfect embodiment of the principles under which he was condemned.

Shogo kills people for their own good—on the face of it, a mad act. The real madness, however, lies in the society that creates Shogo and then creates its own mythology to explain him. Call Shogo by other names—legislative, executive, or judicial departments (for he performs all these functions)—and call his atrocities capital punishment for the purpose of preserving general welfare, and his acts regain their respectability. Shogo is, after all, a classic case of Freudian success. He has subliminated his antisocial drives and built a society. So long as he can control this society, he is a cultural hero. Alternatively, Hatch, in *The Sea,* reacts to the same pressures by imagining an invasion from outer space and by refusing to help drowning sailors whom he suspects to be double agents. For this, Hatch, who does not control society, is declared mad and is locked up. Yet Hatch killed fewer men than Shogo and his intentions were as good. The moral to this, Bond says, is that society disapproves of madness but only society can decide who is mad.

Bond equates the rise of social institutions with the development of nationalism. His Lear is a renaissance figure, responsible for the transition from a community in which man's primary allegiance was to his fellow man and to his environment to one in which a man's primary allegiance is to a central government. Unfortunately, while in theory, governments may be "for the people," in practice their primary allegiances are, at worst, to their own perpetuation or, at best, to an abstract national ideal. For this reason, Lear is capable of building a wall to protect his people at the same time as he has them executed for accidents that occur in that building; and Shogo is able, with a clear conscience, to execute the peasant who was standing *next* to the man who tried to assassinate him: "I'm proud of him—he was a hero. He died for the city—to protect the rule of law and order."[7] Whether for preservation or principle, the effect of nations is to reduce the importance of individuals. Just as his work in an industrial state becomes only a small part of a total effort, the individual is not identifiable as a whole from a nationalistic viewpoint. The individual is allowed to live only so that he may make a contribution to the nation.

Society's reasoning in these matters is simple, if circular. Social institutions (including government, religion, law, etc.) are designed for the protection of the people. Nevertheless, many people rebel against their restrictions. These actions are antisocial, since it is society who determines social definitions. Since the institutions are inherently good, the rebellion must be unmotivated. Therefore, the men must be inherently bad and they must be restricted for their own protection. It is by this reasoning that Queen Victoria in

---

7. Edward Bond, *Narrow Road to the Deep North* (New York: Hill and Wang, 1968):: I, iv, 29. All subsequent references to this play will be noted within the text.

Early Morning can say with perfect consistency, "this is for *your* good,"[8] even as she strangles Arthur.

The restrictions of society cause rebellion and society punishes that rebellion. However, society does not stop at punishing the socially guilty. It presumes, since all men are naturally evil, that all men are potential social rebels. In other words, since all men *should* hate society, all men *do* hate society and must be punished for it. The precept is occasionally fallacious—as Brecht has pointed out—but society must operate by the rule rather than the exception.

Under such conditions the question of why a people permits the continued existence of unjust social institutions must be raised. In *The Mass Psychology of Fascism*, Wilhelm Reich has argued that economic subordinates allow their leaders to form their social standards, receiving as their only reward the right to enforce upon others the oppression that cripples themselves.

> The fascist . . . is an emotional plague character and stands for absolute authoritarianism. He is the little man who grew up so inhibited and restricted and so dependent upon the father that he requires a father-figure or the fatherland to continue to dictate his life and give him permission to express the brutality and hate he can no longer control. . . . Rigidly armored, he still senses the motility of life within himself but cannot experience it directly. Tantalized, as Reich says, by intolerable longing, he lashes out brutally and with murderous intent toward the living. This is rationalized through his extreme mysticism as necessary and just, to maintain the purity of his race and bring it to dominance over other inferior or contaminated races. He is thus an extreme nationalist and an abject slave to his leader and his country.[9]

Reich's theory explains the intense nationalism of a

---

8. Edward Bond, *Early Morning* (London: Calder and Boyers, 1968): xix, 104. All subsequent references to this play will be noted in the text.

9. Elsworth F. Baker, *Man in the Trap* (New York: The Macmillan Company, 1967), p. 196.

A Summary of Themes and Techniques

Hatch, who has been portrayed in some German productions as a Hitler figure, driven by paranoia to save his country.[10] At the other end of the continuim, it is easy to see why Bond chose Queen Victoria as his symbol for society in *Early Morning*. Besides being monarch of the British Empire for two-thirds of a century, she was a matriarch to most of Europe's crowned heads (by blood that carried hemophilia, ironically), and gave her name to an age of repressions that still affects the world today.

His evaluation of the patriarchial influence as basically corrupt and fascistic goes far to explain Bond's concern for children.

> Our society has the structure of a pyramid of aggression and as the child is the weakest member it is at the bottom. We still *think* we treat children with special kindness and make special allowances for them as indeed most animals do. But do we? Don't most people believe they have a right, even a duty, to use crude force against children as part of their education? Almost all organizations dealing with children are obsessed with discipline. Whenever possible we put them into uniforms and examine their minds like warders frisking prisoners. We force them to live by the clock before they can read it, though this makes no biological sense. We build homes without proper places for them. They interfere with the getting of money so mothers leave them and go to work —and some of them are no longer even physically able to feed their own children. Parents are worn out by daily competitive striving so they can't tolerate the child's natural noise and mess. They don't know why it cries, they don't know *any* of its inarticulate language. The child's first word isn't "mummy" or "daddy," it is "me." It has been learning to say it through millions of years of evolution, and it has a biological right to its egocentricity because that is the only way our species can continue.[11]

10. Irving Wardle, "German Theatre: Rolling in Money and Ruled by Directors," London *Times*, 23 May 1974, p. 11.
11. Bond, Preface to *Lear*, p. 8.

The literal deaths of children are presented powerfully in several Bond plays. In addition to Bond's two most horrific set pieces—the stoning of the baby in *Saved* and the beheading of the schoolchildren in *Narrow Road*—the plays contain several other examples of infanticide and child abuse. These include the bombing death of Pam's brother in the park, a parallel to the murder of her own baby, and the murder by neglect of the magician's son in *Passion*. In addition, there are the deaths of those characters who have managed somehow to carry the moral innocence of children into adulthood: the murders of Alen in *The Pope's Wedding*, Arthur in *Early Morning*, the Soldier in *Passion*, the Grave Digger's Boy in *Lear*, and the suicide of Kiro in *Narrow Road*. The abandonment of Shogo as a baby and the blinding of Lear, the Innocent who is not "born" until he is an old man, should also be included on this list.

Even more important than the literal deaths of these particular children, however, is the spiritual death of humanity in those who survive. Bond has said of *Saved:* "compared to the cultural and emotional deprivation of most of our children its consequences [the stoning of the baby] are insignificant." [12] The vast majority of children do survive physically, but in terms of their humane potential they are but ghosts of what they might have been. Bond literalizes this concept in *Early Morning* by creating a society populated completely by ghosts who are "haunted" by the living Arthur. Georgina in *Narrow Road* also raises ghosts by convincing the residents of the city that they are sinful and therefore must be governed. When the administration of this philosophy fails to save the children, she becomes haunted by the specter of sin she has raised and goes mad. To become a living ghost is to believe and *act* according to the principles of social morality. If a socially moralized person accepts as fact that society should control him, the

---

12. Bond, Preface to *Saved*, p. 6.

A Summary of Themes and Techniques

"living ghost" designates himself as an instrument by which society controls others. For example, Len and Joyce are members of a society in *Early Morning* that sets up destructive restrictions over its citizens and then punishes them for breaking those restrictions. Therefore, Len and Joyce eat the man who broke rank in the cinema queue. As Len tells Arthur, "I got a right a be guilty same as you!" (iv, 26). In *The Sea*, Hatch creates in his mind an enemy who threatens society with all the oppression that he himself has suffered. He then sets out to kill all those he believes to be allied with that enemy. In *Lear*, Bodice and Fontanelle realize that their father, the creator of their society, is perfectly capable of sacrificing them (as he does his other "children") to fulfill his national aspirations. Therefore, they propose to destroy him in the same way he has destroyed others, even though in so doing they sacrifice their humanity.

The stoning of the baby in *Saved* thus symbolizes, on one hand, the spiritual and psychological battering all the children of that society receive from their environment and institutions. On the other hand, it symbolizes the loss of identity that makes such battering possible. The dead baby in *Saved* has no name that we know of; it has no sex until the boys remove its diaper in the death scene; and it is sedated with aspirin to remove its sense of its own being. It is therefore not recognizable as human and therefore can be killed without guilt. The same is true of the German soldier that Harry shot during the war, a parallel that reveals society's willingness to permit individual dehumanization and violence if it is in its own interest. The schoolchildren in *Narrow Road* are killed because no one literally can tell them apart. The sixty-nine blacks who are slaughtered in *Black Mass* receive from their killers only a corporate identity as an irritating presence and as a poor substitute for the "mind-cleansing and body-building games" the troops usually engage in on Sunday afternoon: "But it can't hold a candle to wild-fowling. You've shot one man and you've shot them all." [13] *Passion* has two unidentified victims: the Old Woman's son who is taken away to be a soldier and the son of the magician, whose father can never remember his name.

There is a third theme embodied in the stoning of the baby and that is Bond's rejection of the Christian legend. Bond is an atheist, a condition that springs, as much as anywhere, from the religious training of his childhood.

> I don't think one can actually have true religious belief as a child—if you hear the bare facts of the crucifixion, for instance, and are told this is an example of God's love—well, one felt that they were abusing language! I was very puzzled by this, and of course Biblical metaphors were very confusing. But what one *can* have as a child is religious *fear,* and I think I had a certain amount of this . . . yes, puzzlement, bewilderment.[14]

The idea of a Father sacrificing his Son to prove his love for his followers is, after all, a perfectly accurate description of Fred's complicity in the gang's murder of the baby. In *Early Morning,* Prime Minister Gladstone instructs his troops on the proper method to use in kicking his son to death with the admonition: "When 'e dies I'll be the first t' cry. . . . Till then 'e lives by the book" (viii, 53). In *Passion,* the magician sets up a situation whereby his toddler son can not help but have a fatal accident and then goes off to deliver a lecture on, "Science and the Responsible Citizen." Even these examples are far less obvious in their symbolism than the speech of Basho, the new Prime Minister of the city, at the crucifixion of Shogo, the tyrant for whose development he is responsible: "The city is purged. . . . The sin is broken! Let the new city live for ever!" (II, iv, 56–57).

---

13. Edward Bond, *Black Mass, Gambit* 5. no, 17: 51.
14. Bond, as quoted by Hudson, *et al.,* "Drama and the Dialectics of Violence," p. 5.

A Summary of Themes and Techniques

Bond shows how the Christian legend is used to condone inhuman actions in Victoria's speech to the mob after she has murdered Arthur in *Early Morning:* "So he died, to let you eat each other in peace. . . . His last words were 'Feed them'" (xxi, 117). The same theme, society's perversion of the Christian legend, is exemplified in the replacement of Christ on the cross by a fascist trooper in *Black Mass* and by a pig in *Passion.*

It is interesting to note that Bond does not reject Christ, who appears as a decidedly sympathetic character in both *Black Mass* and *Passion,* but he does reject Christianity. That is, he accepts the Man who walked among his fellow men, fed them, comforted them, and taught them compassion, but he rejects the institution that has corrupted Christs's ideals and used His legend for its own glorification. Included within this rejection is God, a bodiless abstraction at best and a homicidal monster at worst.

Christian symbolism is never far away in a Bond play and the images of the Slaughter of the Innocents, the Crucifixion, and the Resurrection are particularly well served. The Slaughter of the Innocents examples have already been described in detail several times and need only be listed here: Scopey's killing of Alen, the stoning of Pam's baby, the eating of Arthur, the beheading of the schoolchildren and the *hara-kiri* of Kiro in *Narrow Road,* the shooting of the blacks in *Black Mass,* the Soldier *in Passion,* and the Grave Digger's Boy in *Lear.* In addition to the literal crucifixions of *Narrow Road, Black Mass,* and *Passion,* Bond (who has a very strong visual sense) has created a number of other Crucifixion images. For example, the drowned Colin lies on the beach, his arms crooked over his head in a dying attempt to remove his jumper. Scopey describes his strangulation of Alen in *The Pope's Wedding* in terms that recall a crucifixion. Alen, who incidentally sings a song about Christ that describes him as a baby nailed to a tree, has other references as a Christ-figure. The villagers credit him with the power of insight into souls and the ability to punish wrongdoers. Despite this, they abuse and stone him, as they do *The Sea*'s Evens who is similarly distanced from society. Finally, he is murdered by a disciple (Scopey) and is resurrected figuratively when Scopey takes his place in the shack. In the first heaven scene of *Early Morning*, the man hung up on a pulley for eating is a crucifixion image. That scene, with Albert first testing Arthur with his sword and then cutting him apart from George, is reminiscent of the image of Christ with his double-edged sword in the Revelations of Saint John the Divine. In such an interpretation, Victoria (who *is* society) would be the "new Jerusalem," the city who is to be the bride of Christ. Arthur's Ascension from the coffin, signifying his triumph over his society, is a Resurrection image, as is the drowning man who saves himself in *Narrow Road*, and the soldier blown from his grave by the nuclear explosion in *Passion*. In a sense, the two deaths of the Grave Digger's Boy are followed by resurrections in the person of Lear: first, by arousing in Lear compassion for his fellow man; second, by coinciding with Lear's attainment of political and moral maturity. As we have seen in the preceding chapter, Death and Resurrection is *The Sea*'s unifying theme.

Bond devotes a major portion of his Preface to *Saved* to still a fourth interpretation of the baby stoning. It is "the Oedipus, atavistic fury fully unleashed." Likewise, the murder of the baby *can* occur because societal restrictions build up tensions for which only a few occupations (for example, censor, policeman, missionary, etc.) allow adequate outlet. "This sort of fury is what is kept under painful control by other people in the play and that partly accounts for the corruption of their lives." [15] When it is released, the results are as spontaneous and horrendus as those of the German V-1 bombs that Bond knew as a child during the war.

---

15. Bond, Preface to *Saved*, p. 6.

A Summary of Themes and Techniques

> I remember once that I was walking along a road and there was suddenly this enormous sort of bang which one can't describe, you know, because it' so . . . a noise almost inside you. I went along to the park and saw all the trees stripped bare, and picked up this little bird with its head blown off. I would think, very much, that was one of the reasons why I wrote that scene in *Saved*. There was always the possibility that violence could really explode.[16]

The same type of Oedipal atavism is displayed in Georgina's obsession with rape after the shock of the children's death drives her mad. Her political suppression of the body as sinful has been a reflection of her own concealed sexual drives and fears. They come to the fore when her mind can no longer control them. In the same manner, Fontanelle, who has always been terrified of her father, moves from excitement to hysteria and active participation while watching the beating of a prisoner.

Other Oedipal aspects are to be found in the works of Bond, the most frequent among them being uterine regression. Alen's shack in *The Pope's Wedding* is a womblike retreat from the world in which he is challenged and eventually replaced by Scopey. On this level, it is an Oedipal triangle in which the son ousts the father as the mother's sexual favorite. On another occasion, when Pat shows Scopey a postcard depicting an impossibly clean town, he daydreams about living in a room whose walls, ceiling, and floor are covered with postcards. The image of cleanliness and beauty unattainable in this world is unmistakably that of the womb. The flat in which Len immerses himself and Mary's skirt, under which he sits while mending her stocking, are symbols of uterine regression. A far more obvious expression is the joy Arthur feels with his bodiless head hidden between Florence's legs or the "sacred vessel" in which Kiro, unhappy over the emptiness of his life, sticks

16. Bond, as quoted by Hudson, *et al.*, "Drama and the Dialectics of Violence," p. 5.

his head. More along the lines of Alen's shack and Len's flat is the Grave Digger's Boy's house into which Lear tries twice to retreat from life. The most magnificent of Bond's uterine symbols is found in the placentalike waters of *The Sea*, which serve doubly as a source of life and of destruction.

Bond himself objects strongly to the womb designation of the above images, arguing logically that the desire of his characters for protection is not made more meaningful or more valid by labelling it a desire to return to the womb. Indeed, such a designation is made at the cost of each scene's political dimensions. It is worth noting, therefore, that no matter what the characters seek in the above scenes, they do not find it. Scopey discovers Alen's shack to be a literal "dead end." Although Len continues to strive, Harry and Mary's flat is scarcely promising. George sniffs out Arthur's head from under Florence's skirt. Kiro nearly suffocates in the sacred vessel. The soldiers twice penetrate the house of the Grave Digger's Boy. The sea from which Willy saves himself drowns Colin. The Golden Age is dead. Once one has left it, the womb no longer suffices even as a metaphor.

In any event, repressed violence and uterine regression makes up only a part of the Oedipal symbolism to be found in Bond's plays. The assumption of clothing is an effective indicator of rivalry. Scopey, who initially believes Alen to be his wife's father (a parallel with Len and Harry in *Saved*), feels "bigger" when he is given Alen's greatcoat to wear. Jealous over the affection that Lear shows to her younger sister, Bodice puts on her mother's dress. As Scopey sees Alen as a rival for Pat, Len finds himself put into a position where he is in constant Oedipal conflict with Harry.

> The first scene is built on the young man's sexual insecurity—he either invents interruptions himself or is interrupted by the old man. Len has to challenge him, and get him out of the house, before he can continue. Later he helps the old

man's wife, and this is given a sexual interpretation by the onlookers. Later still the old man finds him with his wife in a more obviously sexual situation.[17]

The near seduction of Len by Pam's mother in *Saved* suggests an incestual relationship and a similar passion is consummated in *Early Morning* between Len and Joyce. In the same play, Arthur's unwillingness to act against Victoria parallels the Len/Joyce relationship. At the same time, in one of those literary jokes that Bond likes to play, it parallels the relationship of Hamlet to his mother. When the "heavenly" mob goes berserk after imagining themselves poisoned (their fury itself an action of Oedipal atavism), Arthur is carried along in the frenzy and eats his father. When he awakes the next day, Arthur has become old with white hair and a white beard, the symbols of Oedipal guilt.[18] Furthermore, it is not until Lear, like Oedipus, is blinded that he can achieve insight into his own sins and the workings of society.

To isolate all of the Christian and Oedipal symbolism to be found in Bond's plays is probably a hopeless task. It is sufficient to say that in some sense each Bond plot repeats the basic elements of the Christ/Oedipus legend: God/Laius/Society destroys Christ/Oedipus/Innocents in order to save His followers/himself/the System.

Bond's critics look at his plays and call them terrifyingly pessimistic. Bond looks at the world around him and calls man optimistic for trying to live in it. At the same time, this is the only world that man has. If it is not suitable to human beings, the proper procedure is to change the society that controls it, rather than to follow the alternatives that are society's current options: the elimination of man's humanity and the destruction of the earth. Almost all of Bond's

17. Bond, preface to *Saved*, p. 5.
18. The image of Christ in Revelations also has white hair and a white beard. Perhaps in accepting Victoria's ethic, Arthur symbolically becomes her bridegroom.

plays call for this change obliquely. Evens, in *The Sea*, demands it openly: "Don't give up hope. That's always silly. The truth's waiting for you, it's very patient, and you'll find it. Remember, I've told you these things so that you won't despair. But you must still change the world." [19] The protagonists of Bond's plays face society at its most destructive and, if they are never totally victorious, we are nevertheless left with hope for the continuation of man's struggle against inhumanity. Bond's earliest play, *The Pope's Wedding*, may well be his most pessimistic because it's hero, Scopey, destroys himself in order to fulfil an empty abstraction. Even he, however, embodies the desire for a more meaningful existence than the one he knows. In *Saved*, Len "lives with people at their worst and most hopeless (that is the point of the final scene) and does not turn away from them." [20] As for *Early Morning*, in 1969 Bond called that "the most optimistic play" he'd ever written because Arthur "faces things that people do at their very worst, doesn't have to tell himself lies about it, and escapes in the end." [21] Furthermore, both *Saved* and *Early Morning* contain proof of the difficulty of completely destroying the ability to act humanely. Harry, who is continually more and more isolated from other human beings, is nevertheless able to make friends with Len at the end of the play. George, the social half of the Siamese twins cannot eat human flesh because it makes Arthur, the moral half, sick. Arthur also leaves behind a new disciple in Florence, who had previously accepted Victoria's morality. *Narrow Road* would seem to be the most pessimistic of Bond's plays, ending in Shogo's spiritual and physical death and Kiro's despair of ever answering humanity's dilemma. It is a pessimism for the characters, however, not the audience who can see Bond's

19. Edward Bond, *The Sea* (London: Eyre Methuen, 1973): viii, 65. All subsequent references to this play will be noted in the text.
20. Bond, Preface to *Saved*, p. 5.
21. Edward Bond, quoted by Arthur Arnold in "Lines of Development in Bond's Plays," *Theatre Quarterly* (January–March 1972): 19.

answer in the drowning man who saves himself. In *Black Mass*, Christ, like Lear after him, takes overt political action against the murderous regime that uses him as a symbol of their righteousness. In *Passion*, Christ stubbornly refuses to abandon the world: "This is our place. . . . How can we leave this wilderness to its misery and hate." [22] In the same play, the Old Woman understands for the first time her son's suffering and its cause. In *The Sea* Evens withdraws from the corrupting atmosphere of the village, but not before passing on to Willy the admonition to "change the world." Lear, after a lifetime of creating an unjust society, is forced to live in it. Coming to his senses, he takes the first step in the seemingly impossible task of combating what he has built. What Bond has said of that act may well serve for his comment on the optimism of his work in general.

> Lear is old by then, but most of the play's audiences will be younger. It might seem to them that the truth is always ground for pessimism when it is discovered, but one soon comes to see it as an opportunity. Then you don't have to go on doing things that never work in the hope that they might one day—because now you know why they can't.[23]

Each of Bond's plays has a dominant image, in light of which all other actions must be considered. The primacy of the baby stoning to *Saved* need hardly be restated, but not all of Bond's images are so physically apparent. Alen's shack, for example, is central to *The Pope's Wedding* because its existence serves as a comment upon the life of the villagers, stimulating their imaginations and exercising their consciences. The dominant image of *Early Morning* is cannibalism, the ultimate in social competitiveness. In *Narrow Road*, it is the city that symbolizes the question of how man should be related to his society. In *Black Mass*

22. Edward Bond, *Passion, Plays and Players* 18, no. 9 (June 1971): iv, 68. All subsequent references to this play will be noted in the text.
23. Bond, Preface to *Lear*, p. 13.

and *Passion,* the cross is the paramount symbol. In the former it stands for the perversion of Christian institutions; and in the latter it represents the universality of life and the right to life. In *Lear,* the wall represents those social institutions built to protect men that end by perpetuating themselves and destroying mankind. Finally, in *The Sea,* the village and the sea signify, respectively, Death and Resurrection.

One of Bond's greatest assets as a playwright (and the quality that has enabled him to support himself as a screenwriter) is his visual imagination. Much has been written about the cricket match in *The Pope's Wedding,* the carefully controlled and accelerated violence of the baby killing in *Saved,* and the *hara-kiri* scene in *Narrow Road,* but even more important has been Bond's ability to create demonstrated relationships and visual parallels.

Bond has described the eighty or so speaking parts of *Lear* as "one role showing the character of a society."[24] Many of the scenes he has created could be described as 'one role showing the character of a situation." The effect as first noted by Jane Howell, the initial director of *Narrow Road,* is a distancing one. By presenting more than one focal point on the stage at once, Bond forces his audience to pay attention to what is happening rather than to what the characters are feeling. There are some outstanding examples in the later, less realistic plays where the practice was first noticed: the burlesque picnic and revolution scene in *Early Morning;* the argument between Kiro and Shogo on one corner of the stage in *Narrow Road,* while on the other corner the tribesmen try to figure out the rifle that eventually will kill one of them; and Bodice sitting downstage calmly knitting while Fontanelle and the Soldier torture *Lear's* Warrington upstage. The same technique, curiously enough, went ignored in *Saved* when it was mistakenly dismissed as kitchen-sink realism. The supper scene

24. Bond, Preface to *Lear,* p. 14.

A Summary of Themes and Techniques 275

in the flat in which Pam's baby cries offstage throughout while the others bicker, watch TV, or doze, the restaurant scene celebrating Fred's release from prison, and the much-discussed chair-mending scene are perfect examples of multiple-focus scenes. Bond's use of the technique dates from the first scene he ever had produced. None of the loitering farmworkers in *The Pope's Wedding* devotes more than two consecutive lines to a single subject, but the character of the group is caught perfectly.

> BYO. Bloody work t'morra.
> JOE. You wouldn't know what a doo with yourself if it wasn't.
> BYO. I'd know what a doo with you.
> BILL. Five bob. Four bob. Two an' six. One bent shillin'.
> SCOPEY. Put it on the slate.
> BILL. I tried that yesterday.
> JOE. Got a smoke?
> BILL. Chriss, I'd sell my sister if I 'ad one.
> LORRY. Yoo thirsty?
> LEN. If she was anythin' like you t'ent likely yoo get much for 'er.
> BILL. 'Op it. Oi, I saw that Butty girl bendin' down in 'er yard when I come by. Near come off my bike.
> BYO. Yoo like it fat.
> BILL. Soft, mate, soft.
> SCOPEY. Why she bendin' down?
> BYO. That owd stone tore my boot.
> BILL. This week I reckon I'll stow a few bottles under that owd stairs while I still got the dough.
> SCOPEY. That won't still be there Monday.
> RON. Lights off up the vicarage.
> BILL. Now 'e's showin' 'is missis the second comin'. They're all the same in the dark.
> SCOPEY. What?
> BILL. 'Ow old yoo reckon that Butty girl is?
> RON. Seventeen.
> BYO. Big ginger crutch (i, 35–36).

Bond's use of visual parallels also dates from *The Pope's*

Wedding when he uses the actions of Alen inside his shack to forecast the later ones of Scopey. Indeed, Bond makes use of parallels on all dramatic levels. Some are meant to reinforce the emotion of the moment: for example, the parallel between Lear's prison meeting with the shades of his daughters and Blake's *Job's Daughters*. More characteristic of Bond, however, is his use of the original to make an ironic comment on the situation within his own plays, such as the parodies of *Hamlet* in *Early Morning*, the Nō drama in *Narrow Road,* and of the "whodunnit" in *Black Mass*. Not infrequently—Victoria's serving of Arthur's body to the mob in a "Last Supper" and the turning of Florence Nightingale's "Lady-with-a-Lamp" sequence into a whorehouse scene, to name just two—Bond's choice of parallels also reflects his feelings about the philosophy of the original.

Other parallels by Bond are not primarily visual, but are to be found in Bond's characterizations. There is, of course, a straight line of development from Scopey to Willy as Innocent characters. Beginning with *Early Morning*, the Innocent becomes rather more complicated. Thus Len, the Innocent who continues to struggle under what seem hopeless conditions in *Saved,* becomes three characters in *Early Morning:* Arthur, the "moral" Siamese twin who transcends even "heaven"; George, the "social" twin who accepts societal cannibalism; and Len, the Cockney who is tried for a murder as Oedipally violent as the baby stoning in *Saved*. Shogo and Kiro in *Narrow Road* are aspects of the same personality. Kiro is even "abandoned" by Basho on the same river bank where he left Shogo thirty years earlier. Bond experimented even more interestingly with Lear and the Grave Digger's Boy. Lear is the Innocent who is "born" and grows to maturity in his old age. He parallels the Grave Digger's Boy who grows up as an Innocent, then is "killed" and slowly corrupted by society. Willy is Colin, reborn from the sea without the drowned man's restricting village image.

A Summary of Themes and Techniques

Bond also uses character parallels within plays to forecast in what direction a character will develop. Thus, Alen's isolation predicts Scopey's. The estrangement of Harry and Mary precedes that of Len and Pam. The political involvement of the Grave Digger's Boy, Cordelia, and the Carpenter preordains that of Thomas, Susan, and John. Finally, Willy, Rose, and Hollarcut are optimistic resurrections of Evens, Mrs. Rafi, and Hatch. Bond also uses parallel actions to show the effect of power on character. Therefore, although *Early Morning, Narrow Road,* and *Lear* each feature several militarily successful revolutions, the actions and philosophies of the rulers are not altered.

Even apart from the Innocents, there are similarities between characters in different plays. Thus, the queens in *Early Morning* and *Passion* are sisters to such other dominating women as Georgina and Mrs. Rafi. Alen, Harry, and Evens are all recluses from society. So, in a more subtle way, is anyone who attempts to hide from life in the house of the Grave Digger's Boy. The gangs in *The Pope's Wedding* and *Saved* resemble each other. The violent but loyal Len in *Early Morning* becomes Billy Hollarcut in *The Sea*. The sycophantic Lord Chamberlain in *Early Morning* is reborn as the Old Councilor in *Lear*.

No less intriguing than the continuing traits in similar characters is the continuing characteristic of madness that is found in almost every Bond play since *Early Morning*. This trait is not to be confused with mad actions that virtually are the norm among Bond's ruling classes. Madness in individuals is more likely to be the result of societal pressures. Thus, *Early Morning*'s Arthur despairs when he sees that the revolutionaries battling his mother's corrupt regime are no less murderous than she. Driven mad by the horror and misery of the civil war, he determines that men stay alive only to kill and decides to relieve both armies by slaughtering everyone. *Narrow Road*'s Georgina feigns a mad Christian fanaticism in order to force conformity on her charges. She is so successful that Shogo can not tell the Emperor from any of the other children and murders them all. When her system breaks down, so does she. So do Lear and the Prime Minister in *Passion* when they are forced to live unprotected within the societies that they themselves have created. In *The Sea,* Hatch goes mad from a combination of economic pressures and the shock of having the scapegoat he has created to relieve his repressions taken away from him.

Hatch's insanity, as well as that of Georgina and the worst atrocities committed by Lear's daughters, seem to result from and express themselves in terms of thwarted sexual energies. Hatch imagines his customers are trying to seduce him and Georgina that she is about to be raped. Lear's daughters display sexual desires and anxieties toward him, and are later unsatisfied with their husbands. About the time Bond was moving from a naturalistic to a nonnaturalistic form of writing, he became interested in the "armoring" theories of psychologist Wilhelm Reich. The unified front presented by all social institutions against normal sexual development causes in the child a literal, physical rigidity that blocks in man's naturally humane behavior. When sufficient energy is built up to penetrate the armor, it often emerges in a harsh and brutal fashion. In the Preface to *Saved,* Bond describes this kind of explosion as "Oedipal atavism." Armoring also explains the series of monstrous government leaders that populate Bond's plays beginning with Victoria in *Early Morning.* Reich defines the corrupted leadership phenomena as the *emotional plague.*

> This is the social or individual structure that consistently blocks all progress toward natural functioning. No one of us is free of it completely, but there are certain persons who function essentially as emotional pests. They are capable, intelligent, and have a high-energy level, but they are anti-sexual and prone to seek positions of authority where they can dictate rules of living. They are the bulwark of society

A Summary of Themes and Techniques 279

—and they cannot tolerate natural functioning. It creates a longing in them which is intolerable, and so their prime purpose in life is to place restrictions on any natural living thing that might disturb them. At the same time, they rationalize their behavior so successfully that it is accepted as for the common good.[25]

The acceptance of this rationalization by those in socially subordinate positions and their subsequent channeling of sexual energies into its enforcement has been described earlier in this chapter as social morality.

If Bond's memory is accurate, his knowledge of Reich's work dates from "about six or perhaps five years ago." [26] This would place it after either *Early Morning* or *Narrow Road*. Furthermore, since many ideas similar to those expressed in the 1968 plays were also present in *Saved*, we must suppose that Bond found in Reich congenial reinforcement rather than original inspiration. An earlier influence was the English painter-poet-philosopher William Blake.

A number of direct references to Blake are found in Bond's work: the concept of his protagonists as Innocents; the phrase, "Sooner murder an infant in its cradle than nurse unacted desires," in the program of *Saved;* the image of the caged robin in *Lear;* and the posing of Lear and his daughters in prison as a tableau of *Job's Daughters*. Certainly, fundamental to both artists is the fear that the worship of science and untempered reason would lead to an abandonment of purely human sensory needs. This concept was personified by Blake as Urizen, the Zoa of Reason. Urizen stands for inexorable order and the world machine. In his time Bond has seen Blake's fear manifested in mechanized warfare, industrialization, and scientific experimentation that have been both functionally logical and functionally

25. Elsworth F. Baker, *Man in the Trap* (New York: Macmillan, 1967), p. 25
26. Edward Bond, letter to Richard Scharine, 8 January 1974.

dehumanizing. Urizen discovers that to maintain control requires progressively more control. Both Blake and Bond realized, as General Electric does not, that if, "Progress is our most important product," our only measure of value must be material.

Blake previews both Bond and Reich in *The Marriage of Heaven and Hell* where he states: "Energy is the only life, and is from the body; and Reason is the bound or outward circumference of Energy. Energy is Eternal Delight." Blake also created Orc, the antithesis to Luvah, the Zoa of Love. Orc is the demon of restricted Energy and unfulfilled desires. To him belongs the phrase from the *Saved* program. *The Daughters of Albion* further enforces the Bond/Reich platform by calling on humans to give free rein to both masculine and feminine aspects of their personalities.

Finally, another frequently incorporated Bond premise is presaged in Blake's *America, a Prophecy* in which the American Revolution is made to symbolize the eternal sequence of oppression and revolt.[27]

Structurally, as well as thematically, Bond's writing has been remarkably consistent. Although, as we have noted in the previous chapter, he has progressed in his ability to achieve contrast in mood within a scene, Bond still writes in short, staccato units in which a single incident occurs. If it is necessary to know something that contributes to that incident, he writes another scene.

> I think I started by writing a three-acter—one would have done—but I soon discovered that I couldn't tell the truth in that long-winded sort of way any more. It didn't relate to my

27. Much of the material on Blake in the paragraphs above was coalesced from Theodore Roszak's *Where the Wasteland Ends* (Garden City, New York: Doubleday, Inc., 1972), particularly "Blake: The Fourfold Vision," pp. 296–314. It is not presumed to be definitive on the debt Bond may or may not owe to Blake, but merely is a speculation upon sources of inspiration. Ninety percent of these who view or read Bond's work will never have studied closely either Blake or Reich, but will find that his art will stand very well on its own.

A Summary of Themes and Techniques 281

experience at all, which was much more a series of sudden reverses and changes. And I felt it was important not only to know what was happening in the room I might happen to be in, but also what was happening in that room over there, that house down the road. So that in order to say something useful about experience now, one has to keep track of all these things. The plays keep an eye on what's going on, you know —I think that's what my structure does.[28]

"The plays keep an eye on what's going on." By this Bond does not mean that we have to see everything that happens. For example, in the second scene of *Saved*, Pam and Len discuss marriage in a rented, park rowboat. Fred is the attendant. In the third scene, Len appears only briefly to carry some packages for Pam's mother. In the fourth scene Pam has had Fred's baby and he is already beginning to tire of her. Act Two, scene four of *Narrow Road* begins with Kiro announcing that Shogo has captured the city and requested him to return from the deep north. The first person to speak to him on his return is a soldier: "That was last month. The Barbarian had gone to see his people, and he came back up the river with big ships and guns and took the city again" (II, iv, 54). We do not see either battle. This is not oversight. Bond is no more interested in military spectacle than he is in sexual titilation. Nor is he unaware that he could increase our sympathetic identification with his characters by following them more closely.

Bond confused his early critics by spending so much time developing the environment of his characters and so little time telling what happens to them. What the critics failed to realize was that the background *is* the plot. Bond writes about a society, the structure of which causes things to happen. For example, *Saved* is not about the murder of a baby, it is about a society that murders babies as a condition of its own survival. *Narrow Road*, on the other hand,

28. Bond, as quoted by Hudson, *et al.*, "Drama and the Dialectics of Violence," p. 11.

is about the kind of society a murdered baby would build. This is why Bond described the sum of the speaking parts in *Lear* as "one role showing the character of a society."

Bond's intentions of exposing his society went unnoticed precisely because he recreated it so skillfully that his critics could not see the city for the houses. The impression of naturalism was the greatest theatrical triumph of Bond's early plays, for actually they are naturalistic in neither setting nor dialogue. When Bond turned to nonrealism with *Early Morning* and *Narrow Road* in 1968, Simon Trussler recalled in retrospect that Bond had never indulged in kitchen-sink realism.

> Edward Bond's *Saved*—another nod towards Naturalism in a first play, by a dramatist who has since turned to fantasy—scarcely did more than suggest its various settings, though it *could* have survived bird-twittering external realism. Thus, although *Saved* is probably the closest contemporary equivalent to that most exemplary of Naturalist plays, Gorky's *Lower Depths,* it could retain its realistic grip on a bare stage as readily as *The Seagull.* . . . It so happens that Ibsen and Osborne use a functional design to reinforce their sense of realism, whereas Bond in *Saved* (like Chekhov) envokes his surroundings by means of tonal contrasts.[29]

The view of Bond as a naturalistic playwright rests upon his handling of East Anglican dialect in *The Pope's Wedding* and Cockney dialect in *Saved.* Despite a dozen reviews that alternately cursed and blessed the products of "tape-recorder realism," Bond was never other than a thorough craftsman. Raised in North London and the son of transplanted farm laborers, Bond was so able to command lower-class speech that he could manipulate it into a spare, functional poetry. His poetry is almost completely devoid of simile and never contains that self-aware archness

---

29. Simon Trussler, "British Neo-Naturalism," *Drama Review* 13, no. 2 (Winter 1968): 135.

A Summary of Themes and Techniques

that belongs to Christopher Fry at his worst. Bond's characters do not speak poetry. They express themselves. In *The Pope's Wedding* and in *Saved*, no single speech could be called poetry, yet extended exchanges become poetry, exhibiting rhythm, shape, builds, and climaxes constructed from seemingly semiliterate five- or six-syllable lines. No sensitive reader of *Saved* should have been surprised at the haikus Bond composed in *Narrow Road*, for their structures are strikingly similar.

> I think my plays are poetry. You see, this is what I dislike about the poetic drama that one gets nowadays; it's something added to prose. Poetry is what you have left when you take the prose away. Poetry is a simplified form of prose. And that's the other way round you see, because most people try to make their prose clever poetically, and I hate that.[30]

Nevertheless, naturalism or unnaturalism was always irrelevant to Bond's intent. Having been misunderstood in *Saved*, he hoped in his next play to expose his audiences to the same ideas in a context that would arouse fewer immediate associations.

> I think *Early Morning* is essentially about working-class life. I mean, the plays that I am told are based on social realism very often seem to me the wildest fairy stories, and setting them against an immediately recognizable background doesn't make them any truer. So what I wanted to do in *Early Morning* was to take away all the known landmarks that might have led to false assumptions. It's like taking the labels off tins, so that you have to open them up to see what's inside—because so many of the labels were false, anyway. But it's true, the settings change. I didn't choose to write *Saved* about a particular dialect—that was the way I talked and the kind of setting I was familiar with. I now talk differently, and live somewhere different. So it would be

30. Wardle, "A Discussion with Edward Bond," p. 37.

artificial for me to write another play like *Saved* now. . . but that doesn't mean that I'm disowning my past. I *can* still talk like that, but it is too much like a party piece.[31]

Early Morning, like *Saved*, has as its theme the relationship of society to its children. By switching to fantasy, however, Bond was able to personify social institutions in a single character (Queen Victoria) and present commercial competition as cannibalism. The play is in three parts. In the first part, the central character, Arthur, is bewildered by a repressive and self-destructive society, and by the fact that its alternatives seem equally as destructive. In the second part, Arthur accepts societal practice as correct and contrives to kill everyone—thus achieving the ultimate societal goal. In the third part, Arthur recognizes that what social institutions have created is cannibalism, rejects it, and transcends it. *Early Morning* is thus a metaphor for our society. Part one shows Victorian repression and industrial competition. Part two shows the logical culmination of such attitudes to be genocide. Part three reveals our society looked at objectively to be cannibalism.

The language of *Early Morning* is as muscular, as that of *Saved* is spare. According to Peter James who directed the play at Birmingham in 1969, *Early Morning* has no subtext. The dialogue itself is the subtext.[32] It is an interesting observation, but one that should be tempered. When an entire play is a metaphor, all dialogue *must* be subtext. The protagonists of Bond's later plays are more articulate and more sensitive to their situation. Even when they are dreaming or mad, they express themselves in densely written, image-packed parables of which Arthur's description of the mill in which men grind themselves and Lear's sermon on the caged bird are only two of many.[33]

31. Bond, as quoted by Hudson, *et al.*, "Drama and the Dialectics of Violence," p. 13.
32. Peter James, letter to A. J. Coult, 27 May 1971.
33. A measure of the exactitude of Bond's language can be found in

A Summary of Themes and Techniques 285

By contrast, *Narrow Road* is far simpler in both conception and execution, a fact that may also account for its theatrical success. If *Early Morning* is a metaphor whose symbols must be translated to achieve meaning, *Narrow Road* is a simple parable: A man ignores the needs of a child. The child survives to build a society that ignores the needs of men. Finally, the child is overthrown by a more sophisticated religious-military-industrial complex who rules the same society by teaching men that their needs are evil.

Narrow Road was Bond's first critically successful play because it was the first whose form accurately forecast it's author's intentions.

> *Narrow Road* presents situations rather than characters. It shows you people in situations and what they do is very important. One plays *Narrow Road* like a series of facts, the actors do not get particularly emotionally involved in what they do, they always seek to present the situation to the audience in the clearest and most direct way possible. Width of stage is an advantage in this because it is possible to present it almost like a storybook. The actors often stand facing the front, though not always. I find this difficult to explain to you—it is a concept of work which is more clearly allied to political theatre than to method theatre. It seeks that the audience should think as well as feel and that what is presented is always presented as a fact.[34]

Black Mass and *Passion* are exercises in the savagely ironic vein of humor that Bond first mined in *Early Morning*. *Black Mass* asks two questions: (1) What happens when social institutions do not consider men as human beings? (2)

---

the demand for perfection that it makes upon actors. While directing the American premiere of *The Sea*, William Woodman reported that "two weeks into rehearsal, the actors were going crazy—they could not paraphrase *anything*—but day by day Bond's words and ideas revealed themselves" (William Woodman, as quoted by Roger Dittmer in "Bond: Wave of Hope in a 'Sea.'" *Chicago Tribune*, 17 November 1974, sec. 6/7, p. 4).
34. Jane Howell, letter to Richard Scharine, 6 July 1971.

What happens when true religion conflicts with the dictates of social institutions? The answers are that men can be killed without feeling and that precepts of religion will inevitably be corrupted. *Passion* is a William Blake nightmare. Science and industrial capitalism are given free rein and destroy the world. Religion can not save the world because society has determined that institutions are to be saved rather than men. The cost of this preservation is universal suffering.

In *Lear,* Bond investigates for the first time the situation of one of society's architects who is forced to live under the conditions that he himself created. He discovers that the institutions that he has built destroy people rather than protect them. Therefore, he sets out to destroy the institutions. This is Bond's version of *A Christmas Carol,* complete with ghost.

All Bond's plays are means of making us look at ourselves and every society he presents represents ours. Nevertheless, *Lear* marks the beginning of a return to realistic presentation. *Early Morning's* characters were two-dimensional and even their wit had more than a little of *Alice in Wonderland* about it. *Narrow Road* and *Passion* were frankly presentational. *Lear,* however, is generally only surrealistic insofar as the events it describes are phantasmagorical. As a work of art, *Lear* is reminiscent in tone of Louis Buñuel's *Land Without Bread,* a documentary whose surrealism is the product of observed reality. The events of *Lear* are grotesque and difficult to believe. So were those of Buchenwald. The characters, however, have backgrounds, ancestry, and sound psychological motivations. Even the ghost of the Grave Digger's Boy is only seen by Lear when his mind is disordered.

Even this device is abandoned by Bond in *The Sea,* which is something of a summing up of what he has learned to date about playwrighting. As in *Saved* and *The Pope's Wedding,* the setting and dialogue are selectively realistic.

A Summary of Themes and Techniques

While familiar to the audience, it is far enough removed from the present to permit objectivity (as was *Narrow Road*) and neutral enough to prevent confusing associations (as *Early Morning* was not). Like *Black Mass* and *Passion*, it is comic in tone. More important, it is the most accessible of Bond's plays: It is the first Bond play with a *raisonneur;* his most conventionally plotted play; his first play with a successfully culminated love interest; and, finally, it contains his most openly optimistic conclusion.

Bob Peck as Shakespeare in Bingo
(Photo courtesy of the Northcott Theatre, Exeter; photo by Nicholas Toyne, Devon)

Thankfully, it is too early to assess Edward Bond's ultimate effect on either the English theater or his society. The most happy result of Bond's greater audience acceptance is that he has more time to spend writing for the theater. At the time of this writing, Bond has had for the first time a commercial success on the London stage. *Bingo,* subtitled *Scenes of Death and Money,* was first produced by Jane Howell at Exeter in November 1973. Miss Howell also directed the London premiere that opened in August 1974, featuring Sir John Gielgud as William Shakespeare. It has already broken every Royal Court box-office record. Still another play, tentatively entitled *The Fool, Scenes of Greed and Love,* is in the finishing stages. Bond has also recently written an opera libretto for the German composer, Hans Werner Henze.[35] Bond's public is growing and a public acceptance of his plays may foretell a growing public acceptance of his ideas. Whatever his experience, however, it is certain that Bond will continue to be optimistic about man's ability to change his disastrous and self-destructive course, and to search artistically for the means to effect that change.

> I've never experienced hopelessness. If I did, I'd stop writing, of course. Beckett is a pessimist, but even he hopes he will be printed—otherwise why write? I go so far as to hope I will have readers—and that they will be actors not on the stage but the street. So don't ascribe hopelessness to me. On the other hand, I have no courage. It's just I'm constantly enticed by how often experience can be defined in ideas and so made rational, and by the strength and resilience of human beings. The animal I most admire is the fox, not the lamb. No one protects the fox. They protect the lamb—but only because he's good business.[36]

---

35. Dittmer, "Bond: Wave of Hope in a 'Sea.'"
36. Bond, letter to Richard Scharine, 2 October 1974.

Works Cited

Ansorge, Peter. "Director in Interview: Jane Howell." *Plays and Players* 16, no. 1 (October 1968): 69–71, 82.
Antonioni, Michelangelo. *Blow-up.* New York: Simon and Schuster, 1971.
Armstrong, Marion. "Terror and Beauty." *The Christian Century* 88 (September 1971): 1,030.
Arnold, Arthur. "Lines of Development in Bond's Plays." *Theatre Quarterly* 2 (January–March 1972): 15–19.
Baker, Elsworth F. *Man in the Trap.* New York: Macmillan, 1967.
Barnes, Clive. "Theatre: Openly Cerebral." *The New York Times,* 2 December 1969, p. 64.
Basho, Matsuo. *The Narrow Road to the Deep North and Other Travel Sketches.* Translated by Nobuyuki Yuasa. Harmondsworth, Middlesex, England: Penguin Books, Ltd., 1966.
Benedictus, David: "Saved Again." *Plays and Players* 14, no. 9 (June 1967): 18.
Billington, Michael. "First, a Personal Note." *Plays and Players* 19, no. 4 (January 1972): 18.
Bond, Edward. *Black Mass. Gambit* 5, no. 17: 48–55.
―――. "Censor in Mind." *Censorship,* no. 4 (Autumn 1965): 9–13.
―――. "The Duke in *Measure for Measure.*" *Gambit* 5, no. 17: 43–44.

———. *Early Morning.* London: Calder and Boyars, 196p.
———. *Lear.* London: Eyre Methuen, 1972.
———. Letter to Richard Scharine. 23 March 1971.
———. Letter to Richard Scharine. 16 May 1971.
———. Letter to Richard Scharine. 8 January 1974.
———. Letter to Richard Scharine. 2 October 1974.
———. *Narrow Road to the Deep North.* New York: Hill and Wang, 1968.
———. *Passion. Plays and Players* 18, no. 9 (June 1971): 66–69.
———. *The Pope's Wedding.* London: Methuen & Co., Ltd., 1971.
———. *The Pope's Wedding. Plays and Players* 16, no. 7 (April 1969): 35–50, 79–82.
———. *Saved.* New York: Hill and Wang, 1965.
———. *The Sea.* London: Methuen & Co., Ltd., 1973.
———. "You Sit and Watch." Unpublished poem, 1973.
Brien, Alan. "The Monster Within." *New Statesman* 56 (12 November 1965): 735.
———. "This Bond has not been much Honoured." London *Sunday Times,* 31 March 1968, p. 55.
Bryden, Bill. Letter to Richard Scharine. 11 August 1971.
Bryden, Ronald. "Bond goes to Japan." London *Observer,* 30 June 1968, p. 27.
———. "Bond in a Wild Victorian Dreamworld." London *Observer,* 16 March 1969, p. 26.
———. "Making Bond a Test Case." London *Observer,* 14 April 1968, p. 27.
———. "Society Makes Men Animals." London *Observer,* 9 February 1969, p. 27.
Cole, Toby. Letter to Richard Scharine. 7 June 1971.
Dark, Gregory. "Production Casebook, no. 5: Edward Bond's *Lear* at the Royal Court." *Theatre Quarterly* 2 (January–March 1972): 22–31.
Day-Lewis, Sean. "Rude Noises from St. James Palace." *Plays and Players* 15, no. 9 (June 1968): 58–59.
Dittmer, Roger. "Bond: Wave of Hope in a 'Sea.'" Chicago *Tribune,* 17 November 1974, sec. 6/7, pp. 2–4.
Esslin, Martin, "A Bond Honoured." *Plays and Players* 15, no. 9 (June 1968): 26, 63.

Works Cited

———. "Bond Unbound." *Plays and Players* 16, no. 7 (April 1969): 33–34, 51.

———. "Early Morning." *Plays and Players* 16, no. 8 (May 1969): 25–27.

Evans, Gareth Lloyd. "*Narrow Road to the Deep North* at Coventry." Manchester *Guardian*, 25 June 1968, p. 6.

Feingold, Michael. "Ensembles." *Plays and Players* 16, no. 8 (May 1969): 62–65, 73.

Findlater, Richard. *Banned!* London: MacGibbon and McKee, Ltd., 1967.

Gaskill, William. Letter to Richard Scharine. 19 March 1971.

Giffin, Kim, and Heider, Mary, "The Relation between Speech Anxiety and the Suppression of Communication in Childhood." In *Basic Readings in International Communication*. Edited by Kim Giffin and Bobby R. Patton. New York: Harper & Row, 1971.

Gill, Peter. Letter to A. J. Coult. 13 May 1971.

Gilliatt, Penelope. "Cackle in Hell." *New Yorker*, 45 (24 May 1969): 121–122.

Gordon, Giles. "Edward Bond." *Transatlantic Review* 22 (Autumn 1966): 7–15.

Hack, Keith. Letter to Richard Scharine. 11 October 1971.

Hall, Edward T. *The Hidden Dimension*. Garden City, New York: Doubleday & Company, Inc., 1966.

Hall, John. "Edward Bond." Manchester *Guardian*, 29 September 1971, p. 10.

Hern, Nicholas. "The Theatre of Ernst Toller." *Theatre Quarterly* 2 (January–March 1972): 72–92.

Holmstrom, John. "*Lear.*" *Plays and Players* 19, no. 2 (November 1971): 42.

Howell, Jane. Letter to Richard Scharine. 6 July 1971.

Hudson, Roger, Itzin, Catherine, and Trussler, Simon. "Drama and the Dialectics of Violence." *Theatre Quarterly* 2 (January–March 1972): 4–14.

———. "Theatresurvey No. 1: Guide to Underground Theatre." *Theatre Quarterly* 1 (January–March 1971): 61–65.

Hurren, Kenneth. "Lord Mansfield's Advice to Judges." *Plays and Players* 19, no. 4 (January 1972): 20.

———. "On the Hallmarks of Failure." *Spectator* 232 (8 June 1974): 712.
James, Peter. Letter to A. J. Coult. 27 May 1971.
Johgh, Nicholas de. "Bond's Lear." Manchester *Guardian*, 9 October 1971, p. 29.
Johnstone, Keith. Letter to Richard Scharine. 25 March 1971.
Kingston, Jeremy. "A Good Year in the Theatre Means a Year of Good Plays." *Plays and Players* 19, no. 4 (January 1972): 20.
———. "At the Theatre." *Punch* 256 (26 February 1969): 320–322.
———. "At the Theatre." *Punch* 256 (19 March 1969): 430.
———. "Childhood's End." *Punch* 261 (12 June 1974): 1,021.
———. "Theatre." *Punch* 260 (30 May 1973): 774.
Kretzmer, Herbert. "Too deep—Bond's Noh play." London *Daily Express*, 20 February 1969, p. 13.
Lahr, John. "When a Playwright is Prophetic." *The Village Voice*, 5 Noember 1970, p. 47.
Lane, John Francis. "Resounding Success." London *Times*, 25 September 1969, p. 8.
Lewis, Peter. "Georgina was not the Only One to Wind Up Haunted." London *Daily Mail*, 20 February 1969, p. 6.
L. G. S. "National *Spring Awakening*." *Stage and Television Today*, 6 June 1974, p. 18.
Ling, Sheilah. Letter on *Saved*. *Plays and Players* 13, no. 6 (March 1966): 8.
London *Daily Mail*. "Drama of Bond Premiere and the Censor." 30 June 1968, p. 14.
London *Observer*. "Production Without Decor." 16 December 1962, p. 24.
London *Times*. "'Arts Council Bursaries to Two Playwrights." 3 February 1969, p. 7.
———. "Censored Play Summonses." 15 February 1966, p. 13.
———. "Censorship Review May be Accepted." 11 February 1966, p. 12.
———. "Critics Hold Teach-in on *Saved*." 15 November 1965, p. 14.
———. "Devine Award for Edward Bond." 31 May 1968, p. 15.

Works Cited

———. "Gaskill Strikes Again." 21 March 1968, p. 10.
———. "Lesbian Charge in Victoria Play." 4 August 1967.
———. "Play sans Decor but not Theme." 10 December 1962, p. 9.
———. "*Saved* continues next week." 16 February 1966, p. 16.
———. "Whiting Award to Barnes and Bond." 14 April 1969, p. 6.
Marcus, Frank. "Once Again, the See-sawing Fluctuations of Fortune." *Plays and Players* 19, no. 4 (January 1972): 22.
Marowitz, Charles. "If a House is on Fire and I Cry Fire." *New York Times*, 2 January 1972, sec. 2, pp. I, 5.
———. "A Modern *Lear* Amid Political Evil." *New York Times*, 24 October 1971, sec. 2, p. 5.
Marriott, R. B. "*The Sea*, Edward Bond's Best Play, Now at the Royal Court." *Stage and Television Today*, no. 4807, 31 May 1973, p. 7.
Morgan, Geoffrey. *Contemporary Theatre*. London: London Magazines Editions, 1968.
Nightingale, Benedict. "Bond in a Cage." *New Statesman* 72 (8 October 1971): 485.
———. "Overdue Awakening." *New Statesman* 77 (7 June 1974): 810.
Oppenheimer, George. "Road to Nowhere." *Newsday*, 7 January 1972, p. 24.
Panter-Downes, Mollie. "Letter from London." *New Yorker* 41 (11 December 1965): 231.
Pasquier, Marie-Claude. "La Place d'Edward Bond dans le Nouveau Théâtre Anglais." *Bref*, no. 136, pp. 3–21.
Plays and Players. "Drama in Court—Act One." 13, no. 8 (May 1966): 66–67.
Reich, Wilhelm. *The Sexual Revolution*. New York: Farrar, Straus, and Giroux, 1969.
Roberts, Peter. "A Last Look at 1969." *Plays and Players* 17, no. 4 (January 1970): 24.
Roszak, Theodore. *Where the Wasteland Ends*. Garden City, New York: Doubleday, Inc., 1972.
Spurling, Hilary. "A Bond Honoured." *Spectator* 222 (7 March 1969): 313.
———. "A Difference of Opinion." *Spectator* 215 (12 November 1965): 619.

Taylor, John Russell. *The Angry Theatre*. London: Methuen, 1969.
———. "Edward Bond: Beyond Pessimism?" *Plays and Players* 17, no. 10 (July 1970): 16–18.
———. *The Second Wave*. London: Methuen, 1971.
———. "Ten Years of the English Stage Company." *Tulane Drama Review*, 11, no. 2 (Winter 1966): 120–131.
Thirkell, Arthur. "Right Royal Mixture." London *Daily Mirror*, 24 May 1973, p. 6.
Thom, Mary V. Letter on *Saved*. *Plays and Players*, 13, no. 5 (February 1966): 8.
Trevelyan, Raleigh. *A Hermit Disclosed*. New York: St. Martin's Press, 1960.
Trewin, J. C. "Saved." *Illustrated London News* 249 (13 November 1965): 32.
Trussler, Simon. "British Neo-Naturalism." *The Drama Review* 13, no. 2 (Winter 1968): 130–36.
Tynan, Kenneth. "Shouts and Murmurs." London *Observer*, 7 April 1968, p. 26.
Wardle, Irving. "Confident Voice of Violence." London *Times*, 25 June 1968, p. 13.
———. "A Discussion with Edward Bond." *Gambit* 5, no. 17: 5–38.
———. "Edward Bond Deals Kindly with his Characters." London *Times*, 24 May 1973, p. 9.
———. The Edward Bond View of Life." London *Times*, 15 March 1970, p. 15.
———. "German Theatre: Rolling in Money and Ruled by Directors." London *Times*, 23 May 1974, p. 11.
———. "An Interview with William Gaskill." *Gambit* 5, no. 17: 38–41.
———. "Muddled Fantasy on Brutalization." London *Times*, 1 April 1968, p. 6.
———. "A Question of Motives and Purposes." London *Times*, 4 November 1965, p. 27.
———. "The Wrong Quarrel over the Wrong Play." *New Society* 56 (25 November 1965): 25–27.
Warner, Marina. "One Distraction Only: Bond Honoured," *Vogue* 126 (1 October 1969): 24, 46.

Weightman, John. "Stage Politics." *Encounter* 37 (December 1971): 29–32.
Williams, Hugo. "Theatre." *London Magazine* 6 (January 1966): 67–68.
Zweig, M. B. "William Reich's Theory: Ethical Implications." *American Imago* 28, no. 3 (Fall 1971): 268–86.

Index

Alland, Alexander Jr., 195
Andrews, Harry, 183
Antonioni, Michelangelo, 17, 83, 159–60
Arden, John, 30
Arnold, Arthur, 33–34, 45
Arts Council Bursary, 19, 83
Awards: the 1968 George Devine Award, 20; the 1969 John Whiting Award, 20

Balcony, The, 91
Barnes, Clive, 156
Basho, Matsuo, 128
Beckett, Samuel, 58, 216
Benedictus, David, 164
Beyond the Pleasure Principle, 195
Biddle-Wood, Clement, 160
Billington, Michael, 185
Bingo, 288
Black Mass, 158, 160, 169–73, 180, 193, 239, 251, 253, 265–67, 273, 276, 285, 287
Blake, William, 23, 43–44, 58, 79, 197, 204, 279–80; Longing for

"The Golden Age," 201–2, 210, 217–18
Bleckner, Jeff, 52
Blow-up, 17, 83, 158–60
Bond, Edward
   Christian symbolism in his plays
      Christ figures, 39, 107–9, 169–70, 172–73, 178–79
      the crucifixion, 42–43, 80, 115, 144, 153, 173, 231, 267–68
      the Father's sacrifice of the Son, 108–9, 115, 266–67
      the resurrection, 39, 151–53, 173, 228–29, 233–49, 268
      revelations, 268
      the slaughter of the innocents, 23, 42, 106, 153, 171, 173, 267
   Dominant images in his plays
      Alen's shack in *The Pope's Wedding*, 35–36, 38, 40, 44, 46, 273

the baby stoning in *Saved*, 67, 75–79, 273
cannabalism in *Early Morning*, 105–9, 113, 118–19, 273
the city in *Narrow Road to the Deep North*, 131, 273
the cross in *Black Mass* and *Passion*, 273–74
the sea and the village in *The Sea*, 229–31, 237, 242, 254, 274
the wall in *Lear*, 191–93, 210, 274
German production of his plays, 19, 21, 26, 52, 90
Oedipalism in his plays
atavistic repression, 70, 77, 116–17, 196–97, 246–47, 268–69
Father/son conflict, 38, 40, 57–58, 116–17, 198, 246–47
uterine regression, 37–38, 108, 116, 133, 152–53, 209
Optimism in his plays, 27, 56, 163, 211–12, 235, 249, 254, 271–73
Recent projects, 288
Screenwriting, 17–18, 158–62, 180
"Season" at the Royal Court theatre in 1969, 19–21, 33, 53, 126: British Council continental tour of Bond "season," 21, 127–28
Sex in his plays, 63–65, 78, 147–49, 167–68, 198–99, 218, 243–44
Symbolism in titles
Black Mass, 170
Early Morning, 90–92
Pope's Wedding, The, 39
Saved, 78
Sea, The, 254
Technique in writing
characterization
the "innocent," 36, 38, 42, 73, 113, 190–91, 240–41, 253, 276–77
"madness," 99–103, 148–49, 191, 204–5, 247, 277–79; as explained in the armoring theories of Wilhelm Reich, 262
methodology, 92, 99, 119–22, 149–53, 176–77, 186, 231, 252
parallels, 67–68, 72–76, 95, 97, 99, 216–19, 231–50, 277
dialogue, 45, 58–63, 118, 156–57, 176, 220–21
naturalistic and non-naturalistic intent and technique, 25–26, 66–67, 118–20, 219–20, 282–87
structure of his plays, 36, 39, 44, 46, 87–88, 103–4, 117–18, 152–55, 165, 215, 251–53
use of "raisonneurs," 27, 43, 253–54, 287
visual techniques
demonstrated relationships, 44–45, 80, 103, 144, 274–75
parallels, 111–12, 197, 275–76

Index

Theme of society's destruction of its children's humanity
  as represented in the saved baby-stoning scene, 265–69
  as resulting in "living ghosts," 42–44, 97, 99, 103, 105–7, 138–39, 152, 198, 206, 211, 228
  by denial of identity, 70, 78–79, 142–43, 171, 177–78, 265–66
  by social institutions, 37–38, 93–94, 110, 114–15, 131–44, 152, 178–79, 193–94, 200–201, 209, 211, 233–35
  by social morality, 27, 41–42, 70–72, 94–97, 100–102, 110–11, 113, 133–34, 141, 145–49, 194–96, 201–2, 208–9, 211, 233–35, 259–65; as explained in Wilhelm Reich's *The Mass Psychology of Fascism*, 262; rebellion against or acceptance of according to Reichian principles, 111, 192, 195–97, 203, 244, 250–51
  by technological dehumanization, 65–71, 177, 237–40, 256–57
Training as a writer, 29–32
Violence in his plays, 22–24, 43, 65–66, 71–72, 75, 133–34, 207–8
Working method, 166
Brave New World, 257
Brecht, Bertolt, 31, 128, 131, 154–55, 158, 162
Brien, Alan, 23–24, 82
Bryden, Bill, 162, 173–74
Bryden, Ronald, 19, 84–85, 87, 125
Buñel, Luis, 286

Caucasian Chalk Circle, The, 131
Censorship
  Abolition of, 20, 51, 86
  Attempted censorship of *Narrow Road to the Deep North*, 124–25
  Of *Early Morning*, 18, 20, 83–86, 124
  Of *Saved*, 18–20, 50–52, 54, 83, 167–68
Chekhov, Anton, 158, 162–63, 165
Chelsea theatre, 21
Cherry Orchard, The, 252
Christ Wanders and Waits, 240–41
Cobbold, Lord, 51
Cortazar, Julio, 159
Cottrell, Richard, 164
Coventry conference on people and cities, 31
Cresta Run, 47
Cross Plays, The, 180
Cuthbertson, Iain, 50

Dark, Gregory, 183–84, 186
Day-Lewis, Sean, 84–85
Devine, George, 30, 47

Early Morning, 18–22, 24, 26, 32, 53, 82–124, 139–41, 147, 153, 160–61, 186, 191, 205–6, 215, 221, 233, 246, 248, 252–53, 262–68, 271–74, 276–79, 282–85
Eine Jugend in Deutchland, 215
Endgame, 58
English Stage Company, 18–20, 29–30, 33, 47, 49, 51, 59, 126, 164: on trial, 18–20

Esdaile, Alfred, 51, 86
Esslin, Martin, 19, 25, 85, 87
Exit the King, 91

Fool, The, 288
Freud, Sigmund, 195

Galbraith, John Kenneth, 256
Gaskill, William, 19–20, 26, 30–31, 33, 45, 47, 49–51, 58, 60, 83, 86–88, 90, 103–4, 124, 162–64, 183, 186; production of *The Sea*, 236
Genet, Jean, 91
Gielgud, John, 288
Gilliatt, Penelope, 19, 45, 48
Gill, Peter, 31–32
Grein, J. T., 48
Griffin, Hayden, 126, 155
Guerra, Tonine, 159

Hack, Keith, 166
Hamlet, 97
He Jumped But the Bridge Was Burning, 31
Henry VI, 118
Henze, Hans Werner, 288
Hermit Disclosed, A, 33
Hobson, Harold, 138
Holmstrom, John, 184
Howarth, Donald, 30
Howell, Jane, 25–26, 52, 90–91, 124, 126–27, 135, 150, 155, 288
    Production of *Narrow Road to the Deep North*
        at the Belgrade in Coventry, 25–26, 52–53, 126, 155
        at the Northcott in Exeter, 25
        at the Royal Court in London, 25

Hurren, Kenneth, 21–22, 168–69, 184

Independent Theatre, the, 48
Invitation to a Beheading, 61
Ionesco, Eugene, 91, 115, 122

James, Peter, 284
Japanese Nō drama, 154–55
Jellicoe, Ann, 30–31, 47, 163
Jim All Alone, 33
Johgh, Nicholas de, 184
Johnstone, Keith, 29–32, 45, 49
Jonson, Ben, 253

King Lear, 21, 157, 181, 183, 216–19
Kingston, Jeremy, 19, 85, 156, 168
Klaxon in Atreus' Palace, 31
Kleist, Heinrich von, 160
Knack, The, 163
Kott, Jan, 216
Kretzmer, Herbert, 48, 126

Lahr, John, 21
Land Without Bread, 286
Laughter In The Dark, 17, 158, 160
Lear, 19, 21–22, 25, 27, 181–222, 239, 243, 260, 264–65, 267, 277, 286
Lesson, The, 115
Lewis, Peter, 127
Life Price, 59
Livings, Henry, 33
Lloyd-Evans, Gareth, 125
Look Back In Anger, 24, 80

McCarthy, Mary, 19, 49
McGrath, John, 32

Index

Marowitz, Charles, 25, 184–85
Marriott, R. B., 22
Maslow, Abraham, 77–79
Mass Psychology of Fascism, The, 262
Measure For Measure, 167, 216, 218
Michael Kohlhaas, 158–60
Morris, Desmond, 195

Nabokov, Vladimir, 17, 61, 160
Narrow Road to the Deep North, 18–22, 24–28, 52, 88, 108, 123–57, 191–93, 199, 206, 233, 239, 245–47, 252–53, 259, 264–65, 267–68, 272–74, 276–77, 281–83, 285–87
Narrow Road to the Deep North and Other Travel Sketches, 128
New Industrial State, The, 256
Next Time I'll Sing to You, 33
Nicholas and Alexandra, 158–59, 161
Nightingale, Benedict, 168, 184–85
Nijinsky, 162
Nureyev, Rudolph, 162

Olivier, Laurence, 19, 49, 161
Oppenheimer, George, 18–19
Osborne, John, 24–25, 80

Panter-Downes, Mollie, 59
Passion, 158, 169, 173–80, 192, 204, 239, 251, 253, 264, 267–68, 273–74, 277–78, 285–87
Pinter, Harold, 24–25, 45
Pope's Wedding, The 18, 22, 24, 29–48, 64–65, 74, 82, 92, 236, 239, 248, 257, 259, 264, 267, 269, 272–77, 282–83, 287

Reich, Wilhelm, 195–96, 244, 258, 262, 278–80
Richardson, Tony, 17, 160
Roberts, Peter, 54
Roeg, Nicholas, 17, 161
Roundheads and Peakheads, 158, 162, 165, 167, 216
Royal Court theatre physical dimensions, 25–26, 185

Salzburg, Harry, 162
Saunders, James, 33–34
Saved, 18–25, 27, 32–33, 47–81, 83–88, 92, 94–95, 114, 119, 124, 126, 193, 196, 220, 236, 239–40, 248, 251, 253, 257, 264–65, 270–74, 276, 278–79, 281–84, 287
Schlöndorff, Volker, 160
Scofield, Paul, 162
Seagull, The, 163
Sea, The, 19, 22, 26–28, 108, 160, 222–54, 260, 265, 268, 270, 273–74, 277–78, 287
Shaffner, Franklin, 159
Shakespeare, William, 21–22, 24, 118, 157, 166–67
Shaw, George Bernard, 253
Simpson, N. F., 47
Soyinka, Wole, 30
Sport of My Mad Mother, The, 163
Spring Awakening, 158, 167–69
Spurling, Hilary, 20, 59, 127

Taylor, John Russell, 18, 21, 25, 32–33, 67, 85, 125
Theater of the Absurd, 25
Theatre Quarterly, 33, 222, 224
Thirkell, Arthur, 19
Three Sisters, The, 30, 83, 158, 162–63
Toller, Ernst, 215
Trevelyan, Raleigh, 33

Trewin, J. C., 18, 48, 164
Two Storms, 223
Tynan, Kenneth, 19, 49, 84, 123

Vernay, Stephen, 123–124

Walkabout, 17, 158, 160–61

Walker, James Vance, 160–61
Wardle, Irving, 20–21, 25–27, 48, 84, 125, 135
Wedekind, Frank, 162, 167–69
Weightman, John, 184
Worth, Irene, 49

Yale Repertory Theatre, 52, 60